W9-ADQ-003

WITHDRAWN
L. R. COLLEGE LIBRARY

CARL A. RUDISILL LIBRARY
LENOIR-RHYNE COLLEGE

GAYLORD

We Offer Ourselves as Evidence

Recent Titles in
Contributions in Labor Studies

We Offer Ourselves as Evidence

TOWARD WORKERS' CONTROL OF OCCUPATIONAL HEALTH

Bennett M. Judkins

CARL A. RUDISILL LIBRARY
LENOIR-RHYNE COLLEGE

CONTRIBUTIONS IN LABOR STUDIES, NUMBER 19

GREENWOOD PRESS
NEW YORK • WESTPORT, CONNECTICUT • LONDON

RC
773
.J83
1986
aug. 1996

Library of Congress Cataloging-in-Publication Data

Judkins, Bennett M.
    We offer ourselves as evidence.

    (Contributions in labor studies, ISSN 0886-8239;
no. 19)
    Bibliography: p.
    Includes index.
    1. Lungs—Dust diseases—Social aspects—United
States. 2. Byssinosis—Social aspects—United States.
3. Cotton dust—Hygienic aspects—United States.
4. Coal mines and mining—Hygienic aspects—United
States. I. Title. II. Series.
RC773.J83   1986   363.1'79   85-24775
ISBN 0-313-24898-2 (lib. bdg. : alk. paper)

Copyright © 1986 by Bennett M. Judkins

All rights reserved. No portion of this book may be
reproduced, by any process or technique, without the
express written consent of the publisher.

Library of Congress Catalog Card Number: 85-24775
ISBN: 0-313-24898-2
ISSN: 0886-8239

First published in 1986

Greenwood Press, Inc.
88 Post Road West
Westport, Connecticut 06881

Printed in the United States of America

The paper used in this book complies with the
Permanent Paper Standard issued by the National
Information Standards Organization (Z39.48-1984).

10 9 8 7 6 5 4 3 2 1

To Mildred Mallory Judkins, 1912–1977

Contents

Preface

On December 17, 1980, seventy-five retired and disabled textile workers from the mill villages of North and South Carolina came to the campus of the prestigious Duke University. Their cause was education; they presented themselves as both teachers and texts to Dr. Phillip Pratt, a pathologist at the university's medical center. Two months earlier, Dr. Pratt and a colleague, Dr. Siegfried Heyden, had published an article in the *Journal of the American Medical Association* which used the evidence of autopsies from forty-four former textile workers to conclude that chronic lung disease in cotton textile workers was primarily a result of smoking rather than of exposure to cotton dust. Extensive newspaper coverage of this study presented a serious threat to the millworkers' efforts to obtain recognition of byssinosis, a disabling, obstructive pulmonary disease caused by the inhalation of cotton dust into the lungs. In a direct challenge to the Pratt/Heyden research, the millworkers who came to teach brought thirty-six living former cotton textile workers, all nonsmokers, and all diagnosed as suffering from byssinosis, or, as the textile workers called it, "brown lung." Behind these demonstrators a large banner proclaimed their reason for being there: WE OFFER OURSELVES AS EVIDENCE.

It was a profound statement, symbolic of the coalition they represented: the Brown Lung Association was a grassroots organization of 7,000 retired and disabled textile workers fighting to clean up southern cotton textile mills and to secure compensation for those already afflicted by byssinosis. The demonstration was similar to those of the previous decade, when retired and disabled coal miners of the Black Lung Association confronted the state of West Virginia and the federal government for recognition of another dust-related occupational lung disease—coal worker's pneumoconiosis, or "black lung." In both struggles, members of America's working class offered themselves as evidence of the cost to human life and health demanded by participation in our nation's economic system.

This book is about these two movements. It is about the struggle of coal miners, textile workers, and their supporters to convince industry, the government, the legal and medical professions, the news media, and the public of the existence of occupational diseases, the need to compensate those already afflicted, and the importance of protecting workers in the future.

Although this study is limited to only two groups of workers, the problems of occupational health are not. Estimates of disabling occupational diseases range as high as 390,000 new cases per year, with a possible 100,000 deaths during the same period. Despite disagreement over the validity of these estimates, the problem is of sufficient magnitude to have attracted the attention recently of many industry, labor and government organizations. Much of this attention has resulted from the successful efforts of coal miners and textile workers to bring national consideration to their plight. As more worker groups organize around occupational health issues, and as government and industry plan preventative policies, it is important that we reflect on the experiences of the coal miners and textile workers who initiated this broader occupational health movement. It is to this goal that the present book is directed.

The seminal idea for this research developed in early 1973 with the collaboration of Thomas C. Hood, now Chair of the Department of Sociology at the University of Tennessee. An academic appointment the following year at Marshall University in Huntington, West Virginia, provided me the opportunity to spend considerable time as a participant observer with the Black Lung Association in 1973 and 1974. From 1974 to 1976, while on the faculty at A and T State University in Greensboro, North Carolina, I became similarly involved with the emerging Brown Lung Association, a process which has continued to the present since my move in 1976 to Belmont Abbey College in Gaston County, North Carolina, the heart of the southern textile industry.

This book would not have been written if it were not for the generosity of many people who shared their time and ideas about these two emerging movements and the roles they played in relation to them. I would especially like to thank the members and staff of both the Black Lung and Brown Lung Associations who consented to my endless questioning as well as shared with me written documents about their movements.

Much credit for the completion of this book must go to its major supporter, the National Endowment for the Humanities (NEH). In 1980, an NEH Fellowship enabled me to spend a year in the Department of History at Brown University in a research seminar, "The New Labor History," under the direction of historian Joan Scott (who is now at Princeton). It was during this year that the idea for a book comparing the black lung and brown lung movements emerged. Additional support was provided by NEH in the summer of 1982, when I received a fellowship to attend a seminar on southern culture at the University of North Carolina at Chapel Hill, under the direction of John Shelton Reed.

For reading various parts of the manuscript in its early stages and for their suggestions, I would like to thank Jean Moore, Joan Scott, John Shelton Reed, and Tony Oberschall. I would especially like to thank Jan Bronstein for her critical analysis of Chapter 2 and for her substantial contributions to the final draft. Gale Warlick served as an excellent typist for the initial draft. A special note of thanks is due to Karen Brunt, who served as the editor for the final draft. Without her perseverance and patience, as well as her excellent skill in the construction of the English language, this book would not have gone to press.

A very special acknowledgement goes to historian Phillip Scranton, now at Rutgers University, who has provided encouragement and support as both a friend and a colleague in the struggle to understand and change the world around us. I would also like to thank the following individuals for unique contributions that only they would understand: Michael Betz, Carl and Mary Ann Hand, George Hopkins, Star Godfrey, Susan Smith, and Pearl and George Hartgrove. Belmont Abbey College provided small grants to assist in the typing and editing of the manuscript. Finally, I would like to acknowledge the important role that my mother played in my interest in this subject. An occupational health nurse in both the textile and coal industries, she taught me the importance of people, respect, and dignity. Although she never understood my love for sociology, she had a love for people that any sociologist would envy. It is to her, and her work, that this book is dedicated.

Part I

INTRODUCTION AND HISTORICAL BACKGROUND

1

Introduction

A Brooklyn manufacturer inquired recently if the ventilation bill which was introduced in the state legislature last winter had become a law. When informed that in common with several other measures it had failed to pass, but that up-to-date information on ventilation had been collected and could be mailed to him, this manufacturer said, "No, I don't care to know anything about that. I only wished to make sure that I was within the law."

John B. Andrews, "Protection Against Occupational Diseases,"
Academy of Political Science II, no. 2, (1911).

This is a book about the struggle for occupational health, a struggle which involves not only industry and its workers, but, increasingly, the powers of state and federal governments, the medical and legal professions, and the nation's research and educational institutions. The passage of the Occupational Safety and Health Act of 1970 by the U.S. Congress set the stage for continued government involvement in the search for solutions to the occupational illnesses problem and provided a political framework for many of the battles of the 1970s and 1980s. This law itself was the result of actions taken by many workers and their unions to draw the powers of the federal government into the struggle. But the work of the Occupational Safety and Health Administration (OSHA) has in turn increased workers' awareness of potential health threats in America's workplaces and consequently prompted many workers to speak out against hazardous working conditions.

Much of the struggle has been directed through the traditional structure of the nation's unions. But a very important role has emerged for those who have already been victimized by unhealthy workplace environments, the retired and disabled workers of our nation. This study is directed to that aspect of the occupational health movement. It focuses specifically on two industries which have encountered increased government involvement and increased pressure from retired and disabled workers regarding occupationally-linked diseases: the coal mining industry in southern Appalachia and the cotton textile industry in the South.

"Black lung," or coal worker's pneumoconiosis, is a chronic lung disease caused by the inhalation of coal dust; it generally arises out of employment in an underground coal mine. "Brown lung," or byssinosis, is a respiratory disease associated with the inhalation of cotton, flax, or soft hemp dust; it generally affects workers in the southern textile industry. Although the symptoms of both of these illnesses have long been recognized, little attention was given to them in the United States until the late 1960s. Medical research has not produced a cure, but rather a continuing controversy about the detection, causes, and even the actual existence of the diseases. Consequently, both workers and industry management have taken political action to resolve the major issues involved.

One of these issues is the reduction of dust levels in the workplace followed by monitoring to maintain a safe workplace. The cost of both processes can be extremely expensive to the industry. For example, the textile industry estimated that the cost of a proposed cotton dust standard could run as high as $2.6 billion. But the cost of compensation to those workers who have already been disabled also can be, and indeed has been, high. Since the passage of the federal Black Lung Benefits Program for coal miners afflicted by pneumoconiosis, the cost of benefits has risen to almost two billion dollars annually. It is perhaps the excessive cost of occupational health that has encouraged industry to oppose most reform legislation to clean up the workplace and liberalize the compensation process. On the other hand, the potential benefits of a clean workplace and compensation for occupationally induced diseases have equally encouraged the nation's workers to push for significant changes in both the law and their workplaces.

In the late 1960s, retired and disabled coal miners in West Virginia came together to seek reform in the state workers' compensation laws. Their goal was simply to force the legislature to recognize coal worker's pneumoconiosis as a compensable disease, as it had done thirty-five years previously for silicosis, a similar lung condition related to underground mining. Their efforts resulted in the formation of the Black Lung Association (BLA) and the emergence of a movement that not only brought the coal industry of West Virginia to a temporary standstill, but eventually brought about the passage of the first federal program to compensate workers for an occupationally induced disease.

The success of this movement spread to several other coal mining states; equally important, it became a role model for retired and disabled worker movements in other industries. One of the most successful of these was led by the Brown Lung Association, which began forming in the cotton textile industry communities of North and South Carolina in the spring of 1975. It eventually spread to six southern states and reached a peak membership of over 7,000 by 1980.

The black and brown lung movements were two of the most visible and successful in the recent struggle for occupational health. In many ways, however, they were unique in the history of American labor. First, they were composed primarily of retired and disabled, rather than active, workers. Although unions have frequently acknowledged workers' rights to health and safety, these issues have traditionally been sacrificed in the process of collective bargaining. Second, because withholding of labor (which has been a main strategy for labor unions) was not a feasible tactic for retired or disabled workers, the movements sought influence and power by bringing third parties, particularly the government, into their struggle. Third, the movement organizations which emerged were quite different from traditional labor organizations in both structure and operation.

These unique factors suggest several important sets of questions about the experiences of these movements. First, why did retired rather than active workers play such an important role? Do retired workers have more to gain in immediate benefits from compensation, or do active workers have more to lose from the potential loss of jobs? Or is health a low priority when workers are young and actively working? What role did unions play in this struggle, and what was the relationship between these organizations of retired and disabled workers and the traditional union structure?

Second, why did these movements emerge when they did? What were the societal conditions that encouraged a social movement as the vehicle for social change? Why did coal miner's pneumoconiosis and byssinosis not simply remain medical problems rather than becoming political problems with political solutions? What political and financial roles did the government play in supporting these movements, and what was their relationship to other movements of the sixties and seventies?

Third, what were the internal structures of these movements like? How important were both internal and external resources to the success (and failure) of these movements, particularly in terms of funding, manpower, and political support? What type of strategies and tactics were effective in achieving their goals? Although the movements were addressing similar issues, in what ways were they different from each other? And, finally, what was the impact of these movements on the retired and disabled workers who participated in them and on the broader communities of which they were a part?

OUTLINE OF THE BOOK

These were some of the initial questions which prompted my original inquiry into the black and brown lung movements. They seem to have both practical and theoretical significance. What has happened to retired and disabled coal miners and textile workers reveals much about the underlying problems of occupational disease in America's workplaces and perhaps may provide us with a preview of the future as other workers in other industries begin to struggle with similar issues. Theoretically, these movements provide important information about modern social movements in general, and can serve as case studies of collective efforts for social change. Although the purpose of this book is not of a theoretical nature, the analysis of both movements is influenced by issues of relevance to the contemporary sociological study of social movements. In this respect, the following chapters include pieces from a complex puzzle, and their organization, internally and externally, reflects an attempt to make sense of that puzzle.

Part I of the book provides an introduction to the general issues of occupational health and discusses some of the historical circumstances which have affected both coal miners and textile operatives. Part II is devoted entirely to the black lung movement from 1969 to the present. Part III covers the brown lung movement from 1975 to the present. Finally, Part IV is a reflection on the relation between the theoretical and practical issues raised by these two movements.

PART I

Although the guiding framework for this analysis is sociological, I have attempted to make it historically informed. Chapter 2 deals specifically with the way illness has been viewed in American society in the present century and the implications this view has had for the development of concern for occupational health. The way that health and illness are perceived in a society influences not only the responses of the medical institutions, but also those of the political and economic systems to health needs. As was indicated earlier, much disagreement over the cause, diagnosis, and even existence of both coal worker's pneumoconiosis and byssinosis persists in the medical profession because of the unique character of these, as well as other, lung diseases. But it must also be recognized that the health of America's workers has, until recently, been given low priority by industry, the government, the medical profession, and even the workers themselves. If the government fails to provide the necessary funds for research, if the medical profession shows little interest, if the industry professes indifference (or opposition), or if the workers and their unions are more concerned about other, more immediate issues, the many years that are necessary for the diagnosis and prevention or cure of occupational diseases will undoubtedly be increased. This seems to have been the case for the first half of the present century in the United States. This is significant because it resulted in a crisis situation in the late 1960s which encouraged the formation of uninstitutionalized political social movements to resolve the problems of cleaning up our nation's workplaces and providing compensation for afflicted workers.

Another factor which influenced the framework within which these diseases would be addressed pertains to the historical development of coal mining and textile manufacturing as industries and the relationships which were established between the industry owners and the workers. The annals of labor history document repeatedly the collective struggles of both coal miners and textile workers to escape the oppressions of their occupations. Many writers have suggested that these oppressions resulted from a form of colonization, whereby external forces controlled, and perhaps molded, the form of organization and culture that emerged. Chapter 3 compares the experiences in the early coal mining camps and textile mill villages and the subsequent efforts at unionization in both industries which laid the foundation for the present economic, political, cultural, and social conditions.

The chapter develops three major premises. First, central Appalachian coal miners and southern cotton textile workers experienced very similar conditions which limited alternatives for collective action but, at the same time, also established shared experiences which provided a structural and ideological framework for their lives and the world around them. Second, while the coal camps and the mill villages did much to alter the traditional (pre-industrial) values and behaviors of the workers, many cultural traditions were maintained. Third, these cultural and historical experiences provided the foundation upon which contemporary occupational health movements have emerged and greatly influenced their structure, ideology, and tactics.

PART II

Part II is devoted entirely to the black lung movement. Chapter 4 covers the early stages of the movement from late 1968 to early 1970, the formation of the West Virginia Black Lung Association, and the resulting confrontation with the state legislature over a new compensation law. Of crucial importance to the success of the early movement was the medical information provided by physicians about coal worker's pneumoconiosis, as well as the efforts of three physicians to organize retired and disabled miners. The formation of the West Virginia Black Lung Association was a daring venture that put those involved in conflict with the administration of the United Mine Workers of America (UMWA). The passage of the compensation law, however, required the participation of active miners in a well-tested strategy, the strike, utilized in an innovative way. Instead of being directed against the industry, the walkout was aimed at the state legislature, whose members would have to suffer the consequences of a long period of inactivity in the state's largest industry.

Although the miners were successful in their quest for a compensation law in West Virginia, the intensity of the struggle, coupled with a major mine disaster, encouraged the U.S. Congress to pass legislation also. In December of 1969, less than nine months after the West Virginia bill was signed, Congress passed the Federal Coal Mine Health and Safety Act. In addition to substantial legislation on coal mine safety, the act also established the first federal program to compensate non-governmental workers afflicted by an occupational disease. Titled the Black Lung Benefits Program, it was implemented by the Social Security Administration. Problems in the implementation of the program, however, resulted in the revival of the dormant Black Lung Association in West Virginia, which quickly spread to several other coal mining states. The rebirth of the movement and the formation of a regional Black Lung Association is the subject of Chapter 5.

The dynamics of the confrontation between the Black Lung Association and the Social Security Administration is the focus of Chapter 6. The contrast between the uniquely unbureaucratic Black Lung Association and the highly bureaucratic Social Security Administration provides an interesting backdrop for the efforts of miners to liberalize the process for receiving benefits for black lung.

PART III

The brown lung movement was in many respects similar to the black lung movement. Both addressed problems associated with occupational respiratory diseases, the membership in both movements was mostly retired and disabled workers, their goals were similar, and both focused their strategies primarily on the government and its agencies. Both movements were also dependent upon outside personnel (doctors, lawyers, activists, etc.) to facilitate their activities. However, there is one significant difference between these two occupational groups: coal miners have a history of relatively successful union experience, whereas southern textile workers do not. Although the historical failure of unionization affected the formation of the Brown Lung Association, the organizers were able to acquire substantial funding from the federal government, religious charities, and other foundations which at that time looked favorably on movement organizations that were supporting social change. Most funds were spent to pay a professional cadre of mainly young, educated, healthy activists to guide the Brown Lung Association. This dependence on external funding and professional staff greatly influenced the structure, ideology, and strategies of the movement both during its growth and during its eventual decline, as is documented in Chapter 7.

One of the major battles fought by the Brown Lung Association was over the issue of compensation to those afflicted by byssinosis. Although the retired and disabled textile workers did at one time seek a federal benefits program similar to that established for coal miners, this effort never succeeded. The major struggles occurred on the state level, where laws regarding compensation differed widely. Chapter 8 evaluates the efforts of the Brown Lung Association to attack the compensation problem in North and South Carolina, the two largest textile-producing states.

The second major issue regarded efforts to clean up the mills. Although a cotton dust standard had already been proposed prior to the emergence of the Brown Lung Association, the efforts of retired and disabled millworkers played a significant role in the final implementation of the standard, in its approval by the U.S. Supreme Court, and in an attempt to prevent the Reagan administration from decreasing the standard's effectiveness. Chapter 9 focuses on this part of the struggle with attention given also to the response of the textile industry.

PART IV

The last two chapters of this book are essentially interpretive in nature. Chapter 10 uses the black lung and brown lung movements as examples for exploration of the complex interrelationships which make up the internal structure and dynamics of the modern social movement. Particular attention is focused on the role of both "insiders" and "outsiders" in the success or failure of a movement.

"Insiders" are those people who generally make up the membership of the movement and who benefit from the achievement of the movement's goals. "Outsiders" are those people, particularly professional lawyers, doctors, and activists, who do not directly benefit from the movement's success, but who contribute important resources necessary for the growth and survival of the movement and its organization.

Industry management frequently claims that labor movements are orchestrated by nonworker outsiders, thereby challenging both the legitimacy and the goals of these movements. Conversely, many supporters of these movements suggest that these are purely "workers' movements," and that outsiders play only minor, insignificant roles. Obviously, both interpretations have political implications, which makes the work of the serious observer both difficult and suspect. The conclusions which are reached here show that the success of the black lung and brown lung movements was dependent on both workers and professional cadre.

Chapter 11 looks critically at the future of occupational health struggles, with a reflective eye on the experiences of retired and disabled coal miners and textile workers. What can be learned from the black and brown lung movements that may help us to address the health problems of active workers in other industries? Will unions provide the most effective vehicle through the process of collective bargaining, or will the role of the government and its agencies continue to be the focus? Will the recent trend toward worker ownership of industry and economic democracy encourage greater attention to health and safety in our nation's workplaces? More generally, how much is human life worth in our economic system, and who is responsible for seeking solutions to the fundamental conflicts between the economic health of industry in a modern industrial society and the work environment that preserves the physical health of its employees?

2

A Historical Perspective on Occupational Health

The emergence of a social movement around an occupational health issue depends on the availability of medical information. Although miners and millworkers experienced the symptoms of lung diseases, as well as disability and death, they were not always aware that their problems were occupationally induced. And the knowledge which they did have, accumulated from years in the workplace, was not recognized as legitimate. The lack of medical information in the United States on both coal worker's pneumoconiosis and byssinosis was primarily due to two factors: (1) the culturally conditioned perceptions held about illness in our society, which slowed recognition of the scope and nature of occupational diseases, and (2) the influence of powerful interest groups in defining occupational health problems and allocating resources to solve them.

THE MEDICAL MODEL AND OCCUPATIONAL DISEASE

From the time of the Greeks through the mid-nineteenth century, Western medicine regarded disease as a lack of harmony between persons and their environments. As Europe became urbanized and industrialized, diseases widespread in factories and slums became more evident. Observers trained by the traditional medical system assumed there was something wrong with these environments. In early-nineteenth-century Europe and Britain, there emerged a radical public health movement to stop disease by cleaning up the environment. Much of the seminal work on occupational diseases was done during this time.

However, the traditional concept of health and illness in society was challenged by the growth of rationalism and positivism in Western Europe. By the mid–1870s, the philosophical groundwork for the acceptance of microbiology had been laid. Findings by scientists such as Louis Pasteur and Robert Koch that germs, rather than environmental forces, cause disease established the paradigm of "specific etiology": every different disease has a specific causal agent and a specific treatment. The view that environment causes disease was debunked as nonscientific. Consequently, research and treatment efforts shifted from alteration of unhealthy environments to isolation of particular disease mechanisms and discovery of "magic bullet" treatments.[1]

The germ theory model was adopted and promoted by university-trained physicians, who were at this time competing with midwives, homeopaths, and other healers for control of the patient marketplace. In the United States, in particular, university-trained physicians were heavily outnumbered and had to fight for recognition and control. Gradually, the physicians gained state endorsements, set up licensing requirements, and closed down a large number of medical schools which did not meet scientific standards. With the adoption of the recommendations of the Flexner Report of 1910, "nonscientific" medicine was effectively made illegal. From this time, all physicians were trained to use the specific etiology model in diagnosis, treatment, and research. While the germ theory model was dominant in Europe as well, a public health orientation and a focus on environmental and occupational causes of disease remained respectable. In the United States, however, the public health viewpoint was virtually absent from medical education and practice, at least until the 1970s.[2]

The primary activity of modern American medical practice, then, is differential diagnosis, or identification of particular diseases and therefore particular agents or causes of illnesses, that patients experience. This search for specific agents or entities affects the approach taken to research on diseases. For example, research on nutritionally related diseases was for a long time limited to the search for a specific vitamin deficiency; studies of total nutrition as it relates to total health are relatively recent.

In the case of environmentally related diseases, this model demands a search for specific toxic agents.[3] Observations that miners or textile workers get lung diseases from their work situations will probably not result in the identification of a particular disease until a single toxic agent can be agreed upon. If substances in the work environment are believed to be inert, then claims that a disease is induced by the workplace are discredited, despite evidence of workers becoming ill.

The development of a treatment for a disease caused by a specific toxin is necessary for a distinct labeling of that disease. Because there is no treatment for byssinosis which differs from the treatment of asthma or bronchitis, there is no practical medical incentive to label it as a distinct disease.[4]

The impact of the germ theory model is also felt in the process of diagnosis and treatment. Because it implies that a particular agent has attacked an individual patient, laboratory tests and physical examinations, rather than patient descriptions of the health problem, are thought to provide the best information. Little information is collected on patients' backgrounds, perhaps even less on their working or living environments. Even if occupations are recorded, no information is gathered on tasks or substances worked with. Therefore, it is unlikely that the occupational origins of clinical problems will be identified, or even suspected.

Because disease is considered an individual problem, very few centralized records are kept on the incidence of different diseases in a population. For example, only recently are tumor registries yielding information on unusual rates of particular cancers in different populations. No data bank can provide information on comparative rates of upper respiratory syndromes or toxicity reactions to different populations.

Finally, research and treatment establishments are geared to address problems of diseases fitting the germ theory model: those ailments which come on rapidly and acutely and can be treated by neutralizing the causal agent. Diseases with multiple causes which come on slowly over many years, or have long latency periods between exposure to the agent and the observable reaction, are likely to be chronic and incurable because less public attention and research is devoted to these less dramatic problems. Doctors tend to see chronically ill patients only when their symptoms flare up and become acute; medical insurance pays for acute care, but seldom for long-term care or rehabilitation. In general, the medical establishment has little sense of the scope of chronic disease in the population and can offer little information or relief.[5]

THE MEANING OF ILLNESS IN AMERICAN CULTURE

In contrast to the abstract models by which the medical establishment confronts disease, instances of disease in individual, everyday lives are concrete experiences which are socially interpreted according to established norms and values. These interpretations are often termed "illness" and contrasted with the biomedical interpretation of the same incidents, which are labeled "disease."[6] This same contrast may be set up between "impairment," the physical effects of disease, and "disability," the interpretation of impairment as it affects particular people in particular situations.[7] For example, a back injury may disable someone who is trained only to do heavy labor, while it may be considered only an annoyance for a university professor. Both people have the same disease, but entirely different illnesses.

Because sick people occupy special positions in society that affect their normal participation in the social structure, health maintenance is an important need at both the level of the individual and the collectivity.[8] Consequently, society has a functional interest in the control of disease and illness. If it incapacitates victims to a certain extent and prevents usual participation in the structure of roles that go to make up the social system, illness is sometimes classified as deviant behavior.[9] Health, on the other hand, is seen as the state of optimum capacity of individuals for the effective performance of the plurality of roles in which they have been socialized.[10]

Interpretations of illness fluctuate in accord with the different norms and values held to be important in particular cultures. Social and cultural factors may play important roles in the broader societal definition of just what disability is, and illness and disability may be defined differently in different situations and for different purposes. According to medical sociologist David Mechanic, this is so because of the larger system of which the disability is a part:

It will be helpful if [sick people] and the medical facilities are viewed in the context of the larger system of which they are parts. Parsons has pointed out that adequate health on the part of most group members, most of the time, is a functional requirement of any social system. A definition of disability which is too lenient would interfere with the smooth functioning of the system; it is necessary, therefore, to control socially the definition of disability to insure that not too large a proportion of the population is released from its usual social responsibilities.[11]

This sociological concept of illness, then, is one which identifies two potentially conflicting forces—individuals, who are sick and unable to perform their social and economic roles, and the society, which discourages illness and works to define it in such ways as to minimize the dysfunctioning of the system. Regardless of the motivation of the actors, illness and disability are potential modes for the evasion of social responsibilities.[12] While on most occasions the medical definitions of illness and disability may be more or less congruent with lay definitions, exceptions do occur. On certain occasions and under certain conditions, the requirements of the social system itself, or its parts, can take precedence over purely medical and humanitarian considerations and thereby provide a different basis for defining illness and disability.[13]

In American society there is a strong emphasis on individual achievement through hard work and independence. The emphasis among the problems of illness goes to those which affect the capacity for this individual achievement: "The obligation to accept the need for help is stressed, but this also becomes the primary threat of illness, for dependency is alien to the patterns of mastery and the ideals of the good society."[14] This is in contrast to Great Britain (which has generally recognized and addressed occupational health problems ahead of the United States), where the emphasis is more on integration and on the threat which illness poses to individuals' status as acceptable members of society. There exists in Britain a political ideal that people have a right to care when ill and a sentiment that "illness, far from jeopardizing individuals' status, in fact gives them special claims on the collectivity."[15]

Because nonproductivity and dependence are such culturally threatening behaviors, we have to make sure that people are "really sick" before they are allowed to play the "sick role." Friedson suggests that there are two criteria which are used to judge the illness experience in our society: the degree of seriousness and the absence of responsibility for the illness.[16] People are not "really sick" if the symptoms are not debilitating, and therefore they are not allowed to assume the sick role over other mandatory roles. Likewise, if people make themselves sick on purpose (i.e., attempt to commit suicide) or stand to gain from being sick (i.e., by avoiding responsibilities and by collecting compensation), their claims are treated with suspicion.

These norms affect both individual and institutional attitudes toward ill persons and make it especially hard for people with occupationally related illnesses to receive recognition. Often, working people cannot get sick pay or welfare help until their illnesses are certified as serious by doctors; they do not have the resources to make independent decisions about their own health. This means that they usually work until they are completely debilitated; therefore, the early stages of many occupational diseases are seldom seen by physicians. As soon as people suggest that their illnesses may be occupationally related, they face charges that they are exaggerating their problems for the purpose of financial gain or for the sake of shifting the blame, and, perhaps, that they bear the responsibility for their own illnesses because they continued to work voluntarily at hazardous jobs. They are treated with suspicion in doctors' offices and in compensation hearings. The compensation system is set up so that workers must bear the burden of proof about the causes of their illnesses.[17] Workers may avoid taking action or even recognizing the occupational origins of their illnesses in order to avoid this experience.

SOCIAL INTEREST GROUPS AND OCCUPATIONAL HEALTH

Medicine, from its inception, has generally been concerned with individual patients who present themselves to doctors who take histories, make examinations, state the diagnoses, and institute treatments.[18] Public health, in contrast, has been concerned with those matters which affect the lives of large numbers of people. Thus, the control and prevention of communicable diseases has been a high priority in public health. In modern industrialized nations, the major public health problems have been chronic diseases, mental illness, and accidents. Occupational health, a recognized subspecialty of public health, has been concerned primarily with the hazards of work. Although there is evidence of concern for the hazards of the workplace which goes back 5,000 years, it is generally accepted that occupational health had its birth around 1700, when Barnardino Ramazzini, an Italian physician, described many job-related illnesses and injuries.[19]

For many reasons, however, the major thrust of occupational health programs has been directed at injuries and safety, with very little attention, until recently, to the problems of occupational illnesses.[20] According to Dr. Lorin Kerr, former Director of the Occupational Health and Safety Division of the United Mine Workers of America:

Both by definition and actual practice occupational health programs are limited to the prevention, detection, and control of industrial illness and injury; the provision of services to select and place the worker in a manner acceptable to management; and fostering physical, mental, and social ideas to increase productivity. The treatment of disease or injury is restricted to those emergency measures necessary for the worker to complete, if possible, the work day. Any expansion of these services has been impossible primarily because of the economic conflict between the industrial doctor and the personal physician. While management has, in most instances, agreed with this restricted point of view, there are some spokesmen who realize the value of comprehensive health maintenance for the worker and his family but, thus far, they have been unable to overcome medical resistance.[21]

Ideally, of course, an occupational health program should operate free of these constraints. According to the American Medical Association's Council on Occupational Health, the objectives of an occupational health program are: (1) to protect employees against health hazards in their work environments; (2) to facilitate the placement and insure the suitability of individuals according to their physical capabilities, mental abilities, and emotional makeup in work which they can perform with an acceptable degree of efficiency and without endangering their own health or safety or that of their fellow employees; (3) to assure adequate medical care and rehabilitation of the occupationally ill and injured; and (4) to encourage personal health maintenance.[22] But even the Council on Occupational Health expresses its own biases and perhaps indirectly influences others by the qualifying statement that "health maintenance is primarily the responsibility of the individual."[23]

This attitude has been an implicit assumption of the U.S. Public Health Service, state health administrators, industry officials, the medical profession, and even the workers themselves.[24] But attitudes are not created in a vacuum, and an explanation of the knowledge about the incidence of occupational diseases requires a more comprehensive approach. In *Death on the Job*, Daniel Berman suggests that many of the problems we are experiencing today in both work safety and health can be traced back to the first two decades of this century. Responding to high workplace death and injury rates and pressures for reform from labor, government, and public interest groups, monopoly corporations set up what Berman calls a business-controlled "compensation-safety apparatus."[25] It is a complex of mostly private, corporate-dominated organizations which are concerned with compensation, workplace inspection, standard setting, research, and education in occupational health and safety:

It is called the *compensation-safety* apparatus because it emphasizes compensation over prevention and safety over health in its activities. It is an *apparatus* because it has executed the policies of business and insurance interests for decades as the only organized constituency in occupational safety and health. Only in the last ten years has its dominance been challenged by workers, unions, and their progressive allies.[26]

According to Berman, business-funded institutions were the only organized constituencies in occupational safety and health until the end of the 1960s. They include such organizations as the National 315Safety Council, the National Council on Compensation Insurance, the American National Standards Institute, the Industrial Health Foundation, the American Occupational Medicine Association, the American Industrial Hygiene Association, and the American Conference of Governmental Industrial Hygienists. Berman indicates that differences in philosophy between these organizations are few, even when their membership is made up of governmental rather than private employees, and they rarely express public disagreement with the positions on health and safety taken by the Association of Manufacturers or the U.S. Chamber of Commerce:

These organizations share common interests in that they are funded by big business and insurance sources; they believe in voluntary action by the private sector rather than government regulations of working conditions; they support common ventures and do not criticize each other publicly; they hold similar positions on those issues on which they take a stand; and they claim to be disinterested and scientifically neutral between management and labor. All of them subscribe to a common set of doctrines... about the causes and solutions for health and safety problems, and share industry's concern with keeping its costs to a minimum.[27]

One example of the influence of the work of these organizations is the fact that medical schools have paid little attention to the issue of occupational health. In 1968, Harvard Medical School graduated a class which had received only one lecture on the subject in four years of education.[28] A similar situation was evident at Duke University Medical School as well.[29] This may be partly the result of the influence of big business on medical school boards of trustees, who might be prone to neglect research into dangerous conditions in industry.[30] However, occupational health has traditionally been a poorly funded endeavor. According to Kerr, the National Institute for Occupational Safety and Health needs at least one dollar per year per employed worker for the effective detection, control, and prevention of occupational disease. In 1972, the appropriation of $29.1 million amounted to only $0.36 annually for each worker, and only about one-third of this was devoted to respiratory diseases.[31]

Physicians specializing in occupational health have generally come from private practice and reflect the basic values of the middle class, which assumes "that somebody must do the dirty and dangerous work."[32] They have entered into what Berman refers to as the "ghettoized institution of company medicine, in which the industrial physician [becomes] the company's advocate in compensation claims, backed by an infrastructure of lawyers and corporate sponsored research findings that [discount] job hazards."[33] In *Peril on the Job*, Ray Davidson argues that conflicts of interest are inherent in the management system.[34] At every managerial level, the overwhelming pressure is to maximize production; thus health and safety are at risk whenever there is conflict between production and precaution. These pressures put the company doctor in a peculiar position:

If he tells a worker that his illness is job caused, the employee may sue the company for workmen's compensation and subpoena the doctor to testify. At best, the typical medical man dislikes when he is put in the position of testifying against the company which has paid his fee.[35]

Unions have historically been of very little help in advancing issues of occupational health. Management has generally been considered responsible in both tradition and law for providing a "safe" workplace. Even when health has been an issue in collective bargaining, workers have generally been aware that improvements could be attained only at the expense of the wage and benefit demands. According to Nicholas Ashford in *Crisis in the Workplace*:

Both labor and management have difficulty balancing the concrete and immediate costs of health and safety against their own indeterminate and long-term benefits. Short-term and known considerations usually win out. This often means that actions are taken to limit injuries, which are dramatic and whose costs are reflected in immediately perceived pain and in workmen's compensation premiums, but that improvements related to health are limited.[36]

Limited knowledge about occupational illnesses in the medical community has also limited information available to workers in industry. Even when medical knowledge has been available, industry has restricted workers' access to that information primarily through company health programs. Workers who have complained about health conditions in the workplace have been either ignored or risked being fired. Gersuny reports from his research on the early New England textile industry that even though company physicians received numerous verbal reports of adverse conditions, official complaints had to be in writing and signed by the workers, thus minimizing, if not eliminating, their occurrence.[37]

EVOLVING ISSUES IN OCCUPATIONAL HEALTH

This brief historical overview of occupational health in the United States reflects a climate of neglect—by the industry, the government, the medical profession, and even the workers' unions. Why did this situation begin to change in the 1960s and 1970s? Perhaps the most significant reason was an increase in the number of injuries and illnesses. In the decade prior to the passage of the 1970 Occupational Health and Safety Act, there was a 29 percent increase in the reported injury rate in industry.[38] The National Safety Council reported in 1970 that two million workers were injured annually on the job, and of these, 14,000 were killed immediately or died later.[39] Higher estimates indicated twenty to twenty-five million job-related injuries and over 25,000 deaths.[40] Two million workers were either permanently or totally disabled, and seven million lost a day or more of work because of injuries on the job. Also, the rate of injuries per million man-hours worked rose steadily during the 1960s, a fact that many workers attributed to the lack of adequate safeguards and the generalized speedup which occurred through all industries.[41]

If these increasing occupational injuries were an important catalyst to the occupational health movement, figures on worker illnesses also gave cause for alarm. In 1972, *The President's Report on Occupational Safety and Health* predicted that at least 390,000 new cases of disabling occupational disease developed each year and that there might be as many as 100,000 deaths per year from occupationally caused diseases.[42]

At about this same time, both the workplaces and the workers began to change in ways that encouraged attention to occupational health. The changes in the workplaces were negative: new chemicals, new productive processes, and new forms of stress were introduced at an increasing rate.[43] The changes in the American workforce were more positive: increased educational levels and incomes in the manufacturing sector encouraged workers to shift the priority of demands from wages and benefits to job safety and health.[44]

Two issues began to dominate the concerns of American workers with regard to occupational health: cleaning up the nation's workplaces to prevent the occurrence of work-related diseases and providing compensation to those workers who were already afflicted or who might be so in the future. The two were related in that one of the historic arguments for workers' compensation was that the cost to industry would induce it to maintain a healthy work environment. This has not necessarily proven to be true.

Cleaning up the workplaces involves setting priorities for industry which may conflict with the major goal of maximizing profits. Improving the health and safety of work environments also requires some cooperation on the part of workers themselves. In addition, because of the increase in new chemicals introduced into workplaces in the last few decades, management, government, workers, and the medical community are still ignorant of which environmental conditions cause which diseases. Nicholas Ashford, referring to this part of the dilemma as the "information problem," argues that the systematic researching and establishing of safe levels of exposure for every chemical product in commercial use is simply impossible in any practical sense.[45]

Legislative solutions to the problem are further compounded by the different standards of truth in scientific and legal communities. When it comes to safeguarding rights under the law, a "scintilla of evidence" may justify legal sanctions, controls, and even the establishment of liability. The law thus attempts to make the best decisions on the information that exists. Absolute certainty or even consensus is not always required. What is required is an opportunity for all the available evidence to come in and for all parties to be heard.[46]

This principle of operation is confusing to scientists, whose research is used for policy making, as well as to those parties who are adversely affected by any legal ruling. Ashford suggests that in such situations demands are generally made for "scientific proof" that is not available, and it is very unlikely that sufficient scientific proof will *ever* be available—or even possible—with respect to some occupational health issues.[47]

Most of the research which is available is epidemiological in scope, which means that the links of diseases to workplaces are not directly causal or correlational. What data have been collected suffer from a number of problems of validity and reliability: "the small universe of studies which have developed in an ad hoc fashion, the over emphasis on mortality data, standardization problems, and the limited ability to make generalizations on the incidence of the disease in the population at risk."[48] In addition, only fragmentary data are available on the exposed population and the duration and severity of the response. However, because physicians have not generally been trained to diagnose occupational diseases, regulators must rely largely on this type of research.

Obviously, the limited availability of medical evidence on work-related illnesses impedes the development of governmental health standards. However, the standard-setting agency is also required to determine the economic and technological feasibility of control measures. According to the *1980 Interim Report to Congress on Occupational Diseases*, the issue of economic feasibility has been a subject of considerable controversy because the legal requirements for OSHA to demonstrate economic feasibility are not yet fully resolved and because there is difficulty in obtaining comprehensive and reliable cost and economic data.[49]

In turn, this has prompted industry to challenge many of the governmental health standards. The result has been prolonged and costly legal proceedings, best exemplified by the many years of litigation over OSHA's cotton dust standard for the textile industry. And even when a standard has been established, opportunities still exist for industry to avoid implementation. A recent National Occupational Health Survey indicates that one in every four workers (approximately 25 million) in the United States is exposed to some OSHA-regulated health hazard. However, there are only 500,000 workers in worksites inspected by OSHA health inspectors each year.[50]

The maximum penalty for violation of an OSHA standard is often a minor cost for a firm faced with major expenditures for environmental and engineering controls.[51] Thus, industry is not given sufficient incentives to reduce exposures to industrial health hazards. However, there are other economic incentives which encourage firms to actually withhold information about any emerging health hazards in workplaces. Firms that notify their workers and/or the federal government of potential health hazards may encounter regulatory pressure from OSHA or the Environmental Protection Agency. They also risk workers' compensation payments, product liability lawsuits, increased worker dissatisfaction, or union demands for clean up.[52] It is not surprising, then, that firms may withhold information.

The problem of gaining access to information from employers encouraged several government agencies to move in a new direction in the late 1970s. New health standards issued after 1976 contain important provisions which encourage the involvement of workers in occupational disease prevention. These provisions provide worker access to medical records and environmental data, participation in the environmental monitoring process, and education and training regarding hazards and related health effects.[53] In 1979, OSHA initiated the New Directions Program, which provided grants to institutions for the purpose of developing and implementing worker education and training programs. However, that program did not survive long into the Reagan administration.

Industry has traditionally emphasized compensation over prevention. The essential argument is that it costs less to compensate those workers who can successfully negotiate the compensation system than it does to eliminate the conditions that cause the health problems. Prior to 1910, the only legal obligation industry had to workers with regard to occupational health was through criminal courts, in cases in which injured workers sued employers. The criteria for such suits were stringent, and damages rarely awarded. With the tremendous expansion of industry and the influx of migrant labor, workplace deaths and maimings rose dramatically. Progressive reformers and the labor movement pushed for legislation to hold employers automatically responsible for care and pensioning of injured workers. As public sentiment became sympathetic to this position, industry became fearful that it would be held liable for unpredictably large sums through criminal suits.

Consequently, industry representatives sought a way to regulate the costs of occupational health. Their version of compensation insurance was generally adopted.[54] Workers gave up their right to sue in return for automatic payments for medical coverage and pensions. Whole industries pooled their risks and regulated their costs, at the same time maintaining tight control over the criteria for compensation awards. The payments were to be predetermined (generally about two-thirds of the lost wages for the duration of the disability), to be delivered promptly in order to relieve employers and employees of uncertainty, and to eliminate wasteful litigation. The legal principle was liability without fault. Employers were to bear the costs of work-related injuries not because of any presumption that they were personally to blame, but because industrial employment was inherently hazardous.[55]

Compensation programs were set up at the state level, but few have worked well. In 1972, the National Commission of State Workers' Compensation found serious inadequacies in the compensation system. A federal task force found that the system for compensating work-related total disability and death resulted in excessive litigation, long delays in payment, subsequent high rates of persons without employment, and little relationship between benefits awarded and the actual wage loss.[56] Even after federal legislation was constructed on the basis of recommendations from these groups, many state laws were not reformed. As of 1978, not one state had come into compliance with all of the nineteen essential recommendations (reduced from an original eighty-four). The states had reached, on the aggregate, a level of only about 60 percent compliance.[57]

The first workers' compensation laws did not deal explicitly with occupational disease. Statutes generally treated claims for illnesses as "accidents"; the disability had to be traced to an unexpected occurrence at a definite place and time. Judicial pressure eventually forced states to explicitly cover certain diseases. But the mold had been formed and its impact upon concern for health issues was significant. A pervasive safety bias affected legislation, the setting of standards, enforcement, manpower development, employer and employee education, technology development, and attitudes toward occupational disease and illness.

The losers in this whole system have been the American workers. Occupational disease is often painful as well as emotionally trying. Workers may be forced to accept lower paying jobs because of their disabilities, or may be completely unable to work for extended periods of time. The incomes of workers' families are often drastically reduced, and the families must often face the burden of paying for medical and rehabilitative services.[58]

There are winners, however. In addition to reduced costs to industry, insurance companies profit handsomely. They regularly pay out only about 40 percent of what they take in on compensation policies. Lawyers also benefit, because of the high rates of litigation, something which the original statutes had hoped to eliminate. In a recent study of the workers' compensation system, the researchers found that 84 percent of compensated dust cases were contested by the companies responsible.[59] They also found that in occupational disease cases in general, the claimant had formal representation 67 percent of the time, as compared with only 15 percent for accident claims.[60]

Our society's ability to recognize occupational disease, then, is complicated by a number of factors. The medical model tends to emphasize germ theory and focus on patients as individuals. Thus, little attention is given to environmental causes or patients as members of worker groups. Workers who do develop occupational illnesses are influenced by societal norms and values that view such illnesses as deviant behavior; consequently, they are reluctant to acknowledge their plights. Industry is also unlikely to be a prime advocate of worker health because of the potential for interruption of operation and the financial costs. Finally, the traditional concern for compensation, rather than prevention, has deflected interest from the identification of occupational diseases and their ultimate causes. The histories of both coal worker's pneumoconiosis and byssinosis illustrate many of these barriers to the recognition of occupational disease.

COAL WORKER'S PNEUMOCONIOSIS

The disease which we now call "coal worker's pneumoconiosis" has a long history. In *The History of Miner's Diseases*, G. Rosen suggests that as early as 1813 physicians were reporting the occurrence of black lungs in autopsied miners.[61] It was only a few years later that the condition was first identified as a disease associated with coal mining.[62] In 1880, Emile Zola described black lung and what it did to a miner, his family, and the community in the novel *Germinal*. Martin Agronsky suggests that by 1900 it was well known what coal dust did and that the condition would worsen and "only a welcome death in the end would stop the miner's suffering".[63] The cause was also well known to doctors, public officials, and laymen. But, according to Agronsky:

With recognition there came the usual reaction. No one really cared. Coal was being mined and at a good price. If there was a bad conscience, it was balanced by good profits. And the conscience was salved, too, by the tried and true placebo . . . "it is an occupational hazard and you will have to live with it."[64]

In the United States, another reason for the lack of concern for this miner's ailment came from the medical profession itself. Until the end of the nineteenth century, most physicians generally accepted coal dust as the primary cause of the respiratory problems in miners. However, at the turn of the century, conditions outside the coal industry dramatically turned the spotlight of public interest on silicosis,[65] a chronic condition of the lungs caused by the inhalation of air containing finely divided particles of silica.[66] Mass x-rays of workers in industries using silica were initiated in 1912, and soon silica was labeled in scientific journals as the most harmful industrial dust and silicosis as the only important dust disease. One of the reasons so much attention was focused on silicosis was its relationship to tuberculosis. Another was the passage of legislation in West Virginia which made silicosis compensable in 1935. The definition of silicosis which was adopted at that time was subsequently accepted by most states providing workers' compensation for silicosis. However, the definition excluded all other dusts and was so lacking in clarity that it denied compensation to many workers.[67] Some medical professionals have suggested that the medical and scientific community's concentration on silicosis was the outstanding obstacle to the recognition of pneumoconiosis as an important and distinct disease.[68]

While American investigators were concentrating primarily on silica and silicosis, the British scientists continued to act on their long-held concern for diseases associated with coal dust. By 1927, British doctors were reporting x-ray differences between silica and coal dust exposure.[69] By 1930, British investigators were reporting radiographic differences between silica and coal dust exposures and a respiratory disability which could not be attached to silicosis.[70]

In 1936, studies were initiated by the Committee on Industrial Pulmonary Diseases of the Medical Research Council in Great Britain on chronic pulmonary diseases among coal miners, particularly in South Wales. The first report identified a new type of dust disease as "coal worker's pneumoconiosis." It was first established as a clinical entity in which the accumulation of coal dust in the respiratory bronchioles leads to "a coal macule with minimal fibrosis, compensating emphysema and ultimately, in a small but significant proportion of cases, to progressive massive fibrosis."[71] In 1941, coal worker's pneumoconiosis, as distinct from and in addition to classical silicosis, became a compensable occupational disease in Great Britain.[72]

One of the more significant developments in the concern over coal worker's pneumoconiosis in Europe was the establishment in 1952 of the European Coal and Steel Community, which initiated a coordinated effort to study and prevent the disease. By 1962, large sums of money for research in industrial health, with major emphasis on silicosis and other pneumoconioses, had been allocated. Many research laboratories were developed, and their investigations added much to the fundamental knowledge of the pathology and physiology of all dust-induced diseases, with a special emphasis on pneumoconiosis. In 1970, according to Henry N. Doyle, a professor of occupational health at the National Institute of Health in Stockholm, Sweden, preventive measures employed in European mines differed in detail from country to country, but all had in common environmental control and medical surveillance of individual workers. In most European countries, the primary responsibility for environmental control was vested in the mining companies. In Belgium, France, Germany, the Netherlands, and the United Kingdom, there were extensive research programs in dust evaluation and control, usually under the sponsorship of a government agency.[73]

Also in most European countries, a great deal of emphasis was placed on the medical control of individual miners, which included examinations prior to employment and periodically thereafter. According to Doyle, once individuals developed early pneumoconiosis, medical practice required that they be placed in areas of "safe dust" concentration, and if the disease continued to progress, they were removed entirely from dust exposure.[74]

There is some evidence to indicate that Britain has been quite successful in its attempts to control the problem of pneumoconiosis. In 1955, nearly 5,000 new compensation awards were granted for coal worker's pneumoconiosis, but by 1965 this number had dropped to 1,007.[75] In addition, the annual reports of the British National Coal Board since 1959 indicate a gradual reduction in the percentage of British miners with x-ray evidence of the disease.[76] According to Dr. Lorin Kerr, the success of the outstanding British achievements has been the result of cooperation among the British National Union of Mine Workers, the government, and the people:

The union has been well aware of the problem and the need for continuing action. In fact, they, along with other segments of the industry, have known that the British government and the British people would not allow coal mining to continue to extract its price of death and disability if there were reasonable alternative sources of power.[77]

In the United States, until recently, there was no body of information on coal worker's pneumoconiosis comparable to that existing in Europe and the United Kingdom. Of the information which existed before the 1950s, one of the confounding factors associated with the identification of pneumoconiosis in America was the distinction between anthracite and bituminous mining. Anthracite is a hard coal, which gives much heat with little smoke; bituminous coal is a soft coal which yields pitch or tar when it burns. Before 1952, many investigators assumed that bituminous coal did not produce a disabling pneumoconiosis, although pneumoconiosis among anthracite miners had been studied.

The first studies of chest diseases in the United States were conducted between 1928 and 1931 among the anthracite coal miners of eastern Pennsylvania. From these studies, pneumoconiosis that resulted from breathing air containing the dust generated in the various processes involved in the mining and preparation of coal was designated as "anthrasilicosis," a modified form of silicosis caused by the inhalation of silica dust intermixed with considerable amounts of carbon dust. Not only did this definition associate pneumoconiosis with anthracite coal, but it also linked the disease to silicosis.

In 1942, R.H. Jones attempted to demonstrate that silicosis in soft bituminous coal miners was not a rare disease and that "miner's asthma" and anthrasilicosis were one and the same disease. He did this through a study of eighty-six West Virginia bituminous coal miners with evidence of silicosis. His results also indicated that the type of occupation in which one was engaged was just as important as the number of years spent in mining, as had been reported in earlier studies.[78]

By 1949, it was becoming apparent that pneumoconiosis was a major health problem among bituminous as well as anthracite coal miners. One study reported in considerable detail the pathological, clinical, and physiological aspects of anthrasilicosis and pneumoconiosis. Anthrasilicosis was defined as the "condition of progressive pulmonary fibrosis with conglomeration of nodules in the advanced stages, caused by the inhalation of carbon and silica, and characterized clinically by dyspnea [difficult or painful breathing] with varying degrees of disability". The broader designation "coal work-er's pneumoconiosis," a term which was used less frequently at the time, referred to the "bizarre and varied lesions of pulmonary fi-brosis, with emphysema, marked areas of conglomeration, and dis-tention of the bronchi and other thoracic structures."[79] By 1952, studies were reporting the presence of a disease in bituminous min-ers similar in appearance to that found in British miners.

During the next two decades, the number of studies on diseases associated with miners' lung and chest problems increased. How-ever, the medical evidence revealed many inconsistencies which were to have a great effect on how the disease was perceived by the medical, industrial, legal, and legislative communities. In one series of investigations from 1959 to 1961, significant differences in the rate of the disease were found between central and western Pennsylvania—two different sections of the same bituminous coal region. The one common thread was that the disease seemed to increase with age and length of exposure. However, in both studies, subjective symptomatology (the symptoms of the disease) and roent-genographic findings (x-rays) did not necessarily agree. A larger percentage of miners who *did not* have pneumoconiosis than of those who did have the disease complained about shortness of breath. In addition, emphysema was not a prominent finding. Although the results of the study were inconclusive, they did indicate that Penn-sylvania had a problem of greater magnitude in its bituminous mine population than was previously believed.[80]

Partly because of the greater interest in silicosis in the United States and the original identification of pneumoconiosis as anthra-silicosis, many physicians believed that pneumoconiosis was not a new and different disease. One of the first studies to indicate the contrary was conducted in 1957. An environmental study of dust exposure in fourteen bituminous coal mines in central Pennsylvania made a crucial finding regarding the relationship between silica and pneumoconiosis. Of the more than 300 dust samples collected in the working environment, 90 percent showed less than 2 percent silica.[81]

These inconsistencies in medical and scientific findings continued for several years and had a dramatic impact on the medical com-munity, as one physician reported in 1970:

One of the really striking things about this is the tremendous confusion by physicians in the field about the reality of the disease, its character and the various components that contribute to the disability. As a result of these honest uncertainties, in the coal communities themselves, physicians are often not only confused and puzzled, but polarized. There are those who are in fact usually on record publicly, because they have either testified one way or the other, or refused to participate in disability hearings.[82]

While there was wide acceptance of the belief that continued inhalation of coal dust led to progressive stages of pneumoconiosis, many doctors were still skeptical of the directness of the link. Disease is very rarely a result of one causal element, but is produced by a constellation of things. Working conditions are not only a matter of dust concentration. Fatigue, heat, humidity, isolation, and other physical and psychological stresses enter into the patterns of health and illness. Therefore it is not always possible to incriminate a single element, although its presence may be necessary for the illness or disease to develop.[83]

Significant disagreement in the medical profession concerning the identification, cause, and prevention of black lung greatly affected its recognition as a legitimate occupational disease. First, in the area of compensation, physicians' knowledge and attitudes affected their reports on death certificates. As early as 1915, one physician writing on industrial pneumoconiosis observed:

When the condition advances further, the working capacity becomes seriously impaired, but I have been astonished to note how long a man exhibiting all the symptoms in an accentuated degree will continue to work. ... They complain only when the disease interferes with the ability to pursue the occupation. Finally, however, the overtaxed heart dilates and the picture changes, the cough becomes more bronchitic, oedema of legs and ascites supervene, and the end from heart failure is in sight, after which chronic bronchitis on the death certificate gives out little indication of a death from occupational disease.[84]

More recently, Dr. Lorin Kerr related his own experience during his early years with the UMWA Welfare and Retirement Fund:

I can vividly remember . . . the constant stream of wheezing, breathless miners coming to the area medical office in Morgantown, W. Va., seeking relief from the struggle to breathe. I can also remember how overwhelmed I felt. Never in my earlier professional experience had I observed or heard of a single industry with so many men who seemed to be disabled by their jobs. I say "seemed to be disabled by their jobs" because doctors said these men rarely had silicosis and it was unusual to find a physician who even suspected that coal dust might be dangerous. The disability was miner's asthma and it was accepted by miners and doctors as part of the job.[85]

The significance of death certificates is that they failed to give any indication of the extent of the problem for many years. Furthermore, the attitudes of medical practitioners also influenced the response of lawyers, government officials, and legislators. What has been referred to as an "ill-informed complacency" on the part of physicians resulted in not only a lack of medical research on coal workers' pneumoconiosis, but also in an almost total absence of legislative action to address the problem until the 1960s.[86]

BYSSINOSIS

In 1700, physician Barnardino Ramazzini published a work entitled *The Diseases of Workers* in which he discussed the problems of workers in the wool, flax, and hemp industries. According to Ramazzini, "A foul and poisonous dust flies out of these materials, enters the mouth, then the throat and lungs, makes the workmen cough incessantly, and by degrees brings on Asthmatic troubles."[87] Although many descriptions were given to the chronic respiratory diseases suffered by textile workers through the years, such conditions as identified by Ramazzini were reported in France in 1822 and 1827, and in England in 1832.[88] In an official report to Parliament in 1860, a physician described the illness we now know as byssinosis, but credit for coining the term "byssinosis" belongs to another British physician, Adrien Proust, who identified the syndrome in 1877.[89] The word "byssinosis" became even more familiar after its use by Sir Thomas Oliver in 1902 and 1908 in his books on occupational diseases. Although byssinosis was first described as a disease caused by the inhalation of cotton dust, it also occurs among hemp and flax workers and the term has continued to be used in this context.[90]

In Great Britain, textile workers' unions complained of chronic bronchitis and emphysema among workers in the carding rooms (where the initial stage of breaking down the raw cotton was performed) as early as 1908.[91] A government study performed in the early 1920s found that British cardroom workers died much more frequently from respiratory diseases than did the general population. In 1927, the British Home Secretary appointed a committee to investigate the relationship between dust in the textile mill cardrooms and diseases.[92] Following intensive study, byssinosis was made compensable as a work-related disease under workers' compensation laws in 1941.[93]

The existence of byssinosis in the United States, however, was not acknowledged until very recently. Although there was some evidence of a concern in the U.S. Bureau of Labor for the dusty conditions in textile mills in Massachusetts in 1913,[94] a study of workers in a southern cotton mill conducted in 1933 by the Public Health Service yielded negative results and led to the conclusion that the problem of serious dust diseases among cotton workers in the United States hardly existed.[95] In turn, this conclusion had a significant impact and discouraged further research until the 1960s. It was not until 1968 that the Public Health Service, then a division of the Department of Health, Education, and Welfare of the federal government, publicly reported that its earlier study had been in error, according to the testimony of one of its key administrators:

For years, it has been maintained by many that byssinosis—the lung disease caused by inhaling cotton dust—was not a problem for American textile workers. In Britain, where textile plants use American cotton, byssinosis has been recognized as a serious problem. There has never been a thorough study of the health of American textile workers but for some reason—largely, I believe, on the basis of x-ray studies made years ago—we have had the comfortable illusion that byssinosis was not a threat to American workers.[96]

In 1960, two British researchers conducted a study in two American mills to discover how byssinosis could be absent here when it presented such a serious problem in Britain. Their results, published in the *Journal of the American Medical Association* in 1961, confirmed the existence of byssinosis in the United States. However, the researchers themselves did not consider the study to be a proper epidemiological survey, because of the very small groups of working people studied.[97] In 1964, the late Arend Bouhuys, a noted international authority on byssinosis, received a grant from the U.S. Public Health Service to study cotton mill workers in Georgia. The textile industry's lobby attempted to discredit him and to stop the study.[98] T.M. Forbes, Executive Vice President of the Georgia Textile Manufacturers Association (GTMA), wrote the President of Emory University, where Bouhuys was then teaching, to suggest that the study was a waste of the taxpayers' money. He then sent a confidential memorandum to GTMA members urging them to contact Emory alumni or trustees whom they knew. If this failed, he stressed that their participation in the study was not compulsive. Consequently, Bouhuys was not admitted to a single plant in Georgia and was forced to conduct his study in the cotton mill at the federal penitentiary in Atlanta.[99]

The results of his research, published in 1969, showed that 29 percent of the workers in the carding and spinning rooms of the Atlanta mill had byssinosis. Similar results were found in a study conducted jointly by the Duke University Medical Center and the North Carolina State Board of Health in 1970–71. The research found a prevalence of byssinosis among cotton mill workers of 38 percent in preparation operations (opening, picking, and carding) and 15 percent in yarn production (spinning, winding, twisting, spooling and warping).[100]

The initial symptoms of byssinosis are chest tightness, cough, wheezing, and dyspnea in varying degrees of severity. The classical symptoms, however, involve what is referred to as a "Monday morning syndrome," which has become a controversial part of the identification process:

After working for five years without appreciable trouble except a cough, [the victims] notice either a sudden aggravation of the cough, which becomes dry and exceedingly irritating, or peculiar attacks of breathlessness. These attacks usually occur on Monday, whilst the rest of the week finds them in fairly good condition. For a time the trouble may be almost or entirely limited to this "Monday fever," but gradually the symptoms begin to spread over the ensuing days of the week; in time the difference disappears, and they suffer continuously.[101]

One reason posited as to why the disease is initially worse on Monday is that the cotton dust releases a substance already in the lung called "histamine." Histamine produces acute changes in air flow because of its bronchioconstrictor and edemagenic activity. Daily exposure the remainder of the week prevents the reaccumulation of histamine in the cotton workers' lungs. Once it has been released, it takes time to build up again;[102] therefore, workers have a more severe reaction on Monday after a weekend in which the histamine has been built up, but a lesser reaction on subsequent days, at least initially.

In 1963, Dr. R.S.F. Shilling, a British physician with the Institute of Occupational Health in London, suggested a system for grading byssinosis which has become the standard classification for epidemiological surveys:[103]

GRADE ½ The worker occasionally feels chest tightness or coughs on the first day of the working week.

GRADE 1 Chest tightness is experienced on every first day of the work week.

GRADE 2 The worker feels chest tightness on the first and other days of the working week.

GRADE 3 The worker has grade 2 symptoms and shows evidence of permanent ventilatory impairment.

However, this diagnosis is heavily dependent upon subjective data from the workers' own descriptions of their symptoms. Unlike other occupational diseases (such as coal worker's pneumoconiosis), byssinosis does not cause nodules to form or create a fibrosis which can be diagnosed by x-ray or autopsy. Therefore, questionnaires are generally used to determine symptoms. But there are several weaknesses in this method of diagnosis. First, the validity of the questionnaires depends on whether the examiners are able to elicit truthful and complete responses from the workers. The diagnosis of occupational lung disease is difficult because of the need to know details of the production processes at the workers' factories and the type of agent present in the specific work environments. Also, the doctors must possess enough knowledge of textile production and byssinosis to know both what questions to ask and what the answers reveal.[104] Until recently, few doctors knew enough about byssinosis to diagnose it correctly. According to medical students at Duke University in 1976, "Brown lung is an example of a disease that is not taught about. . . . It's mentioned rarely as one of the occupational diseases, and you never hear about prevention."[105]

A second issue is the accuracy of the workers' responses to questioning.[106] Schilling has noted that textile workers with byssinosis often forget their early symptoms and are therefore diagnosed as suffering from nonoccupational respiratory disease.[107] The industry has charged that dependence upon subjective symptoms encourages workers to claim the symptoms in order to get compensation. However, George Perkel, Director of the OSHA division of the Amalgamated Clothing and Textile Workers Union (ACTWU), suggests a different response:

If a worker is dependent upon his job for his livelihood, and of course this is a typical situation, we are dealing here with workers who work towards the bottom of the wage ladder . . . they are generally poor people, and . . . they rely upon their jobs and are fearful of losing their jobs. Therefore, when they are asked by a company doctor about symptoms, they tend to deny them, even though they have coughed or felt tightness in the chest on occasion or had difficulty in breathing.[108]

Because of the unreliability of questionnaires by themselves, Dr. Bouhuys and others have developed an alternative method of diagnosis which is based on the amount of air captured during the first second of expiration before and after exposure to cotton dust. If workers show a decrement in lung function after exposure to cotton dust, they are graded with one of the various stages of byssinosis. However, this method is inadequate for workers who have already been exposed to cotton dust over a long period of time. A high percentage of individuals exposed to cotton dust, not just those who may be susceptible to the disease, experience some decrement in their lung function. Also, for severely disabled individuals, further exposure to cotton dust is ethically unwise and practically impossible, considering the strength of breath required to measure breathing on the machine.

The medical debate over byssinosis continued into the 1970s because of disagreements over four primary issues. First, subjective answers to questionnaires were necessary for diagnosis. Second, the substance causing byssinosis had not been identified (and at this writing still has not). Third, there was a lack of clear evidence linking levels of dust exposure to the disease. Fourth, and perhaps most important, there was an absence of characteristic findings in physical examinations, chest x-rays, pulmonary function studies, and even lung biopsies which were specific for the diagnosis of byssinosis.[109] There are no pathological hallmarks of byssinosis; it is merely chronic obstructive lung disease, that is, chronic bronchitis and/or emphysema.

In many respects, this continued ambiguity favored the industry's position to litigate against compensation claims and reinforced its opposition to lowering the dust levels in the mills. Reform legislation was difficult to pass without strong support from the medical profession. Afflicted textile workers not only continued to suffer, but confronted a maze of roadblocks that limited their abilities to deal effectively with this disease on an individual basis. The very nature of the disease, with its "Monday morning symptoms," often allowed workers to dismiss the respiratory ailment in its early stages. And when the illness became more pronounced, fear of reprisals could prevent workers from reporting early symptoms to their supervisors. Company doctors did not always inform workers when lung dysfunction was detected, nor did they advise them that their jobs were to blame. Often doctors also sidestepped the compensation issue by shunting workers with disabling breathing problems to the Social Security system, where it was not required to prove that their disabilities came from work in order to obtain benefits. When workers sought medical attention outside the mill, they were often treated by a medical profession that was trained to believe that there was no such thing as byssinosis. And if they turned to an attorney, they found that many would not take their cases. As one U.S. Representative so poignantly observed, it became an interwoven conspiracy.[110]

A NOTE ON TECHNOLOGY AND OCCUPATIONAL HEALTH

It was mentioned previously that advancing technology in the form of new chemicals in the workplace has encouraged the current occupational health and safety movement. With respect to coal worker's pneumoconiosis and byssinosis, the link between technology and the recognition of these diseases may be even more direct.

There is some evidence to indicate that increasing mechanization in various stages of the mining and cotton industries also increased the susceptibility of workers to both pneumoconiosis and byssinosis.

The simplest and earliest technology used in coal mining was called "hand loading." Using this technique, individual miners were responsible for the amount of coal which they could load by hand and, in general, worked independently of other workers. In 1923, a new loading machine became available, and although the coal still had to be cut and dynamited by hand, the machines could load a car much faster than men could.[111] The most recent form of this technology, and the one largely in use today, was introduced soon after World War II. Called the "continuous mining method," this technique does not rely on cutting or shooting of coal. Instead, machines dig into the coal and load it directly onto a waiting buggy or onto a continuous belt.

Henry Doyle suggests that miners in this setting take a secondary position to machines, which become the focus of attention:

In the mechanization process the coal miner is often reduced to the status of an appendage of a machine. The pace at which he works, the contribution he makes, the ability which he brings to bear are determined by machines and not by man. The coal industry for the most part looks to the machine and not to the man. They marvel at the productivity of the machine and talk in terms of systems and engineering and output and somehow forget that the key ingredient remains the man—for only the man can operate the machine effectively and efficiently.[112]

Doyle argues that this man-machine relationship is a complex one which tends ultimately to establish an equilibrium of economic advantages balanced against human and economic risks. In American society, labor, management, government, and the general public agree on the human risks involved in the machine-made tasks and accept these risks as a price of the product. When an equilibrium is attained, there is a great reluctance to alter any component of the system. In addition, the risk to human health is frequently difficult to evaluate because health is not an immediate response to an altered man-machine system.[113]

With regard to pneumoconiosis, Doyle states that while there were several system alterations in other areas, the risk of pneumoconiosis was either ignored or an incomplete analysis of the system was made, even though predictive techniques were available. The increase and the actual speedup in motion of the machines increased the amount of coal dust circulating in the mines. The evidence indicates that the high incidence of pneumoconiosis among bituminous coal miners appears to be directly attributable to increased mechanization.[114]

The impact of modern technology on byssinosis may have been very similar. The danger of dust exposure could have increased because of mechanization in both the cotton fields and the textile mills. The transformation of the harvesting of cotton wrought by the mechanical picker has resulted in increasing amounts of trash in baled cotton (the raw material shipped to the cotton textile mill).[115] A component of this trash, called a "brac," is believed to contain the causative agent of the disease. The brac is the leafy part around the cotton bowl. When cotton was picked by hand, the leaf was generally removed. With the mechanical picker, the leaf remains. After the cotton has been picked and dried, the leaf becomes very fragile and breaks into small pieces. In the gins, the cotton seeds are removed, but brac remains. When the bail of cotton is opened in the beginning process at textile mills, brac particles are broken into even smaller pieces and then released into the work environments. It is these fine particles less than a thousandth the size of a pinhead which are absorbed into the lungs and cause the disease.[116] This is why the rates of byssinosis reported in previously mentioned studies were higher for workers involved in the opening stages of cotton processing. Much more foreign matter is transported from farms to cotton gins and then to textile mills today because almost 100 percent of the American domestic crop is machine-harvested. As one observer concluded, "Machines pick less carefully than human hands."[117]

In the textile mill itself, increased mechanization may have also affected the incidence of byssinosis. One of the new technologies introduced was the high speed carding machine, which can generate more fine dust than the slower machine it replaced. Processing speeds in virtually all the yarn preparation and production operations have been accelerated, with little parallel effort to capture or control dust emissions.[118] In the early 1960s, many mills bricked up their windows and put in air conditioning to provide the necessary atmosphere for the newer, faster equipment. In the old days, relatively slow equipment produced bigger dust particles that blew out the open windows; new equipment produces a finer dust that has nowhere to go.[119]

CONCLUSION

By the late 1960s and the 1970s, coal miners and textile workers confronted not only the problems of black lung and brown lung, but also a hostile occupational health environment. First, the practice of medicine in the United States had reinforced an individualistic approach to illness reflected both in the approaches in disease causation as well as in the interpretation of illness in American culture. With regard to occupational health issues, this resulted in more attention focused on workers themselves and less on the working conditions which may have produced the diseases. Second, occupational health was given only minimal attention by the medical profession, the government, industry, and the unions. The consequence of this neglect was a dearth of information about occupational health problems.

With regard to both coal worker's pneumoconiosis and byssinosis, little research was done on either for many years. The lack of scientific data encouraged a confusion on the part of physicians about the identification, cause, and prevention of both diseases. Increasing incidences of respiratory problems in both coal miners and southern textile workers, however, which could have been caused by changes in the technology of work, fostered a growing concern about occupational health issues on the part of many workers and their advocates.

3

Cultures of Domination

In a recent work on the effects of a major flood on a small community in West Virginia, Kai T. Erikson suggests that the key to understanding modern Appalachia lies not in knowing who the original settlers were and what they did with their land, but in comprehending what has happened since at the hands of outsiders: "Whatever one knows about economic theory, wherever one stands on matters of political ideology, one still must conclude that the men and women of Appalachia are among the most truly exploited people to be found anywhere."[1] Historian C. Vann Woodward has expressed similar sentiments about the South in general and about its working class population in particular.[2] The historical lack of concern for the health of workers in Appalachia and in the South at large is both a function and an integral part of this exploitation.

Indeed, the development of the coal and textile industries in the late nineteenth and early twentieth centuries generated many parallel experiences for miners and millworkers, particularly in the environments in which they had to live, work, and die. Although comparative studies of the coal communities of central Appalachia (in West Virginia, southwestern Virginia, eastern Kentucky, and Tennessee) and the textile communities of the South (in North and South Carolina, Georgia, Virginia, and Alabama) have not been made, it has been suggested that both share similar subcultures and situations of domination.[3]

These two regions are linked together culturally by the traditional perception of them as backward, riddled with poverty, underdeveloped, and extremely resistant to change.[4] It is an image that has encouraged many reform programs based upon a "culture of poverty" approach: that is, one which identifies the internal deficiencies of the lower-class subculture as the major source of problems.[5] In the late 1960s, however, this image of Appalachia and the South came under attack. New perspectives began to focus attention on either the internal features of the economic systems or the relationship between the depressed area and the surrounding dominant society. Many students of Appalachia began to observe the relationship between economic imperialism abroad, racial oppression at home, and the plight of Appalachian people. Appalachia, particularly in the coal mining regions, was described as a subsociety structurally alienated and lacking resources as a result of the processes of the total economic and political system. Lately, similar ideas have begun to emerge about southern textile communities.[6]

THE COAL MINER

Before the development of coal mining, central Appalachia was a land of small farms in dispersed settlements that provided mere subsistence. The population was homogeneous and static, with an organization based on kinship patterns. The church was sectarian and informal. Trade operated on barter rather than money, and work proceeded in a "toot" pattern. People would work very hard for a time and then do something else to relieve tensions or regain equilibrium—that is, go on a "toot."[7]

Mountain people did not generally participate in either voluntary or formal organizations. They rejected formal organization in favor of personal behavior as a legitimate source of authority. Civic and social responsibilities were shunned because the family was the main form of organization. Mountain people placed emphasis on being and existence. Rather than being guided by long-range goals or commitments, they directed their concern toward immediate or specific goals. This resulted in "unplanned, spontaneous emotional actions rather than ordered, planned projects."[8]

Closely associated with this orientation was a sense of fatalism and a fundamentalist religious philosophy which defined the world in simple, concrete terms. Stability was cherished and change was rejected. Fatalism was especially functional in a situation where life had been harsh and difficult, and stability was all that could be hoped for. As sociologist Helen Lewis has noted:

One expects little success and, with little hope, optimism, or emphasis on achievement or getting ahead, failure is accepted and one is satisfied with just getting along. One is not competitive and does not try to out-do his neighbors. There is a logic to these values. They fit a restrictive environmental situation which the native settlers attempted to cope with. Man could not dominate the environment and hard work did not bring success, prosperity or jobs. In order to preserve his self image in the face of adversity, he retreated and quit trying and refused to accept obligations beyond those imposed by family and kinship.[9]

These values were maintained in Appalachia for so long because of its most significant characteristic: economic, geographic, political, and social isolation from the rest of the country. When the growth of the coal mining industry began to remove many of these barriers, the socio-political-economic structure was radically changed. Lewis and Edward Knipe document how these changes resulted in the colonization of the coal miner and the transformation of the Appalachian culture. Following the work of Robert Blauner, they look at four components of this process: the forced entry of the colonizers, the impact of culture and social organization, the relationship of domination, and the resulting social and psychological oppression of those considered inferior.[10]

Many outsiders and natives saw the coal industry as a positive step in the development of the natural resources of Appalachia and expected that the profit from mining would remain in the region. Some mountain people were attracted to the mines as a means of livelihood. Hillside farming produced only a meager, difficult existence; regular wages and mining camp houses were appealing.[11] But others were less enthusiastic, concerned about the danger of mining being forced on a backward community by outsiders: "They [the coal mines] are conducted not primarily in the community's interest but for the benefit of the exploiters. . . . The deadly sin is the thrusting of a ferocious and devouring system upon an unprepared and defenseless people."[12]

Welcome or not, coal mining produced many changes, the most obvious of which was a rapid increase in population. In the boomtown atmosphere, there were 300 to 400 percent population increases in many counties over the first thirty years. Mining camps sprang up near the mines and sometimes in mountains more isolated than the original farming settlements.[13] The fertile bottom land where the best farms had been was often the only suitable land for mine offices and houses. The former landowners either sold at a profit and retired or parted with their land and became laborers.

"Company towns" emerged, where the coal operator usually offered all community services, stores, and housing. These coal camps were never very stable, however. Mines opened and closed according to economic conditions, with people coming and going or shifting from one camp to another. Although the miners felt increasingly helpless about their economic circumstances, they learned to accept their work and the living arrangements as if they were inescapable.[14]

Coal mining benefitted from and helped to reinforce many mountain traditions. Fatalism and the lack of civic consciousness beyond the family facilitated the role of the paternalistic coal manager. Potential leadership in the coal communities was thwarted by maintenance of low standards for education and a resistance to paying any local school taxes.[15] Fatalism also fitted well with the dangerous work environment. Suspicion of outsiders, another mountain trait, was also encouraged by the coal companies, at least after the coal interests were well established in the mountains.[16]

The isolation of the coal mining and mountain settlements was maintained by building roads, railways, telephone lines, and later airway systems that would facilitate the removal of coal but limit transportation and communication for the average person. Unlike manufacturing concerns, mining does little to stimulate other types of economic activities. Since mining is immobile and limited in its one product and since the work is arduous and dangerous, the mining industry must develop a means of controlling labor. One way to do this is discourage the establishment of other, competing industries.[17]

The advent of coal mining, then, did not "open up" the mountains, nor did it move the mountain culture into the mainstream of modern society. According to sociologists Helen Lewis and Edward Knipe, it added social isolation to the already present physical isolation by creating three subcultures which were separate and segregated: the traditional subculture, or rural mountain people, a group formed by the earlier pattern of isolated residence and subsistence farming; the coal mining milieu, formed by the new economic structure and occupational ties; and the middle class town, surrounded by and segregated from coal mining and rural mountain communities and coordinated through activities in occupations, associations, and churches encouraged by the social system of coal mining.[18]

These three subcultures introduced distinctions of social class which were previously unknown to the mountain culture. They also served to reinforce and maintain a form of discrimination against the coal miner that had its roots in the traditional subculture. According to Jack Weller, the mountaineer had become an object of amusement and scorn, represented by the image of "a barefooted man in illfitting homemade clothes, with a jug over one shoulder and his rifle in his hand," who had an "affinity for 'corn in the bottle' which he makes illegally, [and who is characterized by his] shiftlessness and outmoded speech."[19] Lewis and Knipe suggest that this stereotypical image is maintained by natives who become "colonizers" of their own people because they must protect themselves with an even more disparaging evaluation of the people than outsiders make. The native exploiter, they state, "is more apt to denigrate his own, speak of laziness and 'sorriness' or a 'certain class' of people . . . [and] recount stories of the suspicion, untrustworthiness, and unreliability of their workers."[20]

The introduction of mining to the mountains of Appalachia, then, created many changes. For the mountain men who went into the mines, the loss of independence was perhaps most significant. Once in the mining camp, they had few choices. Company ownership of stores, homes, and services functioned as an effective form of control, increasing indebtedness and limiting autonomy in union or other activities. The strong family orientation was replaced by a peer group identification developed from living in a closed homogeneous community and working in a dangerous occupation. There was even an initial positive response to the paternalism of the coal camps and the mine operators. But the absentee ownership of the mines eventually strained this relationship, producing a "cynicism, hostility, and bitterness" that formed the foundation for one of the most violent and bitter struggles in labor history. Miners began to shift the old feelings for family to those with whom they now worked and lived, and those feelings became very "strong, intimate and enduring."[21]

The United Mine Workers of America

One of the oldest unions in the United States, the United Mine Workers of America had its beginning in 1890. But it was under the influence of John L. Lewis, who became President in 1920 and remained in that position until 1960, that many events occurred which laid the foundation for the emergence of an occupational health movement in the late 1960s.

Tom Bethel describes the coal business during this time as a "saga of hostility between management and labor," with almost a dozen years of uninterrupted warfare in the period from the late 1930s through the 1940s.[22] "Which side are you on?" was a serious question, as miners and their families were forced to side with either union or management. The years during and immediately after World War II were particularly eventful. Three times during the war, and a fourth in 1946, national strikes by the UMWA resulted in government seizure of the mines. After a 1947 mine explosion killed 111 men in Centralia, Illinois (while the government still controlled the mines), John L. Lewis declared a week of mourning, and mines shut down all over the country. At almost the same time, Congress passed the Taft-Hartley Act, which, among other things, gave the Justice Department the right to get a court order restraining any union from striking. Between 1947 and 1950, however, the miners were frequently out on strike, and the union, the coal operators, and the government were unable to alter the impasse.[23]

Finally, during a 1950 general strike, when a board of inquiry revealed that the country was down to a two-week supply of coal, public opinion, which had for forty years been extremely favorable to Lewis, suddenly reversed itself.[24] When President Harry S. Truman asked Congress for authority to seize the mines, Congress was glad to accommodate him. However, this action pushed both the union and the coal operators into a common defensive position.

Neither wanted the federal government to dictate to the industry, and they suddenly found it possible to negotiate a contract. On March 6, 1950, the Bituminous Coal Wage Agreement was signed. It was significant for two reasons: it marked the end of large-scale warfare between labor and management and it was the first industrywide contract in the history of coal mining.[25]

The true nature of this agreement was not revealed until several years later. In 1968, a federal grand jury in Lexington, Kentucky, rendered a verdict against the UMWA and the Consolidated Coal Company for conspiring since 1950 to create a monopoly of the soft coal industry, in direct violation of the Sherman Antitrust Act. For the eighteen years during which the agreement was in operation, there had been an intricate collaboration between the union and management.[26] With the agreement, Lewis had relinquished the one weapon that the miners had in their favor—the threat of a paralyzing national strike—by stating publicly that there would be no further crises in the coal industry. On the other hand, the agreement also recognized the United Mine Workers Welfare and Retirement Fund, financed by a royalty on each ton of coal, which made UMWA workers among the first in American industry to receive job pensions and free medical care. However, because this arrangement gave the union a vested interest in coal production, it raised the question whether the fund, coupled with the union's desire to see the industry healthy again, did not cause the UMWA's assistance to the major coal companies to go beyond cooperation to collusion.[27]

The decade of the 1950s brought about dramatic changes in the coal fields. Contracts between the union and coal companies were generally negotiated and signed without publicity. Lewis continued to negotiate for the union, but few knew the terms of the contracts until they were read aloud at union conventions.[28] He made the decision in the early 1950s that the UMWA should permit, and even help finance, the mechanization of the nation's mines.[29] The union recognized the serious economic depression of the coal industry at the time and the threat that this posed to its continued existence. Lewis subscribed to the philosophy that it was better to accept mechanization and have fewer coal miners working than to run the risk of the total elimination of coal mining in America.[30]

Economic benefits in the form of higher wages, medical care

benefits, job security, and pensions for those coal miners who continued to work were substantial.[31] The coal industry profited from higher production. As a result of mechanization, American coal miners produced, on the average, twenty tons per man per day, in contrast to three or fewer tons produced in European countries.[32] Mechanization also seemed to positively affect mining safety, with a significant reduction of both nonfatal accidents and fatalities.[33]

But there is another side to the mechanization story. In 1950, 415,000 men were employed in the coal mines; by 1969, less than 130,000 men were employed.[34] Although the coal industry survived, and the miners who continued working were paid well, the impact upon surrounding communities—unemployment, poverty, loss of revenue, and an almost complete dislocation from the mainstream of American growth—was devastating. Many former miners left the mountains, which is a story in itself.[35] In the decade between 1950 and 1960, the southern Appalachian region lost more than one million individuals through migration, and the following decade saw a similar pattern. But equally worthy of attention was the population left behind—high in disability and unemployment and low in literacy and industrial skills.[36] This population turned to welfare as a way of life and, according to Kai Erikson, developed a sharpened sensitivity to illness which was deeply rooted in the mountain experience:

Welfare provided an ethic, as it were, in which people could come to terms with their everyday troubles by retreating into sickness and making the most of their disabilities. On the one hand, men and women who organize their lives around the dole learn soon enough to offer palpable symptoms when they petition for relief. This makes them eligible for additional benefits and lends a suggestion of concreteness and dignity to what otherwise can be a degrading transaction.[37]

Erikson is quite emphatic, however, that this behavior is vastly different from simple malingering and must not be viewed as voluntary or deliberate:

People who view the world as out of whack and themselves as broken, fragmented, and torn loose from their moorings often use illness as a way to signal to themselves and to others what the nature of their discomfort is. The process is unconscious, hidden from the awareness of even the most perceptive persons, and the pains issuing awareness are every bit as sharp as wounds that leave more visible marks on the body. In a sense, illness and infirmity comes to serve as a recognizable name for the otherwise vague maladies that plague people, an identifying motif for lives that are otherwise empty of substance or hope. To be ill in some defined way . . . is often better than to be nothing at all. . . . To be compensated for injury or illness, then, quite aside from supplying a needed source of material support, legitimizes one's feelings of discomfort and apprehension.[38]

Active miners were little better served by the union than un-employed miners. One of the reasons that secret negotiations of contracts, mechanization and loss of jobs were allowed to continue without much resistance from the miners was Lewis's autocratic domination of the union.[39] Working miners contented themselves with the benefits of the union's Welfare and Retirement Fund and did not protest. However, in 1960, when Tom Kennedy replaced the retiring Lewis, the UMWA released its first annual public state-ment of income, expenditures, and assets, as required by the Lan-drum-Griffin Act of 1959, which was aimed at assuring the democratic operation of labor organizations. The contents not only made front page news but fueled a growing restiveness among the rank and file miners. It revealed staggering assets in both banks and coal com-panies, as well as millions paid out for defaulted loans to coal com-panies which the UMWA had guaranteed.[40]

This discontent was further encouraged in 1963 when Tony Boyle, who succeeded Kennedy after his death, was slow in opening ne-gotiations for a new contract. In the northern bituminous coal region, in Kentucky and Pennsylvania, rebel movements developed. When a contract was finally negotiated, the resulting dissatisfaction pro-duced a protest strike that marked the beginning of a dissident movement in the UMWA and the end of a comparatively long peace in the coal fields.[41]

One of the major issues of concern to the dissidents was the health and safety of coal miners. Boyle had sought no new legislation re-garding mine safety, and the union leadership had failed to apply pressure on the Bureau of Mines to enforce existing regulations. In 1968, 307 men were killed in soft coal mines, 94 more than in 1967, and another 9,000 were injured.[42] Although Lewis had fought hard for better mine safety and working conditions, Boyle essentially considered mine disasters as a normal part of business.

The membership who sought reform confronted a union administration that was uniquely resistant to change. The UMWA was composed of twenty-seven districts; in only six of these were the members allowed to elect their regional officers. Most of the officers of the other twenty-one districts were appointed from the national administrative office in Washington, D.C. This practice went back for years and was legal until the passage of the Landrum-Griffin Act, which required the election of officers in all regional union divisions. Although the law became effective in 1960, through the following decade the UMWA administration made no effort to change its practice of appointing most of the district officers.[43]

Boyle continued the legacy of authoritarianism inherited from John L. Lewis, but Boyle lacked Lewis's charismatic appeal. Consequently, he had to depend even more on the apparatus of his administration to maintain power and to protect himself from the dissident membership. By the late 1960s, he had been accused of bribery, misuse of funds, and collusion with coal operators. The machinery was effective at maintaining control, but a movement was emerging that would eventually tear it down.

THE MILLWORKER

For many southerners the beginning of the textile industry was a welcome venture in modern industrialization, particularly as it followed the defeat of the Civil War and the failure of Reconstruction, which left the South with little industry and farms that were only marginally surviving. Early historians portrayed the rise of the southern cotton mills at this time as an "epic folk movement."[44] According to one writer, many towns were willing to make almost any concession in order to obtain mills, and construction was initially financed by a wide variety of community residents.[45] In some places development of the industry took on the status of a religious movement, as expressed by a minister in South Carolina: "It is imperative that we think of Southern industry as a spiritual movement and of ourselves as instruments in a Divine plan."[46] The minister argued that the textile movement was an opportunity to build a democracy on the ethics of Christianity and as a measure of the power of Protestantism. It was pioneered by "men possessing the statesman-

ship of the prophets of God" and reflected "God's way for the development of a forsaken people."[47]

Historian Melton McLaurin suggests that while the folk movement interpretation holds some truth, it greatly underestimates the
complexity of economic factors that facilitated the development of
the industry, such as railway systems, the need for new outlets for
capital investment, the need to create a large white laboring class
as a safeguard against the large black population, credit extended
by machinery manufacturers, and the availability of cheap labor.[48]
Historian Paul D. Escott also points out that many who came to
work in the mills did so hesitantly, if not unwillingly. He argues
that the small farmer wanted to stay on the farm and to remain
independent. Like the farmer in Appalachia,

[he] cherished a way of life, not just an occupation, and the core of what
[he] valued was independence. Traditionally the yeoman farmer in North
Carolina had enjoyed a feeling of control over his personal life and a large
measure of economic and social safety because he provided for himself and
knew that he was beholden to no one.[49]

Even though their farms were failing, yeomen generally turned
to factory work out of necessity, not out of opportunity or gratitude
to the mill owner.[50] In the early stages of industrialization, the mills
grew so rapidly that an adequate supply of labor constituted a problem. Mill companies offered to move farmers, mountaineers, and
their possessions to the new mill villages. Many had already lost
their land because they were unable to pay taxes, and had become
tenant or crop farmers. The devastation of their lives and pressure
to work in the mills is graphically depicted by Tom Tippett:

They are bound down to a horrible poverty because they do not own their
land, and much of their labor goes to pay the absentee landlord. Between
the small farmer and his market stand the cotton and tobacco brokers. He
must sell to the middlemen, and he must sell at the price they set. In
addition, there are the boll-weevil, the drought and the floods, constantly
to haunt his peace of mind. Life could hardly be lived at a lower ebb than
that of the small farmers of the South. The large number of abandoned
farms that one sees all through the rural section testify to the farmer's steady
march into the mill villages. . . . Large corporations, such as timber and
electric companies, are buying up cheap land, and so are enterprising

realtors who look wisely to the future and put their fences up. As a result
the farmer is not only persuaded but actually compelled to go into the
factory. His bridges are burned behind him by forces outside his control.
He becomes a permanent factory hand.[51]

Not unlike the mountaineers in Appalachia, the southern farmers
found the appeal of wages, the company store, and the mill home
strong inducements:

The mill village with a house that boasted of three or four rooms, not to mention an electric lamp, appeared as a luxury to the young women who had
known nothing but crudely built cabins that often did not have windows or
floors. The mill village store opened up a new world to many country people
who had lived in a culture that knew only products made at home by hand.
The jingle of coins was a new sensation also to many of the men and women
who were brought up far from a money economy. It is not any wonder then
that they walked unsuspectingly and willingly into the factory system.[52]

Once established, the mill villages created their own culture. It
reflected a combination of the constraints of the structure of the
villages themselves as well as values, beliefs, and behaviors which
the millworkers brought with them from the farms and mountains.
In many respects, they were a homogeneous group not unlike their
employers. Individualism, nurtured by solitary life on small farms
and sparsely populated mountainsides, was a hallmark of this culture. It resulted in personal interactions with employers and only
sporadic collective labor action. Their previous experiences had made
them patient and accustomed to working from sunrise to sunset,
with little expectation of reward. They also took it for granted that
all members of the family would work as early as possible, and
therefore did not resist child labor in the mills.[53]

Rapid industrialization produced an influx of workers needing
housing and services, and management was the only source of capital
for construction. The result was the creation of mill villages isolated
from the rest of the community and generally under the complete
control of management. This also encouraged the formation of distinct social classes, not unlike those which evolved in Appalachia,
clearly separated in geographic, economic, and cultural terms: the
small farmers and tenant farmers who were basically dependent upon
agriculture for their livelihoods; the millworkers, who had severed

their ties with the farms and mountains; and the "uptown class," composed chiefly of mill owners and managers, professional and commercial groups, white collar workers, schoolteachers and independent skilled artisans.[54]

This separation into classes affected almost every aspect of the millworkers' lives. And while it is unlikely the villages were originally constructed as a means of control, once established they became very effective in shaping the millworkers' society. Company owned houses, churches, stores and schools not only further isolated millworkers from the rest of the community, but contributed to a relinquishing of control over their lives to the mill owner.

To minimize the cost of company-provided housing, mill owners required that families living in mill houses send more than one member to work in the mills.[55] This, coupled with the important positions of women and children in the mill economy, dramatically affected family structures. The census of 1880 showed that women comprised 49.4 percent of textile workers in the South, and children an additional 24.5 percent.[56] Two family patterns generally emerged in mill villages, both of which were the reverse of those prevailing in the semipatriarchal rural culture. In one, both parents worked in the mill and small children were left by themselves; poor supervision resulted in high rates of juvenile delinquency.[57] In the second pattern, the children became the major breadwinners. The mill system many times destroyed the father's role as an important economic force in the family. As family economic responsibilities were placed on the wife and children, a superfluous male population was created, and these men often became loafers, openly living off the wages of their families.[58] Interestingly, the concept of the "family wage" became part of the industry's argument that the total income of the mill family exceeded that of the farm family, thereby explaining the low wages paid individual mill operatives. Of course, the mill family had to purchase much of what the farm family could produce.

Company stores were perhaps the most blatant control mechanism. Unaccustomed to a cash economy but familiar with the poverty of farm life and the cultural pattern of immediate enjoyment of the fruits of one's labor, millworkers generally spent money unwisely and remained in constant debt. They were encouraged in this pattern by the company's practice of paying workers in scrip which could only be redeemed at the company store. Because many of the early firms faced serious shortages of operating funds, this arrangement provided an opportunity to operate with less cash and to drastically reduce the cash value of southern wages. When the operatives went into debt, the owners would simply deduct from the paychecks. This deprived the worker of financial independence and made him almost completely dependent on management for daily essentials. If union activity emerged, management simply closed the store and left the mill families with no cash and usually a good distance from the nearest town.[59]

Mill churches were also separate entities. Although the Lutheran and Episcopal denominations did not want to build mill churches separate from the community at large because of the potential divisive effect, many Baptist, Methodist, and other Protestant churches were glad to find new converts. The mill owners generally supported Methodist and Baptist churches, both politically and financially. However, sects such as the Pentacostal Holiness and Holy Rollers received no support and in some cases were prohibited from operating in mill communities.[60] Although most sects, like mainstream churches, were generally opposed to unions, there is some evidence that sects were supportive of strikes when they occurred.[61] In other ways, the control was less obvious, yet still effective. Given the low income of mill churches, a gift of a few hundred dollars from a mill owner could be a major influence on church policy, whether or not any conditions accompanied the gift.[62]

At the same time, the churches did provide a separate place for some independence and self-respect, a place where natural leaders from the village could emerge. Through these churches, millworkers had an opportunity for self-expression denied in the mill. The mill village church provided at least the potential for a structure from which social action could emerge.

Mill owners had a particular interest in churches and schools because they wanted a steadier, soberer, hardworking class of people with skills to compete with workers in northern mills.[63] Although there is little evidence of interference or control of the schools by mill executives, probably because most schools were part of the public school system and followed a prescribed curriculum, separate primary schools were established by mill owners for the children of millworkers. Although these children could go to high school with children from uptown families, comparatively few went and those who did so faced strong opposition. Also, many children went to work long before high school. The elimination of children from the mills did not occur until well into the twentieth century, when economic advantage reinforced considerations of moral and social welfare. The depression produced a surplus of labor, workers' compensation laws rendered the employment of children more hazardous on economic grounds, and the creation of a minimum wage made adult labor less costly.[64] Still, as late as 1939, one mill town recorded only 11 percent of millworkers with a high school diploma, compared with 14 percent of rural folk and 38 percent of the townspeople. Only 1 percent had any college training, compared with 9 percent of the rural population and 13 percent of the townspeople.[65]

Finally, the subjugation of the millworker was completed by the emergence of negative community attitudes. The suspicion and scorn with which the rest of southern society viewed the millhands resulted in what historian Melton McLaurin refers to as a "negative class consciousness."[66] The farmers looked down on the millhands because they had deserted the farm and degraded themselves by "working with [their] hands at the command of another." The townspeople labeled the millworkers "lintheads," "factory rats," and "cotton mill trash."[67] Textile workers resented this discrimination and generally withdrew into a further isolation that encouraged feelings of inferiority.

The mill village, then, was paternalistic, with management having much control over the conditions of work and the institutions in which workers lived. It created a class system that further isolated millworkers, encouraged discrimination, and left them with a distinctly negative self-image. All of this served the goals of management by producing a docile and obedient labor force with few alternatives for social change. But like the coal miners, the mill operatives did explore solutions to their problems through unionization. Unlike the coal miners, they were comparatively unsuccessful.

Labor Organizing in the Southern Textile Industry

According to Melton McLaurin, the historical failure of labor organizing in the southern textile industry can be attributed to one primary factor: management's power and adamant resistance.[68] Although the docility of southern millhands is frequently given as the major reason for the failure of unionization, recent research suggests that such tactics as the blacklist, the lockout, eviction proceedings, the use of racial fears, and a surplus pool of laborers enabled management to quell most union drives.[69]

John R. Earle et al. have added to this list the fact that textile operations were characteristically small production units, with ownership dispersed over many individuals, families and corporations. There was also the constant instability of the textile market, which threatened both investments and jobs. Equally important was the fact that much of the industry which immigrated from New England southward did so in flight from unions and continued to make great efforts to resist them.[70]

Nevertheless, there were attempts at unionization. When the Knights of Labor began organizing millworkers in the 1880s, management destroyed the movement quickly. But in the late 1920s and early 1930s, textile workers became involved in a series of strikes that shook the foundations of the southern textile industry and the communities of which they were a part, demonstrating that millworkers were neither docile nor content.[71] During this period management saw the union as a fundamental threat to the very social structure that had brought the mills into being, and the resulting confrontations produced significant bloodshed on both sides.[72] Interestingly, in all of the major strikes during this period, no non-unionists were sentenced for violence against union members, although union leaders or members were fined or jailed in every strike.[73] The violence, suspected and actual communist support for the unions, and the disruption of many communities left an image of unionization that remained strong in the minds of both mill owners and millworkers.

In 1939, the Textile Workers Union of America (TWUA) was formed as a member of the Congress of Industrial Organizations (CIO). By 1940, approximately one-fourth of the one million textile workers in the United States had joined. By the end of World War II, however, the percentage of southern textile workers in labor unions still stood at only 20 percent, compared with 70 percent for their northern colleagues.[74]

Two well publicized labor struggles in the 1950s served to reinforce the failure of unionization. The first occurred in Darlington,

South Carolina, where on September 6, 1956, workers at a Deering-Millikan mill voted for the TWUA by a narrow margin. Before the election, management had threatened to close the plant if the workers voted to unionize. By mid October, the mill was closed and the workers were laid off. It was not until twenty-five years later that the National Labor Relations Board awarded compensation to workers for the illegal closing of the plant.[75] The second event occurred at a Henderson Mills plant in Henderson, North Carolina. A large number of workers walked out on strike in November of 1958, but the company was able to bring in strikebreakers. The strike continued until June of 1961, when the union called it off without any concessions from the company. The cost to the union had been over one and a half million dollars. In both struggles, the human costs in jobs and the monetary setbacks to the union greatly influenced many future organizing activities.[76]

In 1963, the TWUA began an organizing drive in twenty-one plants of J.P. Stevens, the second-largest textile manufacturer in the nation. The TWUA was eventually successful in unionizing 3,400 workers in J.P. Stevens plants in Roanoke Rapids, North Carolina, by the early 1970s, but the company failed to bargain with the newly elected union. It was not until 1980, after an innovative, successful boycott of J.P. Stevens products organized by the new Amalgamated Clothing and Textile Workers Union of America (ACTWUA, which resulted from a merger of the TWUA with the Amalgamated Clothing Workers of America), that a contract was finally signed.[77]

It was anticipated by both union and company officials that this contract would have a domino effect on J.P. Stevens plants throughout the South, and perhaps on the whole textile industry. However, the union's job was made more difficult by sagging union assets, a recession, and job losses to foreign competition and automation. Rather than increasing, union membership dwindled, and continues a downward trend today.[78] But because the struggle at J.P. Stevens lasted so long and was portrayed sympathetically in the news media, the plight of labor in the Southern textile industry was brought to the attention of the American public. During this time, problems of occupational health were also exposed, encouraging many supporters to pursue this issue as an organizing strategy, both in the union and in organizations like the Brown Lung Association.

CONCLUSION

Coal miners in southern Appalachia and textile workers in the South shared many similar historical and cultural experiences. Both were swept from their subsistence farms into the mainstream of industrialization in the late nineteenth and early twentieth centuries. Both encountered similar forms of economic and cultural domination that structured the nature of their workplaces, their communities, and their lives. Coal miners were able to regain some control over their existence through a long, and sometimes violent, struggle for unionization. Millworkers, however, were never able to overcome the many barriers to unionization in the southern textile industry, although efforts to organize continue to this day.

Part **II**

THE BLACK LUNG
MOVEMENT

4

Awakening Miners: The West Virginia Black Lung Revolt

Mike Ritter had been a miner all of his life. He was fifty-three years of age in 1968 when the mine in which he had been working in West Virginia shut down. When a new mine opened, many of his friends were not called back to work because they could not pass the physical examination. Most of them went to sign up for Social Security disability. Mike was fortunate; he got a job. In the meantime, however, he had gone to Charleston, West Virginia, to file for silicosis benefits under the state workers' compensation law. He received 30 percent disability and an award of $5,200. His friends encouraged him not to settle for it, because they said the company would let him go. But Mike did not believe that the company would do that. "They been awfully good to me," he said.[1]

Because Mike Ritter was a poor man, the money looked big to him anyway. So he took the check and cashed it. The mine let him go, and Mike was without a job. When his friends went to the union for help, they found that the company and the union had an agreement. If a miner had over 11 percent disability and he filed for compensation, the company had a right to "cut him off." Without employment, Mike then went to the Social Security Administration to file for disability. They sent him a letter saying they could find nothing wrong with him. Joe Malay, one of the original organizers of the Black Lung Association, states that "he had done been awarded

5,200 dollars for silicosis, and then Social Security said they could find nothing the matter with him, he's still able to work, the company's cut him off, and the union says that they had an agreement that they could cut him off. That was what made us mad and got us into this black lung thing."[2]

Joe Malay and several other miners went to their union officials to see if something could be done about compensation for silicosis. Although they were unsuccessful, one official did mention the name of a physician who had been talking about the health and safety problems of miners in the state, Dr. Isadore Buff. Buff was a West Virginia cardiologist, born and raised in Charleston, the heart of the coal industry. He had become interested in lung problems a few years after the coal companies introduced the continuous mining machine. He had noticed a significant increase in the number of miners sent to him by company doctors with the diagnosis of heart failure, a noncompensable disease. Buff realized, however, that a miner's heart failure was often a result of massive fibrosis (development of excessive tissue) in the lungs, which made the circulation of oxygenated blood extremely difficult. As early as 1959, Dr. Buff had proposed a study of the relationship between the environment and lung disorders, but neither the Public Health Service nor the Federal Bureau of Mines responded positively.[3]

In the early 1960s, Dr. Buff began a crusade to educate the mining communities about the problem. Buff was especially interested in getting into the high schools where the coal industry, funded with a $5 million grant from the federal government, had a program to recruit replacements for the coal miners who were being disabled. According to Buff, industry pressure prevented his entrance.[4]

In 1967, Dr. Buff was appointed to the West Virginia Air Pollution Control Commission, and that position gave him considerable access to the press, a vehicle which he used extensively in his struggle for social change.[5] But even the newspaper did not provide him a direct route to the miners. As one Appalachian observer has noted, "only the ubiquitous television set and, to a lesser extent, the *UMW Journal*, succeeded by penetrating these remote mountain hollows and tiny valley towns to bring in an awareness of life beyond the hills."[6] The primary means of passing news among Appalachian folk was word of mouth. While they may have read about an incident in the paper, they really didn't believe it until they got it firsthand from someone else.[7]

After four miners drowned in 1968 in a flooded mine in Hominy Falls, West Virginia, Joe Malay and several other miners asked Buff to speak about health and safety at a meeting in Clifftop, West Virginia. Approximately 100 miners listened as Dr. Buff discussed black lung and the need for miners to demand compensation and safer working conditions. Out of this meeting emerged an initial strategy to work through the legislature and the governor of the state, but little support was found.[8]

Another physician also working at this time to increase awareness about the pulmonary problems of coal miners was Dr. Donald Rasmussen, a pathologist from Beckley, West Virginia. In 1964, the U.S. Public Health Service had funded Rasmussen and his associates in their research on coal worker's pneumoconiosis. In 1966, however, this project was moved to the state university medical center at Morgantown and put under the direction of Dr. Keith Morgan, a British researcher. Here work did not proceed with the urgency it had under Rasmussen. After two years, and an expenditure of two million dollars in public funds, the Morgantown team had examined fewer than 100 miners.[9] Although Morgan publicly challenged the results of Rasmussen's research, Rasmussen and miner Earl Stafford, who was an early leader in the black lung revolt, made several trips to Washington, D.C., to testify in congressional hearings about health and safety. Urged to get a state compensation law passed first, they returned to West Virginia to help disseminate information about black lung.[10]

A third physician to become involved in the struggle was Dr. Hawley Wells, a pathologist who had worked with Rasmussen from 1964 to 1966. He then became director of the chest laboratory at a hospital in Johnstown, Pennsylvania, and also taught at the medical school of the University of West Virginia in nearby Morgantown. Wells is given credit with first interesting Ralph Nader in the problem of pneumoconiosis. Although Nader did not come to West Virginia, his effect at the national level was dramatic. *The New Republic* carried Nader's scathing article on black lung in February of 1968, which was followed by a continuing confrontation with the Bureau of Mines over its failure to recognize the problem of pneumoconiosis.[11]

Buff, Rasmussen, and Wells were important to the early stages of the black lung revolt because they disseminated needed information about the problems of occupational health to state officials, federal officials, and to the public. Their work intensified when they formed a team in late 1968, brought together by a major mining disaster which provided the major catalyst for the emergence of the movement.

THE FARMINGTON DISASTER

Social reforms in the health and safety of coal mining have almost predictably followed the occurrence of major mine disasters. It is an old adage that "dead miners have always been the most powerful influence in securing the passage of mining legislation."[12] History seems to bear this out. In 1910, after explosions during the three previous years had killed a total of 1,013 men, the U.S. Bureau of Mines was established. A year after a 1940 explosion killed ninety-two men in West Virginia, Congress passed legislation that allowed Federal Bureau of Mines inspectors to actually enter and inspect the mines. The Federal Coal Mine Health and Safety Act of 1952 was passed a year after 119 coal miners were killed in an explosion at a mine in Illinois.[13]

At about 5:15 A.M. on November 20, 1968, in Farmington, West Virginia, a coal mine explosion occurred at the Mountaineer No. 9 mine of the Consolidated Coal Company. Ninety-nine men were underground on the midnight to 8:00 A.M. shift; twenty-one escaped but seventy-eight miners were trapped and eventually declared dead as the mine was sealed on November 30, 1968.[14] It was not unlike previous mine tragedies—"the initial explosion, the long vigil by the miners' families, the final abandon of hope, had all occurred before and would occur again".[15] But the disaster was different in that it captured the nation's attention through the medium of television for over a week during Thanksgiving holidays as the search for survivors continued.

In the month following the disaster, a conference on mine safety called by the U.S. Department of the Interior provided an opportunity for Drs. Buff, Rasmussen, and Wells to meet and discuss their work. They formed the Physicians' Committee for Mine Health and Safety, and began touring West Virginia to speak at rallies organized by concerned miners. The three physicians were an effective combination, explaining the causes and consequences of black lung and denouncing the industry, the union, and the government for allowing the disease to develop.

Dr. Buff would generally attack the coal industry, the inaction and corruption of the UMWA leadership, and talk about the horrors of black lung itself. Although his medical facts were questionable, he generally aroused the emotions of the miners with comments like the following:

You can't cure the black lung, but you can prevent it. You're being killed off. You're dying like cattle. Tell me, you there, brother, how much longer do you think you are going to live? You got the black lung. You can't walk ten steps without resting. You can't breathe. You spit up black juice. You're dying and the killing will go on until you tell them to grant you compensation and clean up the mines or there won't be any coal coming out of West Virginia.[16]

Rasmussen's talks were generally less oratorical and more factual presentations of the disease itself. His expertise legitimized the group and its activities. Wells usually concluded the meetings with a call for political action:

The law as it reads now protects nobody but the coal operator.... If you want the law to do something for you, for the coal industry, and for the future of your children, go to the lawmakers and get something done. If you don't you are sick in the head.[17]

THE WEST VIRGINIA BLACK LUNG ASSOCIATION

The efforts of the miners and the Physicians' Committee culminated in early January 1969 with the formation of the West Virginia Black Lung Association. Because the rank and file miners were concerned about a charge of "dual-unionism" (joining an organization considered dual to the UMWA could result in loss of union membership, employment, pension, and hospital benefits) the activities of the BLA were limited to raising money to hire a lawyer to draft a strong black lung compensation bill.[18] Charles Brooks, a black President of a union local, was the first President of the association.

In addition to raising $10,000 for the lawyer, the BLA continued to work with the Physicians' Committee to arrange meetings throughout January to spread the word. The West Virginia Black Lung Association was officially introduced at a rally in Beckley, West Virginia, on January 19. On January 29, the new association held its first statewide rally in Charleston, West Virginia, which was attended by 3,000 to 5,000 miners.[19]

The ninety-minute rally opened with a song written by James Wyatt of Mammoth, West Virginia, appropriately titled "Black Lung":[20]

> A young miner's lungs may be hearty and pale
> When he enters the coal mines, with his dinner pail
> But coal dust and grime
> In a few years of time
> Fills up his lungs and they begin to fail
> Black lungs, full of coal dust
> Coal miners must breathe it or bust
> Black lungs, gasping for breath
> With black lungs we are choking to death.

The audience was mostly made up of miners, and miners' wives and widows, wearing hard hats with "78-4" imprinted on them in memory of the seventy-eight miners who died at Farmington and the four who died at Hominy Falls. Besides the three doctors of the Physicians' Committee, two other noted people made speeches that attracted media attention: Paul Kaufman, a former State Senator who had unsuccessfully competed for the Democratic gubernatorial nomination in 1968, and U.S. Congressman Ken Hechler, Democrat from West Virginia, who had been an early and strong advocate of mine safety legislation.

Both of these speakers played important roles in formulating an emerging ideology about black lung. Kaufman argued that since doctors could not agree on what black lung looked like, they should presume that a miner has it if he has worked two years or more in the mines and contracted the disease.[21] Representative Hechler read a letter from Ralph Nader which suggested a more radical approach, giving even more authority to the miners themselves:

Your gathering here makes it clear to the coal mine operators and those groups and individuals that do their bidding that no longer are you going to tolerate a situation that makes coal miners cheaper than coal. . . . You are not going to tolerate puppet-like physicians, employed by the coal operators, disgracing their profession by saying black lung is not all that bad and miners can learn to live with it. From now on, the coal miners— whose bodies are being abused and whose lungs are being destroyed—are going to be the ones who say how bad black lung is.[22]

After reading the letter, Hechler also attacked the medical profession, particularly the West Virginia Medical Association, which had previously assailed the Physicians' Committee for questionable practice. He displayed a sign which read, "Black Lung Is Good for You," indicating that it was a secret message from the West Virginia Medical Association. Then, theatrical as usual, he pulled out a twelve-pound slab of bologna and said to the miners, "That is baloney," and the miners cheered.[23]

Officials of the United Mine Workers of America did not attend the rally but later denounced it and its leaders as a "self-appointed group" that was dual to the UMWA. Union President Tony Boyle referred to Nader and Hechler as "instant experts" and "publicity seeking, self-appointed saviors" with devious motives.[24] Instead of supporting the black lung cause, he and the leadership of the union urged the passage of a UMWA sponsored bill much weaker than what the miners wanted. When BLA representatives tried to convince the union to strengthen the bill with the provisions outlined at the January 29 rally, the UMWA told them that it was politically impossible and they would not fight for it. Historian George Hopkins suggests that from then on every major decision or action taken by the UMWA representatives only sparked further revolt.[25]

In February of 1969, a total of nine black lung bills were introduced into the West Virginia legislature. Medical disagreement about the nature of coal workers' pneumoconiosis was evident during the first hearing. As one observer commented, "It was hard to tell that different doctors were talking about the same disease."[26] Although the initial hearing was considered a victory for the coal miners, primarily because most of the witnesses favored some legislation, a week afterwards there was still no bill. Coal miners expected quick action, but the West Virginia legislature was not set up to respond so rapidly. Like most state legislatures, it was composed of part-time Congressmen and Senators. In 1969, the salary was only $1,500.

There was a great deal of turnover in legislators. Therefore, West Virginia never had strong, ongoing committee staffs that functioned on a year-round basis. In addition, because it was not until 1965 that full-time research, reference, bill-drafting, and statutory revision staff were made available, standing committees had to rehire every year what staff were needed.[27]

When a wildcat strike broke out over a job dispute near Beckley, West Virginia, on February 18, 1969, many miners on strike reported that their action was a response to the coal-industry-dominated legislature's delay in passing a black lung compensation bill.[28] Although the BLA did not initiate the strike, it was not unsupportive. Ken Hechler and Paul Kaufman, however, feared the strike was premature and initially opposed it. The momentum grew, however, and by the weekend, 30,000 miners were off their jobs.[29]

To add pressure, the West Virginia BLA staged a second rally on February 26 at the Charleston Civic Center, followed by a mass march of some 2,000 miners on the statehouse with signs reading, "No Law, No Coal,"[30] producing a sight that few, if any, legislators had ever seen before.[31] A reporter for the *West Virginia Hillbilly* described the impact of this strategy:

The panorama was something to behold as the group neared the capitol. The gold dome shone brightly as . . . a thousand hardhats turned toward the majestic edifice. . . . They spread at least fifty abreast as they stormed the statehouse steps in a slow motion pace. A human wall of flesh flattened out against the wall of the capitol at the top of the long flight of stairs that faced Kanawha Boulevard.[32]

Once inside the capitol, the miners spread out into the House and Senate, confronting the legislators. On that day, the House Judiciary Committee reported to the floor of the House of Delegates a bill that satisfied neither the coal industry or the miners. Stephen Young, Vice President of the West Virginia Coal Association, exclaimed that the bill was not workers' compensation but social legislation: "What started out to be a bill to compensate miners for black lung has, in fact, become a signed blank check for the miners to be compensated by the industry on or before retirement, not just for pneumoconiosis, but for every other conceivable respiratory ailment."[33] The leaders of the BLA saw the bill as doing justice only to the West Virginia Coal Association. The problem, according to the BLA, was the fact that the bill did not stress the use of tests other than the x-ray for diagnosis. The position of the coal companies, and the majority of testimony, reflected the opinion that while x-rays were inexact, they were the best tool available in diagnosing lung ailments.[34] Two days later, however, the House passed, 95–0, a bill that included most of what the miners wanted.

Amidst charges of galloping socialism and allegations of pressure on the legislature, the House version went to the Senate. On March 5, the Senate passed its own version, which included the x-ray as the sole diagnostic evidence and also a rewritten presumption clause. Differences were to be worked out in a conference committee, but little progress was made until the very last day of the legislative session. Threatened by over 40,000 miners still on strike and the possibility of an additional special session, the legislators reached a compromise only nine minutes before a mandatory end of the annual session. The new black lung act permitted clinical tests as well as x-rays as evidence of disability and also included a presumption clause allowing those with respiratory illness after at least ten years' exposure to coal dust to qualify for compensation. It was a major victory for the black lung revolt. Of course, the striking miners stayed off their jobs until Governor Archie Moore signed the act on March 11, 1969.[35]

5

The Revival of the Black Lung Association

The passage of a new compensation bill was a major success for the miners of the West Virginia Black Lung Association. Because the leadership of the United Mine Workers of America resisted their efforts, however, much of the energy of the leading participants of the black lung revolt was now transferred to a reform movement within the union. This is a story in and of itself and has been analyzed in several sources.[1] But many miners and their supporters also testified in hearings on mine safety and health convened by the Ninety-First Congress in 1969.

Both the Farmington disaster in November 1968 and the black lung revolt which followed have been credited with significant influence on the determination to pass strong legislation in Congress. As one reporter observed, "The message in that spontaneous rebellion . . . has not been lost on Washington."[2] The coal industry was also supportive of change in the safety laws, or at least resigned to the passage of some legislation. Oil companies, sensitive of their public image, had purchased many of the coal companies in Appalachia. They apparently weighed the cost of safety reforms against the possible losses from a rash of wildcat strikes by safety-conscious miners.[3]

The significance of black lung was evident in much of the early testimony at the congressional hearings. However, the thrust of reform discussion centered around the reduction of levels of coal dust to prevent future miners from contracting the disease. Although Dr. Isadore Buff made a strong appeal for a federal compensation program in March, it was not until September 1969 that an official amendment was introduced to establish federal responsibility for what was to be called "the Black Lung Benefits Program."

The eventual passage of this part of the legislation was facilitated by a number of factors. First, several political struggles and accommodations placed elected officials representing coal mining districts, or sympathetic to the miners' interests, in key positions of power in both the Senate and House.[4] Second, the proponents of a black lung benefits program established a successful argument based upon a philosophy of failure and suffering. According to Robert McGillicuddy, a staff member of the House Subcommittee on Labor Standards, there was the failure of the public health services and the medical profession to recognize the disease earlier. Thus, there was failure on the part of states to amend their workers' compensation laws to provide a working environment free from unhealthy levels of coal dust. There had also been massive suffering from a disease that the Surgeon General had estimated afflicted over 100,000 miners.[5]

Although both the states and the corporations were blamed for part of the failure and suffering, it was the feeling of the Committee on Education and Labor, which introduced the legislation, that the federal government was primarily responsible. The substantial reduction of miners employed in the mines following the introduction of the continuous mining machine had caused a dispersal of men throughout the country. These men took with them an irreversible disease, but were denied benefits because of their locations. The committee recognized that states which are not coal-producing had no desire to assume responsibility for residents who had contracted the ailment mining coal in another state. They also recognized the problems inherent in requiring employers to assume the cost of compensating individuals for occupational diseases contracted in years past.[6]

It was also argued that the federal government's failure to take cognizance of black lung, especially when it was recognized by Great Britain in the 1940s, precluded any attempts by private enterprise to control the coal dust and caused states to neglect the problem when it was in its inception. Although the cost of prevention could have been borne economically at that time by the state governments or private enterprise, this was no longer considered feasible, or perhaps constitutional.[7] Further national responsibility was suggested by the argument that the coal produced by the victims of black lung was sold throughout the United States at prices lower than it could have been if compensation costs had been paid at the time that the disability was incurred.[8]

Finally, the passage of the black lung benefits part of the act was influenced by the presence of the miners themselves. Right after the Farmington disaster, Senator Jennings Randolph from West Virginia suggested that it would be appropriate to hear from those who had actually worked in the mines in the deliberations on coal mine health and safety. Although worker testimony in congressional hearings was not unusual, the miners' testimony on an occupational disease set a precedent for workers in many industries in the coming decade. According to one observer, the emotionally effective recitation of black lung case histories had its impact, even on the most conservative legislators.[9]

The rank and file miner was also represented in these hearings by the leadership and staff of the United Mine Workers of America. However, the response of the UMWA leadership to the problem of coal worker's pneumoconiosis was influenced by the fact that the black lung revolt was, at least in part, a reform movement within the union. The leaders of the revolt requested early in the struggle that the President of the UMWA, Tony Boyle, come to West Virginia to lead their fight for a change in compensation laws.[10] Although the UMWA leaders had proclaimed their intention to fight for a new compensation law, they were also wary of upsetting their long alliance with the coal operators. At the same time, the election of UMWA officers was only a year off, and there was growing discontent and activism on the part of rank and file miners.

Consequently, Boyle staged a series of attacks on those "outsiders" he considered responsible for the revolt: Congressman Hechler, Dr. Rasmussen, and Ralph Nader. During the congressional hearings, he continued to level charges against them:

Where were these so called experts whom we now find running to the TV, radio and newspaper with old information [when I needed them] . . . these overnight experts in mine safety who have never seen a coal mine, never worked a day in a coal mine, never been around a coal mine, [who] have all the answers to coal mine safety now. . . . We find . . . men who have been suffering for 20 and 30 years with black lung, who are not now employed in the coal mines, who have been agitated by others, by outsiders, so to speak, to lead a fight against the union. . . . Am I responsible for it . . . because they got black lung?[11]

Boyle's attacks were made in retaliation to charges by Hechler, Rasmussen, and Nader that much of the failure to protect the miners was due to inaction on the part of the then current union leadership.

These charges against the UMWA were not unfounded. Although the then Assistant Director of Occupational Health for the UMWA, Dr. Lorin Kerr, was an early advocate for the prevention of the dust diseases and a strong supporter for the recognition of black lung, his efforts were generally not recognized or acted upon by the union administration. At the 1968 UMWA convention, Dr. Kerr presented to the delegates specific information about pneumoconiosis, how it differed from silicosis, and why it should be considered a compensable disease. The result was a resolution calling for a massive lobbying effort in every coal state to have black lung included under workers' compensation.[12] Even the *United Mine Workers Journal* reported that the resolution started an all-out drive to bring about a solution to the dust problems in the mines. A strike in October 1968, during the negotiations between the UMWA and the Bituminous Coal Operators Association (BOAC), was made primarily to push for some protection against the disease.[13] However, the negotiated contract made no specific mention of coal-dust–related disease, but merely called for each operator to provide protection and coverage under existing compensation laws.[14] During the congressional hearings, the UMWA continued to show a concern for safety at the expense of health issues by supporting separate bills, apparently for fear that the more controversial health questions would delay passage of safety legislation.[15]

The final bill, the Federal Coal Mine Health and Safety Act of 1969, which included both health and safety components, was passed by the house on December 17 and the Senate on December 18, 1969. Although President Nixon considered vetoing the legislation because of objections to the black lung benefits provision on fiscal

grounds, an unauthorized walkout of West Virginia miners is credited with forcing his signature on December 30, 1969.[16]

THE BLACK LUNG BENEFITS PROGRAM

The purpose of the Black Lung Benefits Program, or Title IV of
the legislation, was to provide benefits to coal miners who were
totally disabled by pneumoconiosis and to the surviving dependents
of miners who died as a result of the disease. It was also to insure
that in the future adequate benefits would be provided to coal miners
and their dependents in the event of their deaths or total disability
due to pneumoconiosis. The Secretary of Health, Education, and
Welfare (HEW) was given the power to determine standards for
total disability, guided only by the presumption that pneumoconiosis
was caused by employment in coal mines if the miner had worked
in underground mines for ten years or more.[17]

The program was initially located in the Social Security Administration (SSA). All claims filed before December 31, 1972, were to
be processed by the SSA and after that by the Department of Labor.
Those successful claimants who filed as of December 31, 1971, would
have their claims paid by the federal government; those who filed
during 1972 would receive government support up to January 1973,
whereupon the burden would then shift to the states and the industry.

Although the Social Security Administration, a branch of HEW,
was a likely choice for the program, Arthur Hess, then Deputy
Commissioner of the SSA, argues that it was poorly prepared to
handle the task efficiently:

Even with the experience we [have] had and the responsiveness that has
been built into the organization, the new responsibilities we were assigned
with the passage of the Federal Coal Mine Health and Safety Act of 1969
represent a major challenge to our capacity and resources. We have never
received a major job to do on such short notice or with so little additional
personnel to do the job. . . . Until the very closing days of the last session
of Congress, we had absolutely no idea that we would be involved in carrying
out some of the provisions of this landmark piece of coal mine legislation.[18]

Although the SSA had carried out more massive programs, such as
the Social Security disability insurance program in the 1950s and

the Medicare program in the 1960s, Hess points out that they had some advantages in getting these programs underway that they did not have under the Federal Coal Mine Health and Safety Act: considerable advance notice, close participation in planning and drafting of legislation, ability to initiate planning for administration of the program, time after enactment to develop a basic body of policies, procedures, and other administrative mechanisms, as well as the opportunity to organize and secure necessary staff.[19]

The SSA had only a few weeks to establish the criteria for determining disability, to develop policies and procedures for administering the program, to inform potentially eligible miners and widows about the program and to advise them to file applications immediately to avoid possible loss of benefits. The last task may have been unnecessary, for within one week of the legislation, 18,000 claims for black lung benefits had been filed. An additional 82,000 claims were filed by the end of the first month. By the end of December 1970, one year after the law was passed, the number of claims was approximately 247,000, and almost 350,000 had been filed by the end of 1971.[20]

As might be expected, an initial problem was the length of time it took to process claims. By the end of September 1970, SSA had completed only about one-half of the approximately 100,000 claims filed in the first month of the program. According to SSA officials, delays were caused by the sheer volume of claims and a lack of medical criteria for determining when miners were totally disabled or when their deaths could be attributed to the disease. In addition, limited medical resources, particularly in the central Appalachian area, meant that medical examination of claimants proceeded slowly.[21]

The initial claims processed showed high approval rates. By September 1970, of the over 200,000 claims which had been filed, 43,000 had been processed and 40,000 of these, almost 90 percent, were approved. This created high expectations in the mining communities.[22] SSA officials later acknowledged that many claimants who did not have black lung were found eligible and were awarded benefits. They argued that an "interim" set of criteria was necessary to carry out the directives of Congress.[23]

The most glaring inconsistency in the Black Lung Benefits Program, however, was the difference in processing and approval rates between the major coal mining states. As of November 6, 1970, only 22 percent of the claims from eastern Kentucky and only 24 percent from West Virginia had been processed, while the national average was almost double, at 43 percent. At the same time, while only 20 percent of the claims in the rest of the nation had been denied, in West Virginia miners were being denied at the rate of 32 percent and in Kentucky at the rate of 57 percent.[24] Even as late as December 31, 1971, the approval rate for Kentucky was only 32 percent and for West Virginia 45 percent, but for Pennsylvania it was almost 68 percent.[25]

According to a government report issued later, there were several reasons for these differences. First, more Pennsylvania miners were employed in anthracite coal mines, which assumedly produced more coal worker's pneumoconiosis. Second, miners as a group were older in Pennsylvania, and certain criteria used by the SSA for determining eligibility allowed a level of lung function that was nearer to normal with advances in age. Third, miners in Pennsylvania also had more mining experience and presumably had more exposure to dust. Finally, Pennsylvania already had a compensation program for coal worker's pneumoconiosis, and miners who filed for federal benefits from that state had extensive medical records available to document their cases.[26]

This information was not available, however, to retired and disabled miners in West Virginia and Kentucky. They could not understand the inconsistencies in the administration of the program, and they were aware, in their own communities, of many people getting benefits who were not eligible.[27] An early issue of the *Black Lung Bulletin* recognized the frustration of the mining population: "Coal miners are worried. The Social Security Administration regulations are a mass of confusion and some men are finding themselves tied up in just the kind of bureaucratic red tape that Congress tried to avoid when the law was passed."[28] The sentiments of many miners were expressed by miner Ray Hubbard at an early organizing meeting in Kentucky: "I thought that the Congress had passed a good black lung law. After the Social Security got aholt of it, I figger they're the ones messed it up."[29]

Although the local Social Security offices were the places where the miners filed their claims for benefits, government workers there merely collected the necessary information from available sources and forwarded this information to the Bureau of Disability Insurance in Baltimore, Maryland, where the final status of the claim was decided. The local offices, however, were the focus of frustration because they were the primary point of contact between the miners and the system. It was here that miners went through the laborious process of completing multiple forms to apply for benefits, and it was here that the denied claimants received explanations for the decisions.[30]

THE REVIVAL OF THE BLACK LUNG ASSOCIATION

The first denials of claims by the Social Security Administration occurred in the summer of 1970. By 1971, fourteen chapters of the Black Lung Association had been established in West Virginia, Kentucky, Virginia, and Tennessee. Most of these chapters were established by a representative from the West Virginia chapter who made contact with miners who had been turned down for benefits.

The original West Virginia Black Lung Association had never developed a strong organization. It consisted only of a few officers selected when the association was formed, and served primarily as a vehicle to draft a black lung bill.[31] Brit Hume indicated it was a movement in every sense of the word: "The Black Lung Association had no members, except its officers. Instead, it had adherents and contributors who went about their chores on an ad-hoc basis. The meetings never had an agenda."[32] The rapid growth of chapters in 1970 created many problems of coordination. The association was loosely held together by a group referred to as the Charleston Office Crew, named after its location in Charleston, West Virginia. It was created by staff members of a federal antipoverty community action agency called Designs for Rural Action (DRA). DRA, formed in 1969 by former Appalachian Volunteers, was responsible for supporting community-related projects to assist people in Appalachia. Arnold Miller, a retired miner, served as a liaison between the miners in the BLA and the DRA.[33] Miller became President of the Charleston Black Lung Association Chapter when the original President, Charles Brooks, had to resign because of his health.[34]

The Charleston Office Crew attempted to tie together all of the activities of the BLA by assisting in coordination and communication between the chapters. It also published the *Black Lung Bulletin*,

sent out newsletters, released press statements, and arranged association meetings. Its function was ideally to help the chapters
accomplish what they wanted to see done. As one communication
stated, "It is not the headquarters of the BLA or the place where
the organization's decisions are made. As we see it, that right and
responsibility belongs to the chapters, meeting together as a body."[35]

It is difficult to determine how successful the Charleston Office
Crew were in meeting their goal. The staff were aware of the problem of a concentration of power in their office and were concerned
that what was done "in the name of the Black Lung Association
[was] always in accordance with policies set by the members."[36] On
the local level, each chapter retained autonomy, and pretty much
went about its activities in its own way. This meant that many
decisions on the state and regional levels were made by the staff
supporters, rather than by the chapters, and much confusion resulted:

The Charleston Office functions as a service for the overall BLA—but in
many ways there is no overall structure of the organization to set guidelines
for our activities, to decide on policies we can then help implement. This
confusion, which arises frequently, gives rise to misunderstandings, sometimes jealousies, and in general leads to a lot of wheel spinning and time
wasting.[37]

The problems in the Black Lung Association were not atypical of
many grassroots movements of the 1960s and 1970s. Government
policies during this period established programs that provided both
financial and personnel support for many social change efforts.[38]
Thus, a number of young, educated activists were able to contribute
their time and expertise to movement organizations like the Black
Lung Association.[39] Although their contributions were important,
their presence could create problems. Of no small significance were
cultural differences between miners and nonminers, for example in
education, which may have been a source of strain. According to
one writer on Appalachia, people there see the attainment of education as reflecting a feeling that one is better than the rest. The
mountain child's socialization "trains its members to be sensitive to
people rather than to ideas. Words are used not to express ideas
but to impress people."[40] Disabled coal miner Arnold Miller, an
early supporter of the black lung revolt, and onetime President of
the UMWA, seemed aware of the implication of this difference:

Coal miners and people in Appalachia don't want you to do something for them. They want you to help them help theirself. And all they need is a nudge in the right direction. But it was very important for them to learn to accept that the skill that was necessary and the educational background was seriously lacking in Appalachian regions. They had to learn to accept people coming from other regions of the country because of their moral concern and decency for people and wanting to help.[41]

The impact of those who came from other regions, particularly the Appalachian Volunteers, and the organizations they spawned are aptly described in David Whisnant's *Modernizing the Mountaineer*. Although he speaks of many positive benefits of these efforts, he concludes that there was little lasting positive effect on the Appalachian region. The Appalachian Volunteers not only responded to the mountain people with a paternalistic attitude, but they maintained a "macho spirit of competition" that prevented the volunteers from encouraging leadership among the local people.[42]

Although the outsiders involved in the Black Lung Association probably were paternalistic, it is important to remember that other factors contributed to an increase in power and decision-making by nonminers in the movement. The retired and disabled mining population of the BLA were frequently unable, because of their illness, to carry out many of the tasks required of an effective movement organization. In addition, mortality rates were high and this affected continuity within the association. One of the most serious problems faced by the BLA was that of keeping a few members healthy and alive long enough to provide leadership.

Goals, Ideology, and Organization

The major goals of the Black Lung Association (with the exception of union reform) were to make coal mining a safe and healthy occupation and to provide benefits to those miners disabled by work.[43] Although historically coal miners had confronted industry directly in their struggles, particularly those for better wages and benefits, from the beginning this movement sought intervention from the government. With regard to compensation for work-related illnesses, the role of the government had been established in the early part of this century. But other factors, relating to perceptions of coal mining as an occupation, may have been equally important.

A 1973 study revealed that coal miners generally see their work as the most difficult and the most dangerous of all occupations. Not only were the miners in this study convinced that they worked harder than people in other occupations, but 94 percent of the respondents were convinced that the mines were more dangerous than the general public thought. Seventy-one percent of the miners said they had the worst job in the United States, and almost 63 percent said they would leave mining if they had the chance. With regard to black lung, only 34 percent of the miners agreed that most coal companies were concerned with keeping dust levels in the mines low. Also, the agencies which were responsible for regulating the dust levels were not seen as concerned. Of most significance, though, was the finding that only 11 percent of the miners agreed that people in Washington were really concerned about the miner and that 96 percent said that government should do more for the miner.[44]

The study also indicated that miners were skeptical of the agencies with which they came into contact when applying for black lung benefits, workers' compensation, or Social Security disability. They maintained a defensive stance and an attitude that they would have to fight for whatever benefits they received. They also seemed unaware of the underlying mechanics of the various agencies with which they came into contact. As the study concluded, "There appears to be a need, not only for a better understanding of the miners by the agencies, but also a better understanding of the agencies by the miners."[45]

It was this better understanding of government agencies, particularly the Social Security Administration, that the Black Lung Association gave to the mining community. In an early issue of the *Black Lung Bulletin*, a complex picture of a bureaucratic structure is presented:

In 1969, Congress gave Social Security the responsibility to administer the Federal Black Lung Program. We would like to presume that the intentions of the SSA bureaucrats were to administer fairly a federal law; however, its actions have led to other results. . . . Study of the administration of the Black Lung Program reveals a failure on the part of the SSA. The regulations passed by the SSA on their administration of the poor have frustrated

Congress's intentions and rendered benefits unnecessarily difficult for deserving people to attain. . . .

Why has this happened? In part, this is because the SSA is the largest Federal "antipoverty" organization in the country. In order to get their work done the bureaucrats running the program divide up work into small parts—for efficiency. Decisions are made on bureaucratic convenience rather than on serving human needs. For efficiency's sake workers in the SSA operate almost like machines. A decision is made, a button is pushed, and the workers do what they are told—losing the ability to understand the people with whom they are dealing.[46]

This picture of the Social Security Administration reflected much of the underlying ideology of both the miners and their supporters who were a part of the movement. Many of the young activists had previous experience in the student, antiwar, or civil rights movements of the previous decade and had already developed a sense of the "bureaucratic contradictions" in their lives. They had already begun turning the personal problems they were experiencing with bureaucratization and its many meanings into political issues for social change.[47] These emerging perspectives were consistent with many of the personal experiences and practical problems of coal miners and their families as they encountered government agencies when applying for either black lung benefits, disability, or even welfare during periods of massive unemployment.

A healthy skepticism of bureaucratic structures developed which influenced not only the strategies and tactics of the movement, but also its organization. Although the staff of the Charleston Office Crew wanted to empower the membership to take control of the BLA, neither the miners nor the staff wanted a highly centralized organization. They wanted decisions made at the local level in each chapter and then by representatives from each chapter when regional or national issues emerged. The main work of the local chapter was primarily to facilitate the claims-filing process through the Social Security system. The fourteen chapters frequently came together, however, to plan strategy for protests against the SSA, for trips to Washington, D.C., and also to address problems within the organization.

One of these problems was funding. The Black Lung Association never had extensive support from outside sources. It was generally dependent upon contributions from members, who sometimes would get large settlements for their black lung claims. But in general these contributions were voluntary and did not amount to a great deal of money at any one time. There were frequent attempts to address the possibility of a centralized fund to which all chapters would be required to contribute dues. But these efforts failed to produce such a fund. Perhaps the reason was expressed by a representative from the Beckley, West Virginia, chapter when she said, "If we have a person who spends all of their time just running around collecting dues, that person is not out in the countryside helping to spread the word."[48] A somewhat different sentiment was expressed by a movement supporter who believed that the BLA could be a national organization if it could get the money. It didn't attain this status, however, because "an organization can only go so far on dues that are collected at meetings and operates on a budget which is ripped off from the Appalachian Regional Commission [one of the original funding agencies]."[49]

CONCLUSION

Denial of benefits by the Social Security Administration and serious inconsistencies in the administration of the program were the primary stimulus for many miners and widows to join the movement. The BLA reported a peak membership of 4,000 miners and widows by 1971. The organization was supported by some external funding but was dependent primarily upon its membership for contributions. The retired and disabled miners and widows were supported in their efforts by several young staff members who, like the membership, were committed to advancing health and safety issues and to challenging the bureaucracy of the Social Security Administration. Although the BLA outwardly appeared loose in organization and lacking in unity or cohesion, internally it had a great capacity for decision-making, for mobilizing resources, and for generating power.

6

Bureaucrats vs. People: The Black Lung Association in Confrontation

The recognition of the contradiction between Title IV of the Federal Coal Mine Health and Safety Act (FCMHSA) as established by Congress and its implementation by the Social Security Administration was a significant step for the development of the black lung movement. Arnold Miller, a former BLA President, and then President of the UMWA, reflected on this point during congressional testimony considering amendments to the act in 1973:

One thing I learned several years ago [is that] it is one thing to pass a piece of legislation to deal with a specific problem. I used to think that regulations were then written to regulate how a law was going to be enforced. It did not take me long in spite of my limited education in the field of legislation to learn that regulations many times were when they went back and took out the intent of the law. . . . This induced the people that I worked with in the last four years to come back . . . and try to amend the law and make it specific . . . to give the people who are going to administer the program a roadmap so that Congress could direct them as to how to interpret the law.[1]

The miners came back to Congress several times in the decade of the 1970s and were successful in passing two amendments to the Black Lung Benefits Program that made it possible for more miners to get claims approved. In addition, the BLA struggled in direct confrontation with the SSA and later the Department of Labor to force those agencies to administer the law fairly.

This new struggle confronted a different target group than in the earlier revolt. Whereas the West Virginia state legislature had a high turnover in personnel every two years, the Social Security Administration had developed a very large bureaucratic structure that maintained the stability of its operations. The state legislature had been pressured to pass legislation; the SSA was pressured to administer legislation already passed. Being an elected body, the legislature responded to economic and political pressures, whereas the SSA did not. However, it was influenced by directives from Congress, the President, and the Department of Health, Education, and Welfare.

The SSA established administrative rules and regulations based upon its experience with its already well-established programs. But, the applicants for black lung benefits were different from applicants to regular SSA programs in at least four ways. First, a large number of applicants came at one time. Second, the people making these applications came from a similar occupational, regional, and cultural background and were in contact with one another on and off the job. Third, the SSA was unprepared to handle this program from both a planning and personnel standpoint. Finally, in the central Appalachian area, where the BLA emerged, there were not enough professional personnel to sufficiently and effectively supply the needed medical evidence to support the miners' claims.

One continuing frustration was the confusion over the detection of black lung. The law assumed that coal worker's pneumoconiosis did exist and was caused by coal dust; however, Congress left it to HEW and SSA to establish the criteria for determining its existence. The BLA considered these criteria too rigid and claimed that they were applied inconsistently. Of particular significance was the use of the x-ray as the sole criterion for denying benefits.

The miners were aware of a division of opinion among members of the medical profession regarding the detection of black lung. One study in 1973 reported that while 80 percent of the miners said that the applicants for black lung benefits should get an x-ray, only 32 percent of the respondents said that x-rays were the best test for black lung. Thirty-six percent of the miners responded that the blood gas test was better, 32 percent stated that the breathing test was better, almost 18 percent said "they should take the miner's word for it," and the remaining 13 percent said that the doctor's word was better. Regarding these results, the report concluded:

Of course, the miners themselves could not be expected to have expert judgement on such strictly medical matters. The series of questions was asked in order to find out the extent to which the miners were aware of the medical controversy over which tests are valid determinants of black lung. . . . It is clear that at least some of the miners were aware of this controversy. . . . They knew that a positive x-ray was proof, but they thought that other tests must be used, if the x-ray was negative.[2]

The lack of a legitimate means for detection of coal workers' pneumoconiosis meant that any program which attempted to distinguish between those miners who did have the disease and those who did not was built on a questionable foundation. The Black Lung Association worked on the ideological assumption that, since no conclusive method for detection existed, there would always be some doubt as to whether anyone who was denied benefits did not have the disease. This was the reason that the BLA fought for a good "presumption clause," as it had in West Virginia. Such a clause would mandate the SSA to presume the existence of coal worker's pneumoconiosis in miners with lung disorders who had worked in the mines for a specified number of years.

The BLA's long-range goal of attaching a presumption clause to the existing law was supplemented by short-range goals to alter the administration of the benefits program by the SSA. Efforts against this complex bureaucracy were focused on two levels: first at the local district office where claims were filed and later at the national office in Baltimore, Maryland, where final decisions were made.

Efforts at the Local Level

From the beginning, applicants for black lung benefits experienced many problems. Most frequently publicized in early issues of the *Black Lung Bulletin* were the needs for complete and impartial examinations, claimant access to information in the files, medical facilities for adequate diagnostic procedures, assistance in filing and processing claims, and clear, complete explanations when miners were denied benefits.

One of the first attempts to address these problems occurred on January 11, 1971, when fifty miners from the Mingo County and Logan County, West Virginia, chapters of the BLA presented a list of demands to the Director of the Logan Social Security Office. He forwarded the demands to the Baltimore office. Less than two weeks later, Baltimore and Washington officials of the SSA came to West Virginia to meet with the BLA about its complaints. This established a pattern of protest operations which was to be repeated several times in the next three years.

When the SSA took no action, however, the BLA continued its protests. In April 1971, Don Bryant, President of the Logan chapter of the BLA, indicated for the first time that a trip to the nation's capital might be necessary:

We have waited two months for Social Security to move on their promises but we see no evidence of changes. . . . Thousands of disabled miners and widows are being treated like dirt. . . . We have tried to work things out but all we get is unkept promises and no action. . . . We want what is right and we will get it even if it takes a trip to Washington.[3]

On April 13, 200 members of the BLA marched for a second time on the Logan office. The meeting ended in a bitter tirade against the SSA, with the following list of demands:

1. Explain why individual miners are turned down for black lung benefits and specify the amount of black lung a miner has in the denial letter.
2. Allow miners to see and to copy their complete files on request.
3. Permit miners to be examined for black lung by doctors of their choice, such as Dr. Buff and Dr. Donald Rasmussen.
4. Pay for all additional medical evidence needed to prove that a miner has black lung and collect all of the miner's evidence, not half of it.
5. Admit that a disabled miner who can't work in the mines is totally disabled and can't work.
6. Treat miners on a first come first serve basis and pay benefits promptly.[4]

On April 29, a smaller group of miners met with SSA officials in Bluefield, West Virginia. The demands were essentially the same, with one addition that became a rallying cry for future protests: "We demand that Social Security treat us like people, not like dogs."

The full implication of this was not revealed until later hearings in Washington, but the miners' experiences with SSA personnel were certainly an important factor encouraging their participation in the BLA:

When we go to Social Security for help we are ignored, insulted and get the run around. The Social Security people won't tell us why we are turned down. They won't let us see our files. They won't help us get new evidence. All they do is try to discourage us and get us out of their office. This had better stop. We want to be treated with respect and we want our money now. We only want that which is ours and that which is ours under the law.[5]

The struggle at the local level was important because it legitimized the activities of the BLA to the local population and to the large government structure. It also served to publicize the issue of black lung in the news media, which helped to build a larger constituency. The marches on the SSA offices were an effective tactic, because, unlike the coal companies or the state legislature, the SSA was not accustomed to such collective action, and was embarrassed by it.

Repeated attempts to arrange meetings with the heads of the Black Lung Benefits Program, the SSA, and HEW were unsuccessful. After Bernard Popick, then head of the Black Lung Benefits Program, failed to keep a promise to attend a meeting with the miners in April, the BLA began planning a national march on Washington to talk to legislators and HEW officials.

Even before the march occurred, the criticism of the Black Lung Benefits Program reached such proportions that both the Senate and the House subcommittees having jurisdiction over black lung benefits held hearings in May 1971 to determine the reasons behind the trouble and dissatisfaction. Representative Carl Perkins from Kentucky drafted several amendments and invited interested parties to testify. The Black Lung Association sent its President, Arnold Miller, and Clara Cody, a BLA member who had been trained by the Appalachian Research and Defense Fund to counsel widows whose husbands who had died of coal worker's pneumoconiosis. Dr. Rasmussen also testified, as did representatives from several supportive grassroots organizations in Kentucky and Virginia. Only one and a half years after the passage of the Federal Coal Mine Health and Safety Act, an amendment seemed imminent.

The First March on Washington

The BLA's trip to Washington in June 1971 was not made primarily to seek an amendment, but to effect a change in the rules and regulations by which the SSA administered the Black Lung Benefits Program. However, in addition to a planned visit with Elliot Richardson, then head of HEW, the BLA also anticipated visits to Congressmen from coal mining states. In contrast to the march on the state capitol of West Virginia in 1969, supported by a spontaneous strike of over 40,000 miners, this was a well-organized march, which took two months of prior planning. There existed quite an extensive division of labor among the BLA members who visited Washington with regard to the roles they were to perform and the activities in which they were to participate.

From the registration forms that the members filled out, the leaders of the BLA were able to determine who the miners were interested in meeting and talking to. From their suggestions, eight teams were developed to carry out specific duties in Washington and to see certain people. Of particular importance was the idea that, divided into groups, the participants could tie up many Congressmen and Senators at the same time. Time schedules were developed and almost every minute was accounted for in the plan.

Advance letters to all Congressmen, Senators, and government officials scheduled for visits alerted many powerful figures who were then able to assist the BLA. While there was an attempt to maintain a centralized source of communication, the leaders of the march encouraged the local chapters to do most of the organizing and to handle most of the publicity. Miners were responsible for expenses and for informing the local news media about the march.[6]

The exact number of people who made the trip to Washington varied according to news reports from 100 to several hundred. Although the BLA had hoped for 1,000 or more, their records show that approximately 150 miners and widows attended.[7]

The mass lobbying tactics resembled those of the West Virginia struggle, and, as evidenced by the following report in the *Washington Post*, seemed to be equally effective:

Several hundred coal miners and miners' widows from four states roamed the corridors of Congress and executive offices yesterday demanding "justice for those who mine America's coal." They got tired, they got hungry, they got lost from time to time in the labyrinths of government. They got some stalling and some fancy words, but they also got respectful hearings from powerful men who promised action.[8]

Ben A. Franklin, a staff reporter for the *New York Times* who had followed the activities of the BLA since its inception in West Virginia, saw the lobbying as conveying a different message: "to warn that much of the East's supply of fuel for the production of power [would be] interrupted by strikes this summer unless action [was] taken on their complaints."[9]

In all, the group met with over seventeen Senators and Congressmen and three high administrative officials, including the head of the SSA. Promises were made and Appalachian Regional Commission (ARC) officials indicated they would set up additional diagnostic clinics in the coal fields. According to the next issue of the *Black Lung Bulletin*, the trip was described as "very effective" and "left no question in the minds of government leaders" that the SSA had not carried out the intent of the FCMHSA. However, the BLA swore to return to Washington if definitive answers were not forthcoming.[10]

The Black Lung Education Fund

The Black Lung Association continued the struggle against the SSA on the local and state level through protest meetings. One of the largest occurred on July 25, 1971, when an estimated 400 miners and widows gathered in West Virginia to air their grievances about being turned down for black lung benefits. They were told that Pennsylvania had twice as many applications approved because it had more clinics, more doctors, and better records for the miners. People in Kentucky and West Virginia, in particular, had been denied their claims because of an inability to gather sufficient medical evidence.

So, over the next few months, the BLA directed its efforts to establishing a clinic program in the coal fields of central Appalachia. The Black Lung Education Fund (BLEF) was formed to raise the necessary money. In addition to making it possible for more claims to be approved, the BLA argued that the clinic program was also one of the most important ways that control of the health care of the people could be taken away from the coal industry and its doctors, lawyers, politicians, and bureaucrats.[11]

In the spring of 1972, the BLEF received word that approximately $1.3 million was available from the Appalachian Regional Commission for black lung clinics in the Appalachian area. The BLEF immediately went to work on a proposal to the ARC for clinics in southern West Virginia and in eastern Kentucky which would be run by the miners themselves. It was a bold idea in the field of health care. Unlike most clinics or hospitals, the ones planned by the BLEF would have a board of directors through which the consumers of the health services (the miners), instead of the suppliers of health care (the doctors), would have a majority voice in running the program.[12]

Unfortunately, after several months of proposal writing and rewriting, meetings with the ARC, and arranging for doctors to run the program, the novel idea failed because the Governor of West Virginia, Archie Moore, would not approve any program sponsored by the BLEF. Even after a new sponsor was found, and even after another health program in Kentucky promised a donation of $80,000 for a program run by the miners, no money was forthcoming. Governor Moore announced that $750,000 of ARC money would go to a mobile testing unit in West Virginia. Both the BLA and Dr. Rasmussen condemned the program because it was considered useless without the laboratory and clinic facilities to back it up.[13]

Although the clinic program fell through, the idea was significant because it advocated a program in which the miners would acquire some control over not only the delivery of health services but also the decisions which were made during that process. The coal miners were beginning to recognize that decisions by the medical profession were influenced by many factors other than purely medical criteria. As one miner reflected on his condition:

They told me I had asthma, miner's asthma. Now I find on my reports that I have different things. One doctor said I had a heart condition. Another doctor said I have pneumoconiosis, and this radiologist went over me, and she could not tell me what it was. Now, how can Social Security be honest?[14]

This lack of definitive criteria distinguishing black lung from other lung diseases encouraged the BLA to think more seriously about the need for legislative reform. It seemed obvious that Congress should spell out more clearly for SSA the procedures for determining disability. And equally important, these rules and regulations should be implemented with input into the program from the miners themselves. In the fall of 1971, the members of the Black Lung Association were again in the nation's capital.

The Return to Washington

Hearings in both the Senate and House occurred frequently between the fall of 1971 and the spring of 1972. The testimony of legislators, physicians, miners, and miners' widows provided valuable insights into the problems of occupational illness in the coal fields. The miners' presence at these hearings reinforced the image of an exploited group struggling to regain some control over their work, health, and lives. Representative Ken Hechler voiced a common theme in the testimony by supporters of legislation that miners and their families were "more honest, hardworking, long suffering, God fearing and adjustable to joys and sorrows, triumphs and tragedies, than the rest of the people in the nation."[15] Other legislators reflected on the constant danger coal miners faced in their work, the possible death by rooffall, explosions, or electrocution. And as one Congressman declared, "Even if [the miner] survives those disasters, and survives the safety hazards, he is indeed the fortunate exception if he can live out his life without, to put it bluntly, coughing up his guts everyday of the week."[16]

Many who opposed legislation criticized the paternalistic description of miners as "ignorant, exploited, semihumans lacking in intelligence or the simple amenities of civilized life" who "live in squalor in a company town and owe [their souls] to the company store."[17] However, at least one Representative did acknowledge that it was easier to promote better working conditions for miners if they were described as something other than ordinary people living ordinary lives.[18]

Much evidence was presented, however, to suggest that the plight of the coal miner was not ordinary, because of exploitation not only by the mine owners and the union, but also by the government agencies with whom they came into contact. Many supporters of legislation strongly believed that the actions of government agencies had been almost as spiritually destructive and crippling as had black lung itself:

> Unfortunately these people, who have had to bear the scars of the traditional violence of the past—the abrupt violence of cave-in, and the slow emaciating violence of the disease, have found recent and unsolicited company from an additional and more insidious form of violence, the violence of government institutions—that of indifference, inaction, obfuscation, and delay.[19]

By far the harshest criticism delivered by those testifying was reserved for the Social Security Administration. Charges ranged from ineptitude to insensitivity, from bureaucrats meddling in affairs not of their concern to failure to inform claimants of their rights in the process.[20] Some problems resulted from medical uncertainty. For example, the SSA denied many of the claims from widows because miners' death certificates listed diseases other than coal worker's pneumoconiosis as the cause of death, even though it was not until the late 1950s that this disease was recognized as a distinct entity in the United States, and even then only by a few medical professionals. The SSA also denied claimants when miners died in cave-ins or some other accident. However, accidental death did not rule out severe affliction by pneumoconiosis, because it was common practice for miners to continue working during illness to provide support for their families. As one widow testified:

> He was telling me sometimes it would look like coal dust or phlegm, and he would say he was afraid he had TB because he had such a cough, and his breath was so short. Then he went to the health department and had x-rays, and they told him he didn't have any TB. I were begging him to quit work, because he had chest pains so bad. . . . He told me that morning, the last morning he went off, that he was going to try to work until he was old enough to retire, to draw miners' pension. He was 53 then. He wasn't old enough to retire. We had no income. It wasn't long until he was killed.[21]

But many perceived not uncertainty in the local SSA offices but cruel and inhumane treatment of claimants. Several miners and widows testified that the attitude of many SSA employees had been unhelpful at best and clearly hostile at worst. A lawyer from the Appalachian Research and Defense Fund (ARDF), an organization that assisted claimants in obtaining benefits, indicated that employees of the SSA seemed to resent the time required to process black lung claims and seldom made an effort to explain the requirements of the complex law or to assist claimants in gathering evidence to support their claims.[22]

Even when claimants were treated respectfully, cultural differences often created misunderstandings in communication and interaction, as the ARDF's analysis of the case of George Workman seems to suggest:

George did not understand the printed notice he received from Social Security. He was convinced of the rightness of his case. After being treated fairly by the Social Security office people, and in particular by the lady he talked to, he felt that the assurance "we'll help you" meant that they would help him win his case. Later when he was turned down, he felt that the Social Security people were like other agencies and other employees he had dealt with who tried to "beat him out of" what was due him.[23]

The report suggests that miners of the southern Appalachian mountains were not used to being treated with enormous respect by middle class people. To the women at the SSA, "we'll help you" meant that they would gather evidence for decision, not that they would help George Workman win, as he had thought. This "we'll take care of it" attitude reflected a feeling that the applicants were incapable of acting for themselves. Consequently, the staff at the SSA spent less time explaining the problems of the claim in comprehensible language. The result was that claimants not only failed to receive benefits, but retained a negative view of the legitimacy of the whole process.[24]

Another possible explanation for the behavior of the SSA personnel came from Congressman Ken Hechler, who implied several times in congressional hearings that President Nixon had sent an order down to the SSA to administer the law in a restrictive fashion, and in particular to avoid a liberal interpretation of the law that favored the applicants for black lung benefits.[25] Although this accusation was never proven, one SSA official did indicate, confidentially, that the staff were generally judged on their ability to successfully deny claims or to transfer the responsibility to another agency. If this philosophy of handling claims was in effect, it would explain why the miners and widows were sometimes made to feel that they were "somehow on the other side of a lawsuit, and it was the U.S. Government against the miner."[26]

The adversarial nature of the claims process encouraged many miners to retain legal counsel, a move that in some states resulted in another form of exploitation. The worst abuses occurred in the state of Kentucky. Of the six million dollars given to the state for black lung relief by the federal government, $3.8 million had gone for the payment of attorneys' fees, and of that amount, $2.4 million had been collected by three attorneys.[27] From 1971 to 1973, four attorneys received over five million dollars for 1,225 cases, which amounted to fees of about $215 per hour for the lawyers. The average attorney's fee in Kentucky in fiscal year 1973 was $4,277 for each award, compared to the average fee of $419 that Social Security had authorized for federal black lung benefits. As might be expected, when Kentucky later established a minimum fee of $750 for lawyers in uncontested claims, the number of applicants dropped from 200 per month to an average of only forty-five claims per month.[28]

In some states, UMWA attorneys handled cases, and in others, the claimants did not have to retain legal counsel. In West Virginia, the BLA formed the Coal Miner's Legal Defense Fund, composed of fifteen lawyers, which supported the claims of miners and widows. Through the ARDF, members of the BLA were also trained in the laws, regulations, and administrative procedures of claims processing and then served as legal representatives for the claimants.[29]

Testimony by miners and their widows about legal and other abuses influenced the legislators. Miners were perceived by themselves and many Congressmen as contributing important knowledge about black lung itself. There was so much contradictory and confusing evidence presented in the hearings by medical and scientific professionals that it was difficult for legislators to determine what was valid. According to one congressional observer, some legislators saw this lack of consensus on the part of the medical profession as further evidence of the neglect of occupational health problems in general and justification for, in the absence of definitive evidence one way or the other, resolving the issue in favor of the miners.[30]

In November 1971, the House of Representatives passed an amendment introduced by Carl Perkins of Kentucky by an overwhelming majority. Among other things, the amendment extended the federal program for two more years, eliminated the x-ray as the sole determinant for black lung claims, and extended benefits to above-ground miners. In December 1972, the Senate began its own hearings in the Subcommittee on Labor and Public Welfare. On January 6, the Senate subcommittee took its hearings into the coal fields of West Virginia, to "hear from [the miners] in the areas in which they live and work." The presence of miners and their widows was important to the final passage of legislation, and excerpts from selected testimonies document some of their frustrations:

I sleep 2 hours a night, just about on the average. Sometime not that much. If I get a little bit of cold, I have to sit up and put a quilt around me. When I lay down, I just rasp, and there is nobody around me that can sleep. I cannot sleep either. Sometime around in the morning, I will get coughed out, and maybe I will doze off and sleep a little bit. When I get up, I ain't got enough wind.[31]

Houston Richardson, West Virginia

My husband died in 1962. . . . When he was working in the mines, they cut him off; and after they cut him off, they called him back; and when they called him back they gave him a physical. . . . They discovered that he had an enlarged heart, which the doctor said it would hurt him to work in the mines, so after that he started working in the small mines, where you did not have to have a physical. . . . In those years, people did not talk about pneumoconiosis.[32]

Helen Groom, West Virginia

I am 37 years old, and I have worked in the mines on a curring machine. I went in the mines when I was 15 years old, and I stayed there until 1970 in April, and I was totally cut out. I went to a job before I was cut out and I was turned down on account of my lungs. I could not pass for another job, and the doctor cut me out, he put me on social security. . . . I signed up on black lung but I was turned down because I had a lung impairment, but it was not total. [Mining] is all I have been able to get done, and I have no education. I cannot read or write. All I can do is sign my name.[33]

Vencil Maggard, Virginia

I know a man that never worked a day in a coal mine in his life, that never worked a day on a mine, and he got paid for black lung. . . . If they want to give it to those boys, let them give it to them, but I think they ought to consider all of us.[34]

William McConnell, West Virginia

The presence of the miners and widows left an impression on the legislators, as it had in 1969. As one observer noted, "the stark reality of the widespread misery, suffering, and woe afflicting the victims of the disease" and the "bureaucratic arrogance and insensitivity which had prolonged and deepened the agony of these people" were presented in strong emotional arguments.[35] What was impressive, as one Senator noted, was that the witnesses were not just statistical facts, but "a human document . . . spread here before the witness table."[36] A Senator from Pennsylvania explained his own intense response to testimony by stating that

one cannot have a hearing on a disease that is the largest occupational killer in the world today without it having some impact upon him. . . . One cannot attend committee hearings, see the pictures, and hear the witnesses, including miners themselves, without getting the message that these Americans have been neglected for years. Only belatedly are we beginning to realize that we all have a responsibility, the industry, the unions, and most important of all, the country.[37]

On April 17, 1972, despite strong opposition by the Nixon administration and intensive lobbying by the coal industry, the Senate passed 73–0 a bill which would qualify thousands of additional miners and widows for black lung benefits. Minor differences between the Senate and House bills were worked out and, again under the threat of a national strike, Nixon signed the bill into law on May 20, 1972. Fifteen months of marching on Social Security offices, writing letters to Congressmen and newspapers, and lobbying in Washington had paid off.[38]

Perhaps the most significant provision in the new act was that claims could no longer be denied solely on the basis of negative x-rays. The federal program was also extended eighteen months, which not only gave the states more time to favorably amend their workers' compensation laws, but also allowed coal companies to avoid financial liability for claims filed during that period.[39] Dependent parents, brothers, sisters, and double orphans could now lay claim to benefits. Widows would no longer have to establish that their husbands died of pneumoconiosis—only that they were totally disabled by it at the time of their deaths. Finally, Congress ordered HEW to develop liberalized interim medical disability criteria consistent with the language and the intent of the amendment.

Realizing that HEW might not fully implement the congressional directive, BLA officials from West Virginia, Kentucky, and Virginia met with SSA officials in Charleston, West Virginia, less than a month after Nixon signed the bill into law. The group presented a list of seventeen demands, the first and most important of which was that a committee selected by the BLA (including miners, doctors, and lawyers) be allowed to participate in the creation of the regulations under the new amendments. With the expenses to be paid by the SSA, the BLA would gain the right not only to participate in making laws, but also to help decide how those laws would be interpreted.[40]

Although initially SSA officials were uncooperative, the resistance widened the BLA's power base to a network of strong branches throughout Appalachia.[41] A subsequent trip to Washington on July 17, where representatives of the BLA met with Bernard Popick, head of the Bureau of Disability, resulted in a minor concession: Social Security would release the regulations to the BLA before they were printed in the *Federal Register*. A later denial of this promise prompted the BLA to picket SSA offices in five cities in West Virginia and four in Kentucky.[42]

While picketing was going on, a small delegation of BLA members met again with Popick, but after an hour the BLA representatives walked out of what they called a "fruitless hassle." A week later the BLA again met with the SSA. However, this time HEW Commissioner Robert Ball, who arranged the meeting, invited the BLA delegation and paid their expenses. As a result of this meeting, the SSA agreed to include the BLA in writing the new regulations and to consult regularly with them at the SSA's expense. According to Bill Worthington, then Vice President of the Regional Board of the Black Lung Association, "This was a real victory for the people of the government. . . . Now those who the program is supposed to be run for will finally have a say in how it's run."[43]

Twelve BLA members, two lawyers, and a doctor flew to Washington, D.C., in August to present their suggestions to Popick. An

CARL A. RUDISILL LIBRARY
LENOIR-RHYNE COLLEGE

initial seven-hour meeting was followed by a stormy eight-hour meeting in Charleston, West Virginia, two days later. The BLA delegation reported to the organization that whether the regulations were positive or not depended on whether Popick kept his promises. According to the *Black Lung Bulletin*, the new regulations, when finally released, ignored the wishes of Congress and allowed the SSA to run the program its own way.[44]

A Continuing Struggle

Up to this point, the leaders of the BLA had assumed that there would be a definite terminating point for the organization and its activities. They believed that a good black lung program—one which could be administered fairly without constant pressure—could be established. However, the inability of even congressional action to alter the basic problems in the program indicated that the battle with the SSA would continue.

When Arnold Miller, former President of the West Virginia BLA, was elected President of the United Mine Workers of America in December of 1972, much of the work of the BLA was incorporated into the institutional structure of the UMWA. Miller also funded and staffed a regional BLA office in Charleston, West Virginia, which maintained much of its autonomy.

A continuing battle was also promoted by a shift in the administration of the Black Lung Benefits Program. Beginning July 1, 1973, all claims for black lung benefits would be filed through the Department of Labor (DOL) and after December 31 of the same year, under an approved workers' compensation program at the state level. The responsibility for payment of claims filed and approved shifted to any coal operators found liable. The UMWA predicted proportionately higher claim denials by the DOL than by the SSA because of the differences in medical standards used by the two agencies and because miners would have to argue their cases before the industry in a new tier of adversarial proceedings.[45] The union was correct in its prediction. By 1976, the rate of approvals by SSA had shot up to approximately 70 percent, but of the 108,000 claims filed with the Department of Labor, approvals of less than 5,000 were granted,[46] and almost 90 percent of these cases were appealed by the responsible coal operators.[47] Equally important was that only 142 of claims approved were being paid by the responsible operators, while the remaining number of beneficiaries received payments from the government.[48]

The *Black Lung Bulletin* reported in 1974, "Whether it's the Department of Labor, Social Security, or the State of West Virginia, without a *continuing fight against abuses* and a *continuing fight for immediate compensation*, miners who are now working won't have black lung benefits when they quit or are forced to quit work."[49] Between 1973 and 1977, the members of the BLA testified frequently in either Senate or House hearings on the problems of the Black Lung Benefits Program. In addition to the high percentage of denials and the lengthy processing time for black lung claims through DOL, no state, as of 1975, had met the federal standards of eligibility for compensation. Also, the stringent requirements for dust abatement in the 1969 act had failed to force coal operators to reduce dust levels to the mandatory limit.[50]

One major thrust of legislative reform, headed by Congressman Carl Perkins of Kentucky, was to eliminate the haggling over claims by instituting an automatic entitlement determined by years of employment in the mines. The coal industry, which had originally supported the Black Lung Benefits Program under the 1969 act (presumably because it deferred the cost to government), now turned to increasingly active opposition. Coal operators warned of high premium rates to insurance companies, bankruptcy, increased coal costs, and inordinately high medical treatment costs tied to a large liability generated by high approval rates.[51] To insure the payment of benefits, operators would have to either purchase commercial insurance, qualify as self-insurers, or obtain coverage from a state insurance fund.

The coal operators also fought back directly through the claims adjudication process. In the August 1974 issue of *Coal Age* magazine, the attorney for the National Independent Coal Operator's Association urged all operators to resist payment of claims. That advice resulted in appeals of over 90 percent of all cases decided against the industry. Interestingly, only 11 percent of those claimants who were denied at the first level of adjudication requested formal hearings. Although inadequate legal representation was one of the reasons, many claimants did not want to submit to the coal operator's scheduled medical examinations (allowed under DOL rules) because of alleged abuses by company doctors.[52]

Four years of congressional review, however, did produce two new laws which eased the coal miners' access to benefits and the financing of the program. The first was the Black Lung Benefits Reform Act of 1977, which went into effect on March 1, 1978. It significantly expanded and liberalized the provisions of the 1972 act. First, it redefined pneumoconiosis to include any chronic dust disease of the lung, including respiratory and pulmonary impairments, arising out of coal employment. It also permitted a change in the medical standards which liberalized the definition of disability and modified the evidence required to prove it. Of particular importance was the acceptance of affidavits as proof of disability in the absence of medical or other relevant evidence.[53]

Even more important was the passage of the Black Lung Benefits Revenue Act of 1977, which went into effect on April 1, 1978. This act created a government-administered trust fund to pay benefits to successful claimants which would be funded by a tax on coal sold or used by producers. The thought behind this was threefold. First, the prevalence of an occupational disease could far exceed even expert estimates, and it was necessary to establish provisions for this. Second, the change supposedly ended federal financial responsibility for the program, but insured that payments would be made to beneficiaries even if the responsible coal operator could not be found. Third, as one observer noted, "it ensured such necessary compensation to afflicted persons by placing the responsibility for payment on the very source of its occurrence . . . the industry."[54]

The trust fund was financed by a fifty-cent-per-ton fee on underground coal and a twenty-five-cent-per-ton fee on surface-mined coal. The intent was to hold coal companies responsible for their past neglect and at the same time to build in an incentive for operators to hold down dust levels in the mines. Coal companies, however, continued to challenge the vast majority of black lung claims even after the 1977 amendment. Consequently, the failure of responsible owners to pay the benefits (at least initially; 85 percent of the claims were eventually upheld on appeal) posed a substantial financial burden for the fund, which had to borrow money from general tax revenues of the Treasury. In the first three years of the fund's operation, it accrued a cumulative deficit of $995 million. The Office of Management and Budget estimated that the total deficit could reach $9.2 billion by 1995 if the law were not changed.[55]

In 1980, controversy over the program was encouraged by a study published in the *Journal of the American Medical Association* (JAMA).[56] Conducted by Dr. W. Keith Morgan at the University of West Virginia,[57] the research suggested that black lung was far less prevalent than had previously been thought. Of the 150 miners studied, none had the truly disabling form of coal worker's pneumoconiosis, progessive massive fibrosis. In an accompanying editorial, a JAMA editor suggested that of all the miners eligible for benefits, only those who had smoked cigarettes would qualify when subjected to rigorous pulmonary function testing. Consequently, the taxpayer would be penalized twice, "first in subsidizing those who grow tobacco and then in compensating those who smoke tobacco."[58]

The study was criticized by many physicians and government officials primarily because of its small sample and its limited representativeness to the universe of black lung claimants. Also, Rasmussen pointed out that while cigarette smoking definitely contributed to breathing impairment, no study, including the Morgan study, had demonstrated that smoking was associated with black lung without occupational exposure to coal dust.[59] The Black Lung Association observed that the study was actually several years old and was simply a rehash of "Dr. Morgan's long time crusade against compensation for black lung victims."[60] However, the study, along with a 1980 Government Accounting Office (GAO) report that 88 percent of the claimants certified as eligible were either not disabled or else could not be proved to have black lung, received extensive media coverage.[61] What was not brought to the attention of the public was that two-thirds of the GAO's sample were older widows whose claims were approved on the basis of their own testimony in the absence of medical evidence either way, which was consistent with the mandate of Congress.[62]

As part of his New Economic Recovery Plan to cut the federal budget, President Ronald Reagan utilized these studies as the foundation for an effort to tighten requirements for black lung benefits in 1981. The response of miners to this proposed attack was overwhelming, reminiscent of the struggle in the late 1960s. UMWA

President Sam Church, who had thwarted Arnold Miller's bid for reelection, asked the nation's miners to strike for two days to dramatize their concern over the proposed Reagan administration cuts.[63] He then led approximately 7,000 coal miners and their supporters in a march on the nation's capitol on March 9, 1981.[64]

In the summer of 1981, members of the Black Lung Association testified at congressional hearings on the insolvency of the Black Lung Disability Trust Fund. Many representatives came from one of the fastest growing chapters in the movement—that of the city of Chicago. It is estimated that some 10,000 former coal miners migrated to the "Uptown" area of Chicago, Illinois, after the massive layoffs in the 1950s. Five disabled miners and widows formed the local chapter in 1976 because of difficulties they encountered in applying for black lung benefits. Apparently, the local Social Security offices were ignorant of their responsibilities for handling black lung claims, and many claims were not filed. Of those that were filed, a substantial portion were denied by local administrative law judges. Many of the migrants also felt discrimination because they were from the southern Appalachian mountains and were not well received in this midwestern city. By 1980, the Chicago Area Black Lung Association had over 400 disabled miners and widows as members.[65]

Apparently, neither the march on Washington or the congressional testimony had much effect in challenging the growing conservative mood at the capitol. On December 28, 1981, President Reagan passed a new black lung law which, according to BLA supporters, essentially wiped off the books all they had fought for since 1969. The fifteen-year presumption clause was eliminated, x–rays could be reread an unlimited number of times, widows would not be paid unless the exact cause of death was black lung, and no consideration would be given to a widow's affidavits about her husband's condition. Because the law applied only to those who filed claims from then on, it threatened a growing association between disabled miners and widows and working miners. Because the key to the future was an alliance of disabled and working miners, the Black Lung Association embarked upon a campaign to inform working miners of the history of the movement and the need for their support. Bill Worthington, now President of the National Black Lung Association, sounded the call:

When we won federal black lung benefits, it was the first time I know of that poor working people wrote their own law and then wrote their own rules to enforce it. Our idea was to make the coal operators pay for black lung disease and make them do something to prevent it in the future. Now they'd like to separate the disabled miners and widows from the working miners and put those of us who have fought for 20 years out to pasture. They're going to find out that they can't do that.[66]

Part III

THE BROWN LUNG
MOVEMENT

Organizing the Breathless: The Making of the Brown Lung Association

Pearl Hartgrove was nine years old when she began to work in the cotton textile mills of Monroe County, North Carolina. The year was 1921. She had just finished the fourth grade when her stepfather forced her into full-time work because he had difficulty keeping a job. It was the last formal education she would receive. She and her older sister became the major providers for the family. When the child labor law passed, her family moved to Gaston County, where her stepfather was able to get the then eleven-year-old Pearl a work card, even though she was well below the minimum age.

She was still working in 1934 when the great wave of union organizing and strikes hit the southern textile industry. The company had helped her family to survive during the early years of the depression and she felt as if she owed it something. She remained loyal to the company and fought the union tooth and nail. She used whatever influence she had to convince other workers not to vote for the union.

In the early 1950s, after nearly thirty years employment in cotton textile mills, she began experiencing lung infections and hemorrhaging. By the early 1970s, the problem had become so bad that she was hospitalized. Although she was asked questions about where she worked and about cotton dust, no one told her that she had byssinosis or that her lung problems were related to her work. So, she returned to the mill, became sick during work one day, and finally the company physician told her not to work anymore. But, after one and a half years out of the mill, she began to feel better, so she decided to return to work on a part-time basis. Her condition worsened, though, and she eventually retired in 1975.

In 1978, she read in a local newspaper about a screening clinic being held by the Brown Lung Association for textile workers who were experiencing breathing problems. Although initially hesitant, she decided to attend. On the basis of her case history and examination, the clinic staff told her that she might have byssinosis, or "brown lung," and that she could receive workers' compensation to help pay her mounting medical bills. It was the first time that she had heard of the disease or the possibility of financial assistance.[1]

Pearl Hartgrove's story was typical, not just because she began work in the mills as a child, or because she opposed the union, or because she developed respiratory problems. What she had in common with so many retired and active millworkers in the South was a serious lack of knowledge about the disabling properties of cotton dust.

This is not to say that information was not available, or that no one knew about the problem. Chapter 2 documents that much research was completed in the 1960s and early 1970s which revealed byssinosis among textile workers in the carding and spinning stage of processing cotton.[2] In 1966, considering previous British studies, the American Council of Governmental Industrial Hygienists proposed a one-milligram-per-cubic-meter-of-air threshold for cotton dust, which became law in 1969 for textile companies doing government work.[3] In the same year, Robert Finch, head of the Department of Health, Education, and Welfare, called for new legislation to control brown lung disease.[4]

The Textile Workers Union of America (TWUA) was also aware by 1969. It urged the American Textile Manufacturers Institute (ATMI) to participate in a jointly sponsored investigation by independent scientists to define the nature and extent of the cotton dust hazard and to develop the means of prevention. ATMI rejected this proposal, however, and hired the Industrial Health Foundation (IHF) of Pittsburgh, Pennsylvania, to determine whether the respiratory problem described as byssinosis might exist among American textile workers and, if so, its prevalence and cause. The IHF, which had done much research for the coal industry on pneumoconiosis, concluded in its study that byssinosis in U.S. mills was not as widespread as had been initially assumed.[5]

Individual textile companies also began research on byssinosis in 1969 in conjunction with medical centers at Duke University, the University of North Carolina, the Medical University of South Carolina, and Tulane University.[6] Later that year, the North Carolina Board of Health reported byssinosis to be a significant occupational health problem, and in 1970, the South Carolina legislature established a joint study committee to investigate byssinosis.

The Occupational Safety and Health Act was passed in 1970, which, although apparently enacted with little fanfare, provided the administrative framework to "assure as far as possible every working man and woman in the nation safe and healthful working conditions." The act created two agencies: the Occupational Safety and Health Administration (OSHA) in the Department of Labor to administer and enforce the requirements of the legislation; and the National Institute for Occupational Safety and Health (NIOSH) to conduct the necessary research. In 1972, OSHA released its list of the five most hazardous workplace substances; one of these was cotton dust.[7]

Why did it take Pearl Hartgrove and many of her fellow retired and disabled workers—those most directly affected by the disease—so long to learn about this problem? The knowledge which existed generally remained in medical research centers and universities, in legislative hearings or government agencies, or in the New York or Washington offices of the textile workers' union. What limited information made it to the national press was very rarely printed in local newspapers, particularly the small-town weekly papers that most textile workers read.[8]

It was not until 1975 that an organized effort was made to inform retired and disabled textile workers about brown lung, about the possibility for compensation, and about the need for changes in the compensation system and in the laws pertaining to healthy work environments.

EARLY ORGANIZING EFFORTS: THE BROWN LUNG SCREENING CLINICS

The success of the Black Lung Association had a significant impact on the early growth of the Brown Lung Association. Early organizers of the Brown Lung Association were involved in a coal miners' strike against Duke Power's Brookside Mine in Harlan County, Kentucky, in 1974. Because the strike lasted so long, many of them came to North Carolina (the home of Duke Power) to collect funds for the strikers and their families. During this period they also had several meetings with Bill Worthington of the Black Lung Association at the Highlander Center in Tennessee. Much discussion centered around organizing and what might be the next issue in the South. As one staff member later indicated, "It was a direct translation or application of what was going on in the coal mines into the rest of the South, where textiles was the dominant industry."[9]

When the strike in Kentucky ended earlier than expected, many organizers began to channel their energy toward the issue of brown lung and the southern textile industry. Building on research at the Center for Health Services at Vanderbilt University in Tennessee,[10] and work done at the University of North Carolina at Greensboro by the Ralph Nader–sponsored Public Interest Research Group,[11] one group began organizing retired and disabled textile workers in Greensboro, North Carolina, and Greenville, South Carolina.[12] Another group began working in Roanoke Rapids, North Carolina, building on the recent success of the TWUA's union drive there.[13]

Initial funding for these efforts came from a number of sources— the Church of Christ, the Campaign for Human Development (a Catholic organization), a grant from the Industrial Union Department of the AFL-CIO, and a grant from the J.P. Whitney Foundation. The money was funneled in through two different organizations—the Carolina Brown Lung Project and the Southern Textile Organizing Project. These two projects eventually merged into an organization called the Southern Institute for Occupational Health (SIOH).

Initial organizing efforts were focused primarily on retired and disabled textile workers. To recruit them, the organizers focused on the most tangible reward they could provide for participation in the struggle—workers' compensation benefits. They set up screening clinics with the stated purpose of examining workers for brown lung. But the clinics were also important events in the development of a coalition of millworkers. They were to show brown lung victims that many people were concerned for them, that brown lung disease was important, and that a doctor or medical professional did believe that they had the disease.[14]

Although much of the initial work of the organizers was to educate people about cotton dust and compensation, the ultimate outcome of the clinics was to be an organization of retired and disabled textile workers who would carry on the struggle themselves. To build this movement, the organizers made the whole process of filing for compensation a collective action. Individual discussion of compensation cases was not considered a unifying idea. Instead, the clinics brought the community of brown lung victims together. As one organizer later related, "People who wouldn't have come together for a meeting, because meetings would seem too foreign to them, had their first public experience in an event where they saw lots of other people there for the same reason, and that was an empowering experience."[15] Those people who were diagnosed as having byssinosis were asked to attend follow-up meetings to learn more about the process of filing for compensation; they became the core groups of local chapters.

THE CAROLINA BROWN LUNG ASSOCIATION

The first screening clinic was held in Greensboro, North Carolina, on June 21, 1975. More than 100 textile workers came for the free examination. Within the next year, additional clinics produced Brown Lung Association chapters in Greensboro and Roanoke Rapids, North Carolina, and Columbia and Greenville-Spartanburg, South Carolina. Although SIOH served as a coordinating agency, there was no real overall organization, and thus some conflict between organizers. Although personality differences were apparently part of the problem, more significant was a disagreement over when, and perhaps whether, the retired and disabled workers would take over the movement.

To attempt a resolution of the problem, SIOH called a meeting of delegates from the four chapters. It was agreed in August of 1976 that SIOH would dissolve itself and give all of its assets to a newly created Bi-State Board of the Carolina Brown Lung Association. The board would be composed totally of retired and disabled textile workers. Its first order of business was to address the internal staff conflict. The final decision was strongly influenced by one of the major funding sources—the Campaign for Human Development (CHD). Continued funding from this source was contingent upon complete membership control, and one of the organizers wanted to maintain greater control of money and decision-making by the staff. The relationship with this organizer was terminated and the Carolina Brown Lung Association took its first step toward worker autonomy.

The Campaign for Human Development was not atypical of funding sources that grass-roots organizations like the Brown Lung Association depended upon. Committed to the goal of "breaking the hellish cycle of poverty,"[16] CHD grants focused on those projects that contained a philosophy prevalent in the 1960s—attacking the root causes of poverty, emphasizing institutional change and greater participation on the part of low-income populations in decision-making processes. The Brown Lung Project was able to convince CHD of the importance of its work by arguing that it would not only provide a tool for pressuring local, state, and federal agencies to address the problem of brown lung, but would serve as a model for what people could do in the Carolinas. In states with low levels of social activism and social services, the project would create a "vehicle for profound social protest and a force for tremendous social change, by challenging the omnipotence of the textile manufacturers head on."[17] This was no small goal for states that were the least unionized in the nation, with workers' wages well below the national average. But the Brown Lung Association was not a labor union, and it was not organizing for better wages or fringe benefits. It was struggling for the millworkers' health.

Becoming Social Activists

Like many other change organizations of the last two decades, the Brown Lung Association could have attained its goal of educating people about brown lung and compensation by having organizers (or staff) do most of the work. But their intent, and that of their financial supporters, was to build a grass-roots organization, composed primarily of retired and disabled textile workers who were knowledgeable about the issues and motivated for social change. As one of the early organizers emphasized,

I like to think of it as a movement, and movements have to have members.
They can't have staff doing it. It teaches a whole different lesson. It is very
nice if there are people like me who are willing to provide a service for
"poor ignorant millworkers," and that would be the lesson of an organization
that was only staff... but if you're a movement, then you have to be about
people learning something and that changing them, and then [trying] to
change the society that has denied them something, and then changing
themselves as they do it, and [including] more and more people, who are
also about changing themselves and changing society.[18]

The issue of workers' health was not sufficient in and of itself to
prompt retired and disabled textile workers into the forefront of
social activism. Although they were angry at the mill owners for not
telling them about the problems of cotton dust, early members of
the Brown Lung Association refrained from making public pro-
nouncements against the industry or any particular company. They
were also hesitant to participate in any form of protest.[19] The staff
had to devise a strategy which reinforced the empowering of collective action but at the same time was acceptable to millworkers
themselves. It also had to successfully draw the public and the
press's attention to the plight of the victims of the disease.

The strategy chosen was the mass filing of compensation claims.
It was to be the first real group-building event beyond the clinics
and the follow-up meeting. Not only would it generate publicity,
but it would stress the significance of collective action in the first
step of the process. Members would see the need for an association,
not just lawyers to file the claim for them. As the organizing liter-
ature emphasized:

Do not let the lawyers just mail in people's forms. If you don't pull your
people together to actively participate in this first event as a group, you
may have lost them to the lawyers. The danger is that their cases will then
become a matter between them and their lawyers and they won't see the
need for the Association.[20]

The first attempt at a mass filing of compensation claims occurred
on November 12, 1975. Approximately forty textile workers from
Greensboro and Roanoke Rapids, North Carolina, went to Raleigh,
the state capital. Although they were unable to file their claims
collectively, they were able to meet with the Industrial Commission,

the body of state government responsible for awarding workers' compensation, about the claims-filing process. At that time, approximately sixty-three claims for brown lung had been filed with the commission. Thirty-six had received compensation, eleven were denied, three were withdrawn, and the rest were still pending. Although the approval rate was relatively high, the time required for processing claims was six to nine months for those that were not contested. The commissioners promised to speed up this process. Protests outside the commissioners' office also received considerable publicity, a very important goal at this early stage in the movement. As Lacy Wright, spokesperson for the group, indicated, "We're down here because we're a people that have never been recognized. We have got to get it across to somebody what is wrong with us."[21]

The failure of the commissioners to uphold their promise brought the Brown Lung Association back to Raleigh in October of 1976. Approximately sixty former millworkers gathered at the North Carolina Industrial Commission, this time to successfully accomplish a mass filing of claims. In addition, placards and statements by the participants demonstrated a more sophisticated understanding of the controversy over brown lung, and of the roles of medical professionals, the insurance companies, and the Industrial Commission.[22]

The mass filing of claims and the accompanying demonstration were revealing experiences for the members of the Brown Lung Association. They communicated the significance of collective, as opposed to individual, action, and taught lessons about a world beyond textiles which was previously unfamiliar to them. It was through these types of events that they began the transformation from passive to active movement participation, a point reinforced for the early organizers:

Every event that people participate in, every meeting is an educational experience and a group building experience. People don't learn from just being told or taught things, they have to *experience* things. And the experiences have to be repeated and they have to build on each other for people to really learn and understand.[23]

The experiences were repeated within the context of a number of institutions. For example, when an economics professor at a southern university published an unfavorable analysis of the process of compensation for byssinosis and its economic impact upon the industry, several members of the Brown Lung Association went to the university to protest.[24] One seventy-four-year-old retired textile worker relates the experience:

When we went to Clemson [University] we couldn't get nobody to talk to, and they said that if we didn't get out of there, they would get the law after us, and we had to get out of there. . . . It's dirty, it's dirty, such things like that is like textile people [owners]—they ain't got no sympathy for those poor people that stayed in there and killed themselves all of their lives.[25]

A similar experience occurred when a physician published a paper indicating that byssinosis could not occur in non-smokers.[26] In response, seventy-five members of the Brown Lung Association went to the hospital where he worked to "offer themselves as evidence" as victims of byssinosis who had never smoked. The same textile worker was among the group:

He put it in the paper that there ain't no such thing as brown lung. It was smoking. Then when we went down to have a talk with him, he wouldn't even come out. We didn't even see him. No, you see, he's sneakin'. He knowed somebody was going to tell him about some lies, and that we had a lot of them there that have never puffed a cigarette in their lives, and they was going to tell him about it.[27]

Equally important for the retired workers was the realization that the mill owners had not been as concerned about their health and welfare as they had for so long believed. A former President of the Bi-State Board of the Brown Lung Association reflected on four years of helping other disabled workers file for compensation benefits:

When I came out, I thought that the mill company had our interest at heart. But my opinion has changed entirely. . . . I was trusting what they said they were, but I found out they are not what they say they are, they're only putting on a big front. . . . I realize now what they are doing to people—in this case and that case—they are trying to get that person off their responsibility.[28]

These experiences revealed to the members of the Brown Lung Association that their own interests were not always represented by

institutions and professionals around them. They learned that confrontation was a necessary part of life. As one experienced retired
worker exclaimed: "You have to challenge everything. I believe you
do. Not demonstrations, necessarily, but challenging people—the
doctors, the lawyers, everybody connected with it."[29]

But the struggle to empower the retired and disabled textile
workers of the Brown Lung Association required more than reve-
lations about the institutions that oppressed them. It required a
transfer of power and knowledge from the young professional staff
that built upon the experiences of participating in clinics, mass
filings, and demonstrations.

Young activists played important roles in many movements of the
last quarter of a century, particularly those that emerged out of the
War on Poverty addressing the problems of the underprivileged and
lower classes. The sheer number of movements, and the availability
of funding, even made it possible for many of these activists to make
a career of organizing. The resulting professionalization of many
movements,[30] however, created an image of increasing control, and
possible manipulation, by the outside organizers. It was an image
that the staff of the Brown Lung Association were quite aware of.
They spoke frequently with one another about how to empower the
membership of the association, how to transfer their knowledge and
skills to the retired and disabled millworkers.

One of the more crucial problems they encountered was frequent
attempts on the part of the membership to defer to the staff—to
leave it to the staff to make decisions, write press releases, talk to
reporters, etc. Some insight into this is provided by Bea Norton,
an early Brown Lung Association member, who suggests that millworkers have basically been told what to do all of their lives and
have never been allowed to express themselves:

People are just like I am. They worked under a dictation [sic] all of their
lives. When they was little, it was mommy and daddy that told them "they
had to do this, they couldn't do that." When they got old enough to go
into the mill, it was dictation there. They had to do this, they had to do it
in a certain way—they couldn't do it this way, they couldn't do it that way;
they was under a dictation. And now they have not got a dictation, they
don't know what to do with themselves.[31]

Like the Black Lung Association, the Brown Lung Association experienced a rapid growth in a relatively short period of time, which caused several problems in coordination. Within its first four years, the Brown Lung Association had expanded into four states (North Carolina, South Carolina, Virginia, and Georgia), with chapters operating in fifteen cities. Its membership was reported at 7,000 retired and disabled textile workers, although less than 1,000 were considered active members. More significant, however, and very much unlike the coal miners' movement, the funding and staff also expanded. From an initial two organizers with a budget of only $5,000 in 1975, the organization had approximately forty staff members in 1981 with an estimated budget exceeding $300,000.[32] As the organization grew, its staff became more specialized. In the spring of 1981, the association supported two full-time lawyers, a medical researcher, a professional fundraiser, an accountant, at least one staff person for each chapter, and several people whose major work was solely with active workers.[33]

Even though policy decisions were made by the retired and disabled workers who served on the state boards and the General Board (which evolved from the Bi-State Board when the organization expanded beyond the Carolinas), the influence of staff at these meetings, as well as in the everyday activities of the association, was significant.[34] A worker-directed organization was the ultimate goal of the organizers, but many realized that the complex issue of occupational health would require contributions from both the professional staff and the millworkers.

The staff contributed to the struggle what one organizer referred to as "trader skills," those skills that come from one's educational experiences as well as from continued interaction with government agencies, corporations, and other professionals. As she said to me, "We know how to write, we know how to plan strategy, and to look at an economic analysis and figure out what is going on. . . . We empower the organization by providing certain skills that help us to deal with the opposition."[35] These were skills that were not easily transferred to the membership. For example, an important part of maintaining the organization was the writing of proposals to foundations for funding. Most of the funding sources, even those sympathetic to the movement, were perceived by the staff as very insensitive to the way the working class world operated. Although they wanted proposals to be "from the people," they also wanted them perfectly typed and superbly written. Rather than taking on the funding world to teach it to be more receptive to working class people, which would require time away from the real struggle, the staff were forced into a compromise of accepting the foundations as they were, thereby failing to empower the membership with these skills.[36]

The complexity of issues also required sophisticated knowledge not possible to transfer to the membership. The association needed skilled lawyers and medical professionals to interpret and clarify legal and medical information for the membership. While it is commonly accepted that industry executives need professionals to simplify complex material for them and to handle their affairs, the involvement of similar people in workers' organizations seems to imply manipulation, or "orchestration," as one mill owner suggested.[37] This impression results from a long-held stereotype, quite unsubstantiated, about American workers in general and about southern textile workers in particular.

Still the differences between the staff and the membership were very real. Retired millworkers had not been the beneficiaries of either the skills one acquires through the process of formal education or the opportunities for personal advancement that accompany it. Meetings of the Brown Lung Association reflected the different views of life that resulted from this. Staff members were also generally "outsiders" in a number of respects. Most came from outside the South, most were not Protestant (as were most southern Christians), and most had very middle class upbringings.[38]

With few exceptions, high turnover in both the staff and the membership inhibited opportunities for working out these differences. Members were usually lost to illness or death, although many remained in the association only long enough to get compensation. As for the staff, low salaries (between $4,000 and $8,000 a year) encouraged many to leave after only one year, although there were usually people waiting in line to take their places. At its peak, the Brown Lung Association became a training ground for people who wanted to go into occupational health careers, medical school, law school, and public health.

A few staff members stayed for years, seeing their work as a career.

The possibility of continued funding made this a real option, as one experienced staff person explained:

I think it is a real honor. I have always thought that this is the kind of stuff you had to do after you made a living, after working eight hours a day someplace else. You could pittle, even if you pittled very seriously. I still think that as long as I can afford to raise my child, that it is a real honor to be paid to fight the bad guys. And then, because every year I get better at it, it's a challenge. . . . We really don't know very much about how to make change happen, even if people have been doing it forever. And so, there needs to be that kind of continuity. I figure by sixty I'm really going to know what is going on.[39]

But this opportunity was never realized, at least within the Brown Lung Association. The funding which had made this movement organization possible was abruptly withdrawn as the country moved in a more conservative direction and a new federal administration began defunding the left.

THE FUNDING OF THE BROWN LUNG ASSOCIATION

The Brown Lung Association received $27,500 from the Campaign for Human Development during its first year, and smaller amounts from the Church of Christ, the J.P. Whitney Foundation, and the AFL-CIO. For several years thereafter, CHD provided approximately $75,000 per year to continue funding the association.[40]

In one of the more innovative uses of government funding, the association in 1977 received funds to hire staff under the Concentrated Employment and Training Act (CETA). Restrictions on hiring and utilization of the staff, however, forced the association to begin keeping extensive records regarding the allocation of funds. Also, because the grant came through the state of North Carolina, and the personnel could only be used there, it dramatically increased the rate of growth of the association in North Carolina. Consequently, North Carolina was able to add three additional chapters, extend its membership, and have more claims filed and approved. Although there was some debate among the membership about whether to accept the funding, Lacy Wright, then President of the

Greensboro Brown Lung Association, convinced the association with the argument that "the more apples in the pipe, the more apples out the other side of the pipe." The essence of this strategy was that if more compensation cases went into the system, more workers would receive benefits. The bad cases would make the good cases look even better, and the situation would be presented in a more dramatic way. As one lawyer stated, "Many were marginal cases. It was just a way to draw attention from the public and the politicians."[41]

The Brown Lung Association was also supported by the Occupational Safety and Health Administration. In the late 1970s, the Director of OSHA, Dr. Eula Bingham, initiated the New Directions Program, which encouraged the education of rank and file workers about occupational safety and health issues. The new program was designed to help institutions develop their own competency to deliver educational services to working populations.[42] The Brown Lung Association received $95,000 a year for three years, which basically allowed the association to hire seven staff members to work primarily with active workers, although the job description allowed sufficient flexibility to continue much work with retired and disabled workers, the main focus of the movement.[43]

Volunteers in Service to America (VISTA) also provided approximately fifteen staff members per year. These generally served as either staff members for the local chapters or worked in outreach, recruiting new members from outlying areas into the organization.

The organization also attempted to raise money from various grassroots approaches such as yard sales, bake sales, raffles, etc. Of the average $5,000 annual operating budget for each chapter, approximately $3,000 was provided through external funds, with the remainder to be collected by each chapter through its own activities. However, through 1981, the records of the association show that less than 10 percent of the association's operating budget came from grassroots funds.[44]

In 1981, when the Brown Lung Association had reached its peak growth, both staff support and external funding began to diminish quickly. With the election of Ronald Reagan and an increase of conservative members in Congress, funds which the association had come to depend on were withdrawn. Both VISTA and CETA were dismantled by the new administration, OSHA de-emphasized the New Directions Program, and many of the foundations which had previously supported the association began to reduce or eliminate their assistance. By 1982, the Brown Lung Association was $35,000 in debt and had fewer than five full-time staff members. Most of its chapter offices had closed down.[45]

In May of 1982, the association listened to a proposal from a representative of the Campaign for Human Development to consider tithing on the basis of successful compensation claims. Pat Spier told the Brown Lung Association's board that they had made a critical mistake that was now coming back to haunt them: they had depended on staff members to obtain funds from foundations and government agencies. Now that this money was no longer available, he suggested that the association request a donation of 5 percent of their settlements from all successful claimants for workers' compensation. The plan was estimated to bring in approximately $13,000 a year. The board, however, rejected the proposal.

They chose to support other projects such as selling cookbooks, running direct mail appeals, operating bingo games, and canvassing door to door. This last project was the most successful, but very controversial. From August 1982 to July 1983, over $100,000 was raised in a canvassing campaign in North Carolina. However, the Brown Lung Association had to stop its fundraising drive because of conflicts with state solicitation laws in North Carolina. The association had registered for a solicitation license with the state as a charitable organization, which under state law could not pay solicitors on a commission basis unless the organization told what percentage of the contribution actually went to the specified charity. According to its records, 79 percent of the funds collected went to cover the costs of the drive itself. This was primarily to pay the canvassers, who received 40 percent of what they raised, plus 50 percent of the amount raised above $360 for each week. What was left went to the Brown Lung Association, mostly to pay back wages to the staff and to pay auditors for financial reports. Virtually none of the money went directly to help brown lung victims, as the canvassers had apparently told the public it would.[46]

8

For a Little Justice: The Struggle for Compensation

The hearing for compensation for a work-induced disease is the most visible element of the politicalization of occupational health. It brings into one arena the industry and insurance company lawyers, the worker, his lawyer and advocates, representatives of the medical community, and all of the state legislative and court regulations that govern the process. The potential for conflict, confusion, and delays is all but written into the script. One lawyer, who had handled compensation cases for work injury for fifteen years, remarked after his first brown lung hearing, "It is a circus, a whole new ball game with its own set of 'rules of the game,' unlike any compensation hearing I have been in before. Lawyers whom I have encountered in other types of compensation hearings behaved totally differently in hearings for brown lung cases."[1]

One of the continuing goals of the Brown Lung Association was to alter, through the legislature and the courts, the workers' compensation process so as to increase the likelihood that claimants would receive benefits. Because compensation programs were different in each state, strategies and tactics were generally constructed on a state-by-state basis. Although the Brown Lung Association eventually expanded into six states, the two major textile producing states, North and South Carolina, are the major focus here.

While the process of filing a claim was similar in both states, several factors contributed to a larger number of claims being filed and paid in North Carolina. First, as was mentioned in Chapter 7, more staff in North Carolina meant that more people had the support of the association in filing claims. Unlike the coal miners, textile workers were not "breaking the doors down" to file claims for byssinosis. As has been discussed, many were not aware of the disease, and even more were unaware of the possibility of compensation. Second, workers in South Carolina had to pay for their own medical examinations, whereas in North Carolina the fees, which could run to several hundred dollars, were paid by the textile companies or the insurance firms representing them. In both states, workers generally retained the services of a lawyer, although fees were not paid initially. They were taken as a percentage of the settlements or awards, usually 20 to 30 percent, depending on whether the cases were contested.

Although the first compensation laws were passed to eliminate the need for legal representation, the recent increase in occupational disease claims has been accompanied by a higher incidence of litigation. According to one recent nationwide survey of 40,086 workers' compensation cases, in nearly 67 percent of the occupational disease cases, the claimants had lawyers, while only 15 percent of accident claimants had lawyers.[2] Attempts to expand occupational disease coverage have historically met with resistance from lawyers who may have a vested interest in retaining the litigation. Even where employers and workers have agreed that such expansion was desirable, trial lawyers have been able to delay such changes. According to Peter Barth and H. Allan Hunt, trial lawyers in North Carolina were able to delay expanding occupational disease coverage for years out of concern for the anticipated reduction of tort actions.[3]

Whether claimants had lawyers or not influenced whether they sought settlements or awards. In both North and South Carolina, workers could negotiate settlements with the industry or the insurance companies—settlements which were usually less than the maximum amount and generally did not include medical benefits. On the other hand, workers could seek awards from the Industrial Commission in cases involving disputed claims. Several factors encouraged settlements rather than awards. The lawyers encouraged them because it meant that they would not have to go to court. The industry encouraged them because it generally meant less money to be paid and no medical benefits. The Industrial Commissioners encouraged them because it minimized their workload to simply approving (or in a few cases disapproving) the settlements. Workers were also pressured to settle because awards could take several years to acquire, years that many retired and disabled millworkers did not have. Claimants also ran the risk that the Industrial Commission would deny claims. The staff, and some of the members, were opposed to settlements, because they were seen as a compromise not only of the compensation involved, but of the health of workers and the goals of the Brown Lung Association.

EARLY COMPENSATION STRUGGLES IN SOUTH CAROLINA

When the organizing efforts of the Carolina Brown Lung Association began in 1975, no one had ever received compensation benefits for byssinosis in South Carolina, whose state motto is "While I breathe, I hope." The state had passed legislation in 1950 which made occupational diseases compensable under the state workers' compensation act, and an occupational disease medical review panel was established to aid in the diagnosis of occupational diseases. However, between 1950 and 1972 the physicians on the panel never made a diagnosis of an occupational disease; therefore, there were no awards for claimants alleging occupational diseases.[4]

Several factors contributed to an absence of awards for brown lung claims. The existence of the disease is difficult to prove and most doctors in the state had not been taught to recognize it. Instead they many times diagnosed emphysema or bronchitis. In a 1979 study of 300 compensation claimants in North and South Carolina funded by the Department of Labor, it was found that while 96 percent were told by local doctors that they did not have a lung problem before going to work in a cotton mill and 71 percent were told that they had a lung disease after leaving the mill, only 15 percent were told that cotton dust might have caused their lung disease and only 10 percent were told that they had byssinosis, or brown lung.[5]

In addition, many workers failed to apply for benefits until it was too late to qualify. In South Carolina, the law required that the claimant file for disability within two years of the occurrence of the disease. Varying interpretations of this law led to one of the points of contention by the Brown Lung Association. Also, the mills usually did not inform their employees about the hazards of cotton dust. As a result, many disabled workers failed to apply within the specified time period.[6]

This and other problems with the law in South Carolina forced the Brown Lung Association to address the law itself, rather than just proper enforcement:

We were told that as long as the law was so bad, we had only two routes to go: into the legislature or into the courts. As hard as it is to work on the legislature, we were assured that the courts are even more expensive, time consuming, and in South Carolina, just plain conservative.[7]

In November 1975, the Brown Lung Association asked the Legislative Study and Review Committee of the South Carolina legislature to listen to their problems. During the same month, twenty-seven workers filed for compensation to test the system.[8] The next several months were important learning experiences for the newly emerging coalition. During the legislative session in January 1976, they were assured that a bill would be forthcoming. Consequently, they went back to organizing chapters in Spartanburg and Greenville. By the end of May, however, when the legislative session was almost over, no bill had been introduced. In June, the Senate voted not to call the bill out to the Senate floor. Shortly thereafter, representatives of the association were invited to dinner by a lobbyist for the textile manufacturers. It was a revealing experience:

We ate his $10 steak and listened to all he said about how he wanted to help us. He told us that he would see that a good bill got passed, and not to worry. . . . But we had learned about *not worrying*. We didn't say anything but we thought to ourselves that we would believe that he would help us when the bill was signed into law and the people began getting compensation. We learned that if we didn't do the work ourselves no one would do it for us.[9]

This experience prompted the association to become more aggressive in its approach to influencing the legislature. By October 1976, a 1977 legislative program was formulated and distributed to all candidates for the legislature. They were asked to sign pledges to support the program if elected.

The program suggested six basic changes in the compensation law. First, under the then current law, people with lung diseases had to be totally disabled before they could receive compensation. The program indicated that compensation should be paid to people partially disabled from lung diseases—just as with any other disease or injury. Second, because a medical board was required to review compensation claims for occupational diseases but was not required in the case of other claims, the program recommended the elimination of the medical board, placing the final decision in the hands of the industrial commissioners. The Brown Lung Association felt that the medical panel, recommended by the South Carolina Medical Association and appointed by the Governor, was prejudiced in favor of industry.[10] Third, the two-year filing time would begin on the date when a medical diagnosis was made. Fourth, all changes in the law would be retroactive to 1941, the year that Great Britain made the disease compensable. Fifth, the Industrial Commission would presume that persons who had worked in conditions which were known to cause an occupational disease and who had the symptoms of that disease were disabled unless the industry could prove that the disability was caused by something else. Finally, the fifty-two-week limit on medical benefits for people disabled by occupational diseases would be deleted, thereby providing all claimants with the same benefits under the compensation law.[11]

The South Carolina Brown Lung Association succeeded in getting forty candidates for the legislature to commit to backing the program. The basic strategy was to bring people into the legislative process who would support the association's goals rather than just to depend on those who were already there. After the election, information about brown lung was sent to all legislators. In December of 1976, the legislative program was presented to the study committee to bring before the next legislative session.[12]

The association spent the first two months of the 1977 legislative session making personal contacts with legislators all over the state of South Carolina. By March 1, no legislation had been introduced. However, the association used a creative strategy to encourage legislation. It sent letters to the top 200 executives in the state's textile mills, asking them to help the Brown Lung Association. Although the association did not expect a positive response, the executives did call their own lobbyists to find out what was going on; those lobbyists in turn got mad at the association's lobbyists and accused them of "not playing fair." News reporters picked up on this and began asking questions about why a brown lung bill had not been introduced.[13]

On April 6, 1977, the study committee recommended changes to the Senate's Labor, Commerce, and Industry Committee. By the end of the month, a bill had been introduced to the full Senate. The Brown Lung Association had somebody at the Senate session every day that they met. As one reporter commented:

And when the measure comes up for discussion, members of the Carolina Brown Lung Association are sure to be there, as they have been many days this year. Generally rather elderly, plainly dressed, coughing and wheezing, the association members present lawmakers with a conspicuous reminder of their cause.[14]

On May 13, the South Carolina legislature approved a brown lung compensation bill which incorporated two of the six recommendations from the Brown Lung Association—it allowed compensation for up to 500 weeks and made the findings of a state-appointed medical panel no longer mandatory in awarding payments for occupational disease. Although the association had pushed for no minimum exposure requirement, the law required exposure to cotton dust for at least seven years.[15]

Although the bill was not all that the textile workers had wanted, it was a beginning. Certainly, the Brown Lung Association had made an impact on the legislators. As Senator Isadore Lourie, chairman of the special legislative committee, remarked, "The Brown Lung Association had a lot to do with crystalizing the attitude of the legislature. If it hadn't been for the association, the bill never would have passed."[16]

COMPENSATION IN NORTH CAROLINA

Until 1963, workers' compensation disease claims in North Carolina were either governed by a list of diseases or through a provision for broader coverage which only included external organs of the body. Nothing about internal diseases which could be respiratory was mentioned. In 1963, the law was amended to provide coverage for both internal and external organs. The law was amended again in 1971 so that the general provision for occupational diseases was greatly broadened and specific coverage was given to diseases such as byssinosis.[17]

The major problem in the compensation system for the claimant was the long delay in processing claims, which could typically last several years. These delays caused many claimants to accept settlements—not a desirable alternative, according to Olive Pankey, an association member from Rockingham, North Carolina: "Many of our people are entitled to five or ten times what the companies are offering. But time to wait for what we deserve is something we just don't have. We have two choices—to settle for blackmail while we're living or fight for justice till we die."[18]

Most of the delays involved the difficulty of diagnosis and administrative problems. One report revealed that the physicians' examinations generally occurred three to four months after compensation claims were filed, that the medical reports were made up to three months after examinations, and that an additional two and a half months passed before any steps were taken to initiate hearings.[19] Although claimants could submit testimony from their own doctors, they were required to be examined by one of ten "panel" doctors who were specifically appointed to examine brown lung claimants. At this point, if a doctor said that an individual had brown lung, the Industrial Commission would ask the insurance company to attempt to settle the case or to admit or deny liability. If no agreement was reached, the employee had a right to ask for a hearing, at which the Industrial Commission could make an award. This award was based on a worker's average weekly wage, degree of disability, educational level, and the job market.[20]

In an attempt to reduce the delays in processing of claims, forty members of the Brown Lung Association from Greensboro and Roanoke Rapids met with the Industrial Commission in Raleigh on November 12, 1975. At that time, sixty-three claims had been filed for brown lung; thirty-six had been approved for compensation. This early meeting was characterized as friendly by both sides and elicited promises from the commission that the claims process would be expedited.[21] It was the first in a series of meetings that would occur between the two groups in the next few years.

Less than a year later, sixty members of the Brown Lung Association again converged on Raleigh with signs that read, "Give Me Compensation, Liberty Mutual, or Give Me Breath" and "Brown Lung—Red Tape: Which Will Kill Us First?" The first placard implied the role of the insurance industry in orchestrating the delays; the second pointed to the length of time required to process claims. None of the thirty-six claims filed during the association's previous visit had been acted upon.[22]

In June of 1977, over two years after the first screening clinic, the North Carolina Industrial Commission sat down with representatives of the Brown Lung Association, the industry, and the insurance companies to discuss the problems of the compensation system. In July, the commission put into effect several new procedures to facilitate the process. First, it broadened the definition of brown lung to say that any lung affliction caused by cotton dust could justify compensation. Second, changes were instituted to make it easier for claimants to get medical examinations paid for by textile companies (or their insurers) and to simplify the form for filing. Third, the commission required that employers supply the medical and work histories of the claimants.[23]

In August, the Brown Lung Association tested the new system by adding fifty new cases to the files in another of its mass-filing strategies. Over 140 cases were already in the system at this time; only six had received awards, and thirty cases had been approved for settlements. By February of 1978, over 300 claims had been filed with the commission, nearly half of these since May of the previous year. The commission was literally "swamped in compensation cases filed by brown lung victims." Chairman William Stephenson was prompted to comment on how curious it was that so many cases were contested by the companies (75 percent at that time).[24]

The already strained system was put under additional stress a month later when the Brown Lung Association, in an ironic dramatization of dissatisfaction with delays in processing claims, staged yet another mass filing with over 160 workers from all over North Carolina. Prior to the filing, the claimants participated in a motorcade billed as a "memorial procession for brown lung victims" and carried signs which read, "Free the Brown Lung 5000," referring to the estimated number of cases of byssinosis in North Carolina, and "Cotton Breathes But We Can't," a response to the cotton industry's advertising campaign.[25]

As they gathered to file at the commission offices, other members of the Brown Lung Association held a press conference to denounce the bureaucratic red tape and the stalling tactics of the mill owners and their major insurer, Liberty Mutual. They then engaged in a three-hour meeting with Industrial Commission Chairman Stephenson, which resulted in his announcement that two additional hearing officers would be hired to handle the backlog of claims. In addition, the Chairman agreed to several other minor reforms. And, like the Black Lung Association, the Brown Lung Association was allowed to comment on the reforms before they were put into effect.[26]

The Hunt Investigation

Because the delays continued, the Brown Lung Association continued to meet periodically with the Industrial Commission until 1978, when the commission refused to have any more meetings. It appeared to the commission that the meetings were being used mainly to obtain publicity for the association and not for the purpose of constructive criticism or suggestions. As a quasi-judicial body, it did not consider it proper or ethical to engage in debate with litigants without the opposing party being present.[27]

In September of 1979, the Brown Lung Association embarked upon a new strategy. Nine representatives of the association met with Jim Hunt, governor of the state of North Carolina, while approximately 100 members demonstrated outside the commission offices. As a result of this meeting, Governor Hunt appointed a Brown Lung Study Committee to analyze the processing of byssinosis claims and to make recommendations to expedite their determination. The committee was made up of seven people—a Dean of the University of North Carolina Law School, a lawyer who represented workers in compensation cases, a lawyer who represented insurance companies, a State Appeals Court Judge, a pulmonary specialist, a representative from the textile industry, and a representative from the Brown Lung Association.[28]

The study committee was important for several reasons, First, its mere existence affirmed publicly what the association had been saying for a long time—the Industrial Commission's policies had many shortcomings. Second, the committee provided an open forum for members of the association and their supporters. Third, the twenty-four recommendations made by the committee, and accepted by the Governor, did address many of the issues which were responsible for delays and inefficiency.[29] However, the report did not address the basic issues which were to become the central focus of confrontation between the industry and the workers. In a minority report to the Governor's Brown Lung Study Committee, Florence Sandlin, the association's representative, outlined the major flaws in the committee's recommendations.

The association believed that the high rate of litigation involved with these claims (over 80 percent were contested) was the major source of delay. According to Sandlin, "Excessive litigation and therefore excessive delay of brown lung claims are caused by the mills' continued resistance to paying valid compensation claims and the Industrial Commission's attitudes and policies that allow the delaying tactics to continue."[30]

To address this problem, the association sought a presumption clause which would give benefits to those textile workers who had worked a certain number of years in the mill and had a breathing problem. The idea of a presumptive diagnosis had been a successful goal of the Black Lung Association, and the Brown Lung Association frequently pushed the same goal in their struggle, although they were never successful.

One of the reasons they did not succeed was the intense opposition from the textile industry. The industry's sentiments were expressed by the then President of the American Textile Manufacturers Institute and the industry's representative on the Brown Lung Study Committee, "I will fight presumptive diagnosis until the day I die. I will be down there with those damn brown lung, sign-carrying nuts until my blood runs out."[31] The main reason for the industry's opposition to a presumption clause was the implication of responsibility for diseases that were not of its making. Most of the evidence to link the textile industry to byssinosis consisted of epidemiological studies which showed a higher than normal rate of respiratory illnesses among textile workers, particularly those involved in the early stages of yarn production.[32] Medical research has not documented the exact cause of the disease, consequently linking it to the workplace. If a law were passed which specified only the number of years worked as the criterion, the industry might have to pay for many who had contracted emphysema, chronic bronchitis, or asthma.[33] On the other hand, to not compensate workers who legitimately had byssinosis would be equally objectionable to the workers and their supporters.

The industry's solution to the problem was called "apportionment." The idea was to divide the responsibility for a particular disability into several possible causal variables. Even the Governor's Brown Lung Study Committee recommended that the examining doctor "quantitate" the degree of respiratory impairment of the worker which was felt to be related to occupational exposure. Although this recommendation did not directly encourage apportionment, it did acknowledge the fact that the issue was still unresolved:

In many cases involving byssinosis claims both cotton dust exposure and other nonoccupational factors may contribute to cause the claimant's lung disease. . . . A serious dispute exists about the extent of the employer's liability for compensation in these cases. Employees contend that when the occupational exposure has made a significant contribution to the claimant's disability the employer's liability for compensation should not be reduced when nonwork related factors have contributed in causing the disability. Employers contend that compensation liability should be limited by the relative contribution the claimant's occupational exposure has made to this disability. These conflicting interpretations of the worker's compensation statute create a major obstacle to easy or early resolution of byssinosis claims.[34]

This and other controversies have prompted some observers to coin the term "legal disease," meaning one whose existence is determined by a political body rather than a medical one.[35] The issues of apportionment and presumption were the foundations in several court battles that dominated the political struggles of the Brown Lung Association and its members.

The Case of Elsie Morrison

When the Brown Lung Study Committee had completed its work, the North Carolina Court of Appeals was already reviewing a case which reflected the problem of apportionment. Elsie Morrison, who had worked for twenty-seven years at Burlington's Erwin, North Carolina, mill, was forced to retire in 1975 because of her breathing problems. A year later, at the age of forty-nine, she filed a claim for compensation.

In 1978, Industrial Commissioner Robert Brown awarded her total disability. The full Industrial Commission overruled that decision, saying that only 55 percent of her disability was due to cotton dust. Burlington doctors contended that the rest was attributable to cigarette smoking and other ailments, including phlebitis and varicose veins. The North Carolina Court of Appeals, however, overturned the commission, and the case went to the State Supreme Court. Morrison's case was one of a growing number of byssinosis claims that had made their way into the courts. In June of 1982, thirty-eight brown lung claims were on appeal to either the State Court of Appeals or the Supreme Court of North Carolina. Many of them were breaking new legal ground by testing sections of the state workers' compensation statutes which had never been clearly defined by the courts.[36]

The *Morrison* case was particularly important to Burlington Industries because it estimated that winning the case could mean a potential savings of $100 million from future claims.[37] Many state business associations also joined the textile industry to fight the millworker's disability claim. On March 11, 1981, almost five years after Morrison had originally filed for compensation, her case came before the State Supreme Court. The courtroom was filled with members of the Brown Lung Association. In addition, a new group was present—representatives of the tobacco industry, which had a vested interest in the outcome of the case. Tobacco was North Carolina's most lucrative cash crop, and second only to textiles as the largest industry. The industry representatives were concerned about the potential implication for liability in compensation cases where smoking was a factor, as well as the bad publicity which might result from a ruling in favor of apportionment.[38]

On October 6, 1981, the Supreme Court ruled in Burlington's favor, stating that workers suffering from brown lung disease could not also be paid for lung damage caused by smoking. They could be paid only for that percentage of their lung problems caused by exposure to cotton dust on the job. In essence, the court majority argued that Morrison suffered from one chronic obstructive lung disease that was job-related and another that was not. However, there was no medical testimony to support the concept of two diseases.[39]

The politicalization of this process was further demonstrated less than two years later when, as a result of personnel changes in the North Carolina Supreme Court, the court ruled in a similar case that a chronic lung disease caused partially or wholly by on-the-job exposure to cotton dust could qualify the victim for compensation, even if other factors, such as longtime smoking, also were present. In the case of *Rutledge vs. Tultex Corporation*, the court essentially reversed the *Morrison* ruling by stating that to insist that inhaling cotton dust be the sole cause of the illness would be excessively harsh to workers.[40]

The textile industry, dissatisfied with the court's ruling, almost immediately attempted to circumvent the law by proposing state legislation to change it. The bill was drafted, interestingly, by a retired Supreme Court Justice who had supported the majority position in the *Morrison* case.[41] The bill seemed to have substantial support until over 100 active and retired textile workers from the then dwindling Brown Lung Association and the Amalgamated Clothing and Textile Worker's Union converged on the Senate committee considering the legislation. Lawyers handling brown lung cases had also retained a professional lobbyist (at a cost of $15,000) to defeat the bill. When the summer session of 1983 ended, the bill had never reached the Senate floor.[42]

The Cases of Lucy Taylor and Grover Hardin

Lucy Taylor was elected the first President of the Bi-State Board of the Carolina Brown Lung Association in 1976. She had worked in the mills from the time that she was fourteen. In 1963, she was forced to retire at the age of forty-nine by a breathing problem. In 1975, she was one of the first members of the association to file for compensation.

The last years that she worked were very difficult. The ordeal was described by her husband in Mimi Conway's *Rise, Gonna Rise: A Portrait of Southern Textile Workers:*

The last seventeen years of our lives have been filled with hospital stays, waiting in emergency rooms, trips to doctors and drug stores, and the everlasting coughing. When Lucy was up in the hospital, the other patients complained because they couldn't sleep. We've bought cough syrup of all kinds by the bucketfull. . . . She coughed a thousand times to my one, and I was smoking four packs of cigarettes a day. For the last ten or fifteen years she coughed every night. Half the time she gets me up with her coughing. Then when she gets quiet, I start to worry that she's dead. I've gone to bed a thousand times like that, half the night sleepless because of her coughing, and the other half worried that she's died. Never a night passes that I don't look and see if she's breathing.[43]

Although in ill health, Lucy Taylor was one of the most active members of the Brown Lung Association, perhaps one reason why the industry continually appealed her case. After three hearings in May, June, and July of 1977, two years after she had filed, she was denied compensation in 1978. The North Carolina Industrial Commission in 1978 stated that she had not proved she became disabled within a year after she was last exposed to cotton dust, a requirement from a previous ruling.[44]

She appealed the commission's decision to the North Carolina Court of Appeals, which overturned the commission's order. J.P. Stevens, the textile company for which she worked, and its insurer, Liberty Mutual, then appealed to the State Supreme Court. In May of 1980, the Supreme Court upheld the compensation claim and returned the case to the commission for further hearings. Although the commission recommended that the claim be paid on August 18, Liberty Mutual had until September 5 to file an appeal.[45]

In an innovative strategy to block the appeal, forty members of the Brown Lung Association gathered at the Raleigh, North Carolina, offices of Liberty Mutual Insurance Company to protest the unnecessary delay in paying Lucy Taylor's claim and to demand that the company abandon any plan to appeal the claim further. Carrying signs which read, "Pay Lucy, Not Lawyers" and "Liberty Mutual Lies, Lucy Taylor Dies," the association demonstrated its awareness of the industry's willingness to pay far more than the disputed compensation figure for appeals and lawyers.[46]

Less than a week after the association's visit to Liberty Mutual, Lucy Taylor (in the hospital for the third time in six weeks) received word that the company had dropped its third appeal and that a check for $12,000 was on its way. Lucy Taylor was discharged from the hospital the next day and, according to an association staff member, she was "secure with the knowledge that after devoting almost her entire time the past five years to helping other disabled textile workers, she too had finally won a little justice."[47] But Lucy Taylor's victory was short lived. On Wednesday, November 12, 1980, only two months after she received her settlement, but over five years after she filed her claim, Lucy Taylor died.

However, Lucy Taylor left a legacy. The strategy of protest was so successful that the Brown Lung Association was encouraged to use it again. The case of Grover Hardin, a cardroom employee of the Dan River Textile Company in Greenville, South Carolina, provides an important example. Lung problems had forced Hardin's retirement in 1962. Although he was told he had a lung disease, no one had mentioned byssinosis. In 1977, he was examined at an association screening clinic and told that he might be eligible for compensation.[48]

Hardin filed a claim in 1978 and was diagnosed by a physician from Duke University as totally disabled by byssinosis. This diagnosis was confirmed by a physician who examined Hardin for Liberty Mutual Insurance Company, and indicated that he had grade 3 byssinosis, the most disabling level of the disease. In March 1980, South Carolina Industrial Commissioner Rosslee Douglas awarded Hardin $10,000 and medical expenses for total disability. Dan River and Liberty Mutual first appealed to the full commission, which upheld the previous ruling, and then to the circuit court.[49]

Dan River's response to the Hardin case reveals some of the strongest public statements by industry representatives to this issue. In 1980, Dan River published a position paper on byssinosis, with arguments similar to those of other industry and insurance representatives. However, it contained strong words about the Brown Lung Association:

The diagnosis of obstructive lung diseases is difficult enough because of the scientifically unclarified relationships between heredity, infection, life style (i.e., smoking) and other factors. The facts of lung disease have been further complicated by an organization that is not medically qualified to make medical assessments. We refer here to the Carolina Brown Lung Association.

The CBLA's clinics have gained widespread publicity in recent times. A great deal of the publicity has reinforced the false impression that *all* breathing problems experienced by textile workers are caused by conditions within the workplace. Indeed, the CBLA has led many workers who suffer health conditions completely unrelated to employment to believe that their condition was precipitated by cotton dust exposure in textile plants. This organization has been successful in generating a great deal of misguided sympathy from many in the media and the federal government. The unquestioning acceptance of this organization's statements by the press and the government is contrary to the best interests of the public who ultimately pay the bill for such unfounded allegations and distortions of facts.[50]

It was this perspective which Dan River carried into the compensation case of Grover Hardin. David Johnston, President of Dan River, not only charged that the cotton mill did not damage Hardin's lungs, but even generalized to all cases:

We don't believe that the people who work for us and get disease had their lungs damaged because they worked in a cotton environment. They got it from cigarette smoking or other natural causes. We didn't create the problem. Therefore, we have no moral responsibility for it.[51]

With regard to Hardin specifically, the company maintained that the statute of limitations to file a claim had expired. They said that there was no evidence that he was totally disabled or that he had a pulmonary disease related to his employment.[52]

On January 26, twenty-five members of the Brown Lung Association from across the state of South Carolina staged a protest and press conference outside the corporate headquarters of Dan River in Greenville. Paul Cline, President of the South Carolina Board of the Brown Lung Association, proclaimed that he was fed up with the textile firms appealing awards made to textile workers who suffered from brown lung:

We are picketing Dan River to bring out into the open what kind of company it is. . . . We got news for them. We're going to fight too. We're going to fight this thing and we're not going to be run over anymore. . . . We think it is a disgrace. They worked him for forty-three years . . . they made him sick, and they don't want to pay him.[53]

On February 16, Grover Hardin received an offer from Dan River for a $12,000 settlement. At the time, he was in a bed at Greenville

Memorial Hospital for the sixth time since April. Facing growing medical costs with a limited income, he decided to take it. According to his wife:

They asked us to settle before, but we always thought it was too low. This time they offered us what we wanted. It suits us right now because we need it, and when you need something, it's different. Its been two and a half years that we've been fighting for it. So we are glad to get it over with. He's not able to fight it anymore and I'm not either.[54]

Although the *Grover Hardin* case ended with a settlement, rather than an award, it raised an issue similar to the *Lucy Taylor* case—the statute of limitations. In most states, a limited amount of time could pass before claims had to be filed. Depending on the laws, the time could count from the date that a person knew about the disease, when he was first informed about it by a qualified physician, or from the time he left the mill.[55]

This problem was exacerbated for those textile workers who lacked knowledge of the disease's existence or were uninformed about the possibilities of compensation. Seventy-year-old Clyde Lingerfelt, who had been forced into medical retirement at age fifty-four, expressed the sentiments of many disabled millworkers when he said, "I just didn't know that there was anything I could do about getting too sick to work."[56]

THE STRUGGLE FOR FEDERAL COMPENSATION

Well, we don't have the money to bribe politicians and we don't feel like we should have to in the first place, but the state legislators have proven in two successive sessions that they are not going to do anything to help the brown lung victims. We've waited a long time and many of us have died waiting. I don't want to die of injustice.[57]

Bea Norton, Brown Lung Association member

From 1975 through 1983, the Brown Lung Association was involved in many court cases and many legislative hearings regarding the state workers' compensation programs in North and South Carolina and then in Virginia, Georgia, and Alabama. Some of these resulted in success and others in failure. Underlying these state efforts, however, was a continuing struggle for some assistance from the federal government in the compensation process. In general, the members and staff wanted to keep the compensation system on the state level. It meant easier accessibility for lobbying and other political activities, an important factor for disabled textile workers. While they were impressed with the Black Lung Benefits Program achieved by the miners, they also recognized that it took two amendments and over eight years to get the program "right," and then the program was weakened by a new administration. They also expressed concern that the government had funded the largest percentage of black lung claims. As one member testified, "We want the medical benefits that workers were entitled to as part of the risk of working in the mills. We think it is up to the textile industries' insurance companies to pay the claims and not to pawn our people off as wards of the government."[58]

Continuing struggles with the state compensation programs, however, brought the Brown Lung Association to Washington, D.C., to seek federal intervention to make state programs equitable. Strongest support for federal legislation came from South Carolina, where the compensation law produced few successful claims. After forty-eight members of the association met with Senators and Representatives in Washington in the spring of 1977, Senator Ernest Hollings, Democrat from South Carolina, promised to introduce federal legislation with the argument, "if the machinery breaks down, they pay the cost of the replacement of the machinery. If the workers break down, they ought to put that in as costs of the product."[59] But the threat of any such legislation was considered so remote that the American Textile Manufacturers Institute did not even take an official position on it.[60]

In the following summer, association members went to the nation's capital to testify before the Senate Health and Welfare Subcommittee of the Committee on Appropriations. The testimony was so convincing that the committee held a special hearing in Greenville, South Carolina, in December 1977. Approximately seventy-five textile workers, association staff members, scientists, physicians, and a few industry representatives, gathered for a full day of testimony.

The personal testimonies of twenty-eight retired and disabled millworkers were a dramatic part of the hearing, and revealed much about the personal struggle of those who have occupational illnesses in our society today. The story of Josephine Newsome, for example, demonstrates the limited alternatives for help available to the textile worker. Even though she was diagnosed in 1951 as having a lung problem that her doctor said was caused by the place where she worked, she did not see an acceptable solution:

Millwork was the only work I knew. If I filed suit against the mill it would be against a very powerful company and if I lost I would be in the same boat as those who tried to unionize, blackballed not only from the mill where I worked, but from every other mill in the country. If you didn't work in the mill, there was no other job, so I stayed out of the mill for 13 years, but in 1964 I had to work again so I returned to the mill. Many will wonder why I did such a thing. Why go back to the place that affected my health? Well, the reason is simple. A person has to make a living and the mills are the only place around.[61]

The experience of Mrs. Lennie Bass from Burlington, North Carolina, reveals how both the industry and the medical profession affected the outcome of her condition. In 1971, when Burlington Mills started giving breathing tests to its workers, Bass was diagnosed as having a breathing problem. She was sent to a doctor at Duke University and, upon her return to the mill, the company doctor recommended that she be transferred to a "less productive area" in the plant. Three years later she was finally transferred, and only then after she and a supervisor pushed for it. Equally important, she was never told what her illness was. In the early years of the mills, it was not uncommon for workers to contract either tuberculosis (TB) or emphysema. On her own initiative, Bass went to a sanitorium to find out if what she had was TB:

The doctor told me—he did not tell me my disease—that if he was me that he would never walk inside of another cotton mill, which at that time I was real sick. So I said to myself, I won't go back and carry these papers to the company because if I do I won't be able to work. So instead of coming home and getting a leave of absence I go back to work the next day, not telling anybody where I had been or what they had told me because I knew that if I did it would cause some trouble.[62]

However, upon her return to work the next day, she became too sick to work and told the supervisor about her visit to the sanitorium.

After the papers from the sanitorium arrived, Bass was sent by the company to a lung specialist in Chapel Hill. In response to her direct question, the doctor told her that she did not have emphysema. Satisfied that she did not have tuberculosis or emphysema, she returned to the mill, only to find that the company doctor declared her totally disabled to work. After pointing out that no doctor had diagnosed her as having byssinosis, he suggested that she file for Social Security disability. She was initially turned down but, with the help of her physician, was finally able to get disability payments. Not long after, the Brown Lung Association came to town:

So the brown lung people came to Erwin, and I guess I was about one of the first people that they visited when they came, and they told me that there was compensation to be paid for diseases that came from the company. And so I filed—well, they had a clinic there and I went to the clinic and one of the doctors from Chapel Hill told me that I had byssinosis. That was the first time I had ever been told that I had it.[63]

The impact of leaving the mills and being out of work was a devastating experience, perhaps one of the reasons that so many continued to work when they were disabled. Beatrice Norton was forced to leave the mills at age fifty because she could no longer perform her job up to the expectations of management:

My job would get behind and they'd call me into the office. They was fussing at me continuously and my nerves started getting bad. I was scared. I knew I wasn't old enough to get social security and there wasn't any pension waiting for me, and I couldn't see how to live except on welfare. I tried to get a leave of absence, but they talked me into quitting. I felt that the world had just turned upside down and left me without a place to put my feet on. I was awfully upset and I realized that the company didn't care about people. They cared only about machines. I had worked in the mills since I was a child, in the Beattie plant for 24 years and suddenly had no job, no money and I was sick, too sick to ever work in my life again. . . . I ain't no doctor and I wish I known what was wrong with me. Until the Brown Lung Association came along nobody was saying anything about cotton dust hurting people. . . . That was the first time I had ever heard about byssinosis. Then I got mad that they had never told me about brown lung before, that the dust in the mills would make me sick.[64]

Sometimes those who left the mill were so debilitated that their spouses had to testify for them. Such was the case with Vinnie Ellison:

My husband worked for Grady mill in Spartanburg [South Carolina]; and he worked in the dustiest part of the mill, the opening room, the cardroom and cleaning the air conditioning ducts. Sometimes he would come home from work and need a hairpin to clean the dust from his nose. Over the years his breathing got worse and worse. He did not know what was wrong with him. He never thought it was the cotton dust in the mill. In the early sixties he started having trouble keeping up his job because of his breathing. In 1963 his bossman told him that he had been a good worker, but he wasn't worth a damn anymore, and he fired him.[65]

Just as important to the retired and disabled millworkers' testimony was the documentation of the slowness with which the state compensation systems were operating, as reflected in the testimony of Evaline Peoples of Cayce, South Carolina:

The mills say, "Oh, these cases are so complicated; we need to study these difficult things. We need to send you to just a few more doctors." They always seem to have new ways of delaying, and the industrial commissioner always lets them do it. I have seen cases where the commissioners have ordered the insurance companies and the mills to get their evidence in within 30 or 60 or 90 days, but nothing happens. Just the same, the commissioners don't seem to do anything to make the mills do it. These delays are some of the most discouraging things about the State laws that we have.[66]

But the impact of these delays and bureaucratic red tape was perhaps best communicated by Lillian Baldwin, who worked for thirty years in the textile industry and had to stop working when she was fifty-five years old:

All I know is this: I lost ten years of my working life. I suffer now from shortness of breath and back discomfort and I was never told about the danger of cotton dust. I think it's wrong that people like me who have been partially disabled can't get workmen's compensation because he came out of the mill before May of 1977. I also think it is terribly discouraging and very strange that different doctors tell me different things about me but nobody tells me the truth. I worked all those years for J.P. Stevens and all

I have to show for it is a plaque of loyal service. I didn't get any pension and it doesn't look like I'll ever get any compensation. You are in a position to help all those people who haven't been helped by the industry or even told the truth about our condition.[67]

In response to the testimony at these hearings, South Carolina Senators Ernest Hollings and Strom Thurmond introduced a bill on January 27, 1978, to establish a federal program to pay textile workers crippled by brown lung. The legislation was patterned after the Black Lung Benefits Act and was justified by the argument that a "conspiracy of neglect" had victimized textile workers for decades, "a conspiracy contributed to by industry, elected officials, and the medical community."[68] Hollings held up the bill for several months to give a recently passed South Carolina law a chance to take effect. By 1979, little evidence was presented to indicate that the processing of claims was improving, so the bill was reintroduced in February. It failed to receive much support, however, and was eventually withdrawn.

Toward a National Compensation Act

Although Congress was hesitant to produce another federal benefits program, it became increasingly aware of the incongruity of state workers' compensation systems. The National Commission of State Workmen's Compensation Laws had filed its first report in June of 1972. Its findings concluded that state programs did not adequately compensate the victims of industrial injuries or diseases. The commission made a series of recommendations for improving state laws and also recommended that if the states did not sufficiently improve their laws by 1975, federal legislation accomplishing basic reforms would be in order. In 1977, a task force established by the Ford administration also studied state worker's compensation laws and concluded that the need for federal minimum standards still existed. The policy group of that task force found that the system for compensating work-related permanent total disability and death resulted in "excessive litigation, long delays in payment, high subsequent rates of persons without employment, and little relationship between benefits awarded and the actual wage loss."[69]

Of the original eighty-four recommendations made by the 1972

Task Force Report, nineteen were deemed essential. As of 1979, no state had come into compliance with even the nineteen essential recommendations. The states had reached a 60 percent level of compliance; that is, of the nineteen recommendations, the states had come into compliance with an average of fewer than twelve.[70] As a result of these findings, Senator Harrison Williams, Chair of the Subcommittee on Labor of the Committee on Human Resources introduced a National Workers' Compensation Standards bill in the spring of 1978. The bill left the state compensation system intact and required that claimants who were seeking workers' compensation first go through the state agencies or courts. A major thrust of this legislation was to address the problems presented by compensation for occupational disease and to develop specific standards dealing with occupational disease compensation. In the fall of 1978, hearings were held, and once again the Brown Lung Association came to the nation's capital.

Essie Briggs, a member of the association for three years, represented the organization. In her testimony she supported the idea of workers' compensation standards but suggested several additions to the bill. Because the association was beginning to organize in Georgia and Virginia, the need for broad coverage in occupational disease cases was important. All states had their own peculiar programs, which resulted in significant inequalities in the compensation system. But the main purpose of her talk was to communicate the extremely long delays in settling the compensation cases. Her testimony revealed not only this specific problem but a great deal about what the retired millworkers had learned during their years of struggle:

Our experience in the Carolinas is that even the most clear cut case of byssinosis takes years to complete. The industrial commissions in both states have allowed the companies to stall these cases in hopes that we would just lose interest and die. Red tape can choke us surely as brown lung. In both North and South Carolina we have seen many Brown Lung Association members die before their cases could be completed.

The original idea behind worker's compensation systems, as I understand it, was to replace slow and cumbersome court proceedings with a simple and speedy hearings procedure. In fact, the industrial commission hearings are just as slow and complicated as going to court. What we need is a system that reduces the need for attorneys. In North Carolina, less than 5 percent of regular worker's compensation cases are contested and require a lawyer. But 90 percent of brown lung claims filed are contested.

Experience has taught us the misery of a bad state system. Experience has also taught us that the states cannot be trusted to do the job well. . . . We know things take time. The Congress has a great responsibility to make certain that a piece of legislation is the nearly best solution to the problem. But, as I have often said, time is one thing we don't have.[71]

Opposition to the federalization of state workers' compensation programs was presented by both industry and insurance companies. The American Insurance Association was particularly opposed to granting broad authority to government agencies in the area of occupational health because medicine was not a precise or definitive science and, therefore, open to many diverse opinions.[72] The American Textile Manufacturers Institute considered it too radical a departure in scope and effect from the history of workers' compensation and liability programs.[73] The Alliance of American Insurers (AAI), however, identified the bottom line of resistance by pointing to the increasing costs of the present system. They wanted change, but in the opposite direction. High benefit levels and more liberal programs for workers' compensation had generated entirely new utilization patterns: the more closely benefit payments came to replacing lost wages, the greater the utilization of the benefits. The AAI saw this as causing serious dislocation to both the business and insurance communities.[74]

Although no federal standards act emerged in 1978, the Congress continued its hearings to explore the problems of workers' compensation. The most extensive of these occurred from April through June of 1979 in the House of Representatives Subcommittee on Labor Standards, chaired by Congressman Edward P. Beard, a former carpenter and painter from Rhode Island. The hearings focused on a wide range of occupational health problems, including byssinosis, asbestos-related conditions, and radiation exposure. Testimony reflected an increasing professionalization of the occupational health movement and in particular of the Brown Lung Association. The previous renditions of personal case histories of retired and disabled millworkers were supplemented by the association's legal coordinator, a plaintiff's attorney, an investigative reporter, a social researcher, professors of occupational health, medical researchers, and OSHA and NIOSH staff.[75]

Equally important as those who were there were those who were not. The leaders of the textile industry chose not to attend and merely submitted a written statement, indicating that little in their position had changed and that dialogue would not necessarily be productive.[76] It was an emerging pattern that frustrated at least one Congressman:

It is very interesting the way we held hearings on asbestosis in the middle of the region where so many workers were affected, basically out in California, where people worked in the shipyards. The industry refused to testify there, too, but they showed up in Hawaii, where there were very few workers. I suspect that if we hold a hearing now in California, maybe the industry will come to testify on brown lung, and I think this is very disturbing.[77]

The industry's opposition to federal intervention remained firm, as did its strategy. Senate hearings in 1980 resulted in the textile industry's conspicuous absence, although legal counsel for the insurance industry did make an appearance. Industry testimony reflected much of what had been said before, a point that led Senator Jacob Javits to comment on the futility of the previous year's efforts to reach any agreement on a federal compensation bill:

I have heard the witnesses testify before, not once but at least more than once—I cannot remember how many times—exactly the same way. It has been seven years. It must be a profitable business to hold this thing off. I think it is a narrow view and I think very adverse and unfair to the working people of this country. . . . Your enterprises are against any Federal action in the field and you are paid to come here and tell us that. . . . I am very devoted to the private enterprise system and I certainly welcome a little public interest from private enterprise. And it is needed in this field, gentlemen. It is almost inhumane. I have heard it many times. I know what you are saying and why you are saying it. There are just too many victims and it is just too unfair. And it is bound to get its reckoning day.[78]

The struggle for federal compensation legislation is yet to have its "reckoning day." A change in the political climate of both the executive and legislative branches of the government, adverse publicity from the costs of the Black Lung Benefits Program, effective lobbying from the textile and insurance industries, and a strategy on the part of the Brown Lung Association which gave more attention to state-level programs all contributed to this failure. The ultimate "justice" for the textile workers, though, came not from compensating the victims of brown lung, but by addressing the problem at its source. One of the underlying assumptions of the workers' compensation system was that the high cost of paying claims would force the industry to clean up the workplace. The ability of industry to hold down the cost of claims through various legal and political strategies, however, encouraged the Brown Lung Association to adopt a second major goal: a federal standard to reduce the cotton dust in the mills.

9

Not Another Generation: The Cotton Dust Standard

The history of a cotton dust standard in the United States began in 1966, when the American Council of Government Hygienists, a group of state and federal specialists in occupational health, proposed a one-milligram limit to cotton dust per cubic meter of air in textile plants. In 1969, the U.S. Department of Labor adopted this standard for textile firms with federal contracts. The one-milligram limit was applied to all textile firms in 1971 under the new Occupational Safety and Health Administration. However, even at that time, government scientists and officials recognized that a more restrictive standard was necessary. Such a standard was opposed by the Nixon administration, which had received substantial contributions from textile manufacturers before the 1972 election.[1]

No major push for a new standard came until 1975, when the Textile Workers Union of America formally petitioned OSHA to set a new standard which would control "respirable dust," that is, dust which could be inhaled and therefore affect the lungs. When OSHA failed to respond, the union filed suit in federal court against the U.S. Department of Labor to force it to establish the standard.[2] In the following year, the newly formed Brown Lung Association joined the struggle with a letter to the Director of OSHA stating that "the time for delay is over. The million textile workers in the United

States know that the Department of Labor has dragged its feet for five years."[3]

The impetus for a new standard came from two directions. First, medical research in Europe and more recently in the United States seemed to warrant a change. Of particular significance was the work of Dr. James Merchant and his associates at the Duke University Medical Center in 1971–72. An extensive study of nearly 3,000 textile workers documented a high correlation between dust level exposure and byssinosis. Previous research had already established that between 17 and 28 percent of textile workers would contract byssinosis at the then current one-milligram standard. Merchant and his colleagues revealed a prevalence of byssinosis among workers in cotton preparation and yarn areas of less than 13 percent at a .2 milligram dust level. They suggested, however, that a reasonably safe level of exposure would be a .1 milligram level, because even at this level almost 7 percent would still get byssinosis.[4]

OSHA's poor enforcement of the then current standard was another indication that reform was necessary. North and South Carolina were two of the twenty-two states approved to administer the federal OSHA program on the state level. However, it was not until 1974 that either state made its first cotton dust inspection. Even six years later, North Carolina officials had inspected only 170 of the 461 plants in the state. North Carolina officials had generally allowed companies that violated OSHA standards an average of almost two years to clean up, twice the time the federal government said was necessary to do the job. South Carolina had allowed an average of two and half years. In both states, labor officials had never gone to court to try to close a plant, and officials routinely levied only modest fines, never forcing a company to pay an overdue fine.[5]

According to research by the *Charlotte Observer* for its Pulitzer Prize–winning series "Brown Lung: A Case of Deadly Neglect," inspectors were many times encouraged to look at the "worst first," meaning that they should scrutinize those areas where the greatest number of accidents occurred, such as construction sites. Cotton dust inspections were relatively low on the list of priorities for an overworked and frequently inexperienced staff. Because of the low pay for inspectors, there was a high turnover in personnel (100 percent turnover in one eighteen month period in North Carolina); many state employees left for better-paying jobs in the industries which they had been inspecting.[6] The situation in South Carolina attracted the attention of federal OSHA officials in the summer of 1978, when a petition filed by the Brown Lung Association and the AFL-CIO asked the federal government to take over the state's inspection program. The association complained of collusion between state OSHA officials and textile owners that supposedly resulted in an agreement not to issue citations, to reduce penalties, not to prosecute, and to make few inspections.[7] Although the Assistant Secretary of Labor threatened to reinstate federal jurisdiction, this never occurred.

The *Charlotte Observer* series did, however, prompt an investigation of the North Carolina program. North Carolina was accused of extending correction dates beyond the time required, not citing violations documented in case files, not conducting follow-up investigations on serious violations, and closing some cases without evidence of abatement.[8] This investigation also failed to reinstate federal jurisdiction, and the struggle had moved onward, beyond enforcement, to the promulgation of an even more stringent standard. It was a standard which meant not only increased federal intervention, but a potential massive outlay of funds by the industry to comply with it.

THE NEW COTTON DUST STANDARD

On December 28, 1976, OSHA finally proposed a new cotton dust standard in the *Federal Register*, and held its first hearings on the standard in the spring of 1977.[9] Under the proposed standard, OSHA would initially require yarn and fabric mills to limit the amount of fine cotton dust to .5 milligrams per cubic meter, the level favored by industry. After four years, the limit would be lowered to .35 milligrams, and after three more years to .2 milligrams. These levels were based in part on a economic feasibility study done for OSHA by North Carolina's Research Triangle Institute. The study estimated that it would cost the textile industry $2.7 million to meet a .2 milligram standard. The .5 milligram level would require about $225 million in industry-wide investment. At the same time, the .5 level would prevent only 3,470 cases of byssinosis (beyond the then present level), a .2 level would prevent 28,750 cases, and a .1 level, which the Brown Lung Association and the union favored, would prevent 46,320 cases.[10]

Retired and disabled textile workers had an opportunity to respond to the proposed standard on April 15, 1977, at a public hearing arranged by OSHA in Washington, D.C. Like the coal miners before them, they made a dramatic impact, aptly described by an investigative journalist in attendance:

> The Carolina Brown Lung Association made its national debut when the fifty member delegation walked into the Departmental Auditorium on Constitution Avenue. For weeks now the room had been filled with well-dressed, high-paid lawyers and lobbyists, medical experts and technicians, each offering testimony on the feasibility of controlling the cotton dust that had already injured countless thousands of millworkers.
>
> No one like the members of the CBLA had come forward to testify in this Chinese green room with its pale gold carpets and draperies, its crafted chandeliers. When the phalanx of old and sick mill workers began their slow procession up the long aisle of supporters, textile representatives, and press, all eyes were on them.
>
> Six blinding klieg lights, set up for the three major television networks and a fourth camera, caused some of the brown lung victims to squint as they made their entrance. The cameras whirred and ranged over the lined faces, the two wheelchairs, the denim overalls, the respirator, the two oxygen tanks. The still cameras snapped at the buttons each member of the delegation wore—a large brown one reading "Cotton Dust Kills" and a smaller yellow one which said, "And It's Killing Me."[11]

One by one, disabled millworkers related their stories to the OSHA panel, a proceeding described as a "relentless witnessing of ravaged lives."[12] They also presented arguments for a .1 milligram standard with no delay in implementation, an increase in the number of inspectors, assurance of accessible medical files, and programs on the state level which would inform and educate employees to the dangers of cotton dust.[13]

At the same time, they also had an opportunity to meet privately with the recently appointed head of OSHA, Dr. Eula Bingham. It was a particularly emotional meeting, as Dr. Bingham expressed the importance of rank and file workers coming to testify. Reflecting on the constant stream of mill owners and lawyers who had come to Washington, she stated, "It is very difficult for me to get people in government to understand that we're talking about a rule or regulation that deals with people."[14] She then broke into tears. In a rare moment, the head of a government agency responsible for the health of our nation's workers "shared with these disabled mill-workers the impact of their own lives, the fearsome, cruel, and inhumane reality of what had happened to them."[15] This dramatic moment received extensive press coverage. Although certainly an atypical event, it cut through the statistics and data which had been presented in official testimony.

These hearings were to have resulted in the implementation of a final cotton dust standard by the end of 1977. However, in part because of the 5,000 pages of testimony, OSHA miscalculated how long it would take to complete the process. Also, OSHA wanted to produce a standard that would be acceptable to both workers and industry, thereby hoping to avoid a lawsuit which might postpone implementation.[16] The deadline for release was repeatedly changed, with the final and most significant delay coming in May of 1978, when President Jimmy Carter ordered a delay until the standards had been thoroughly reviewed by the Regulatory Analysis Group, an interagency panel created to keep a rein on the economic costs of regulation.[17] Strong response from the Secretary of Labor, Dr. Eula Bingham, and several members of Congress, as well as tele-grams and letters from members of the Brown Lung Association, forced him to reconsider. On June 19th, the long-awaited cotton dust standard was announced.[18]

OSHA was not successful in its effort to avoid a delaying suit, however. Somewhat unexpectedly, though, both the Amalgamated Clothing and Textile Workers Union of America (ACTWUA, which had resulted from a merger of the Textile Workers Union of America with the Amalgamated Clothing Workers of America in 1976) and the American Textile Manufacturers Institute (ATMI) filed suit in the U.S. Court of Appeals to have the regulation reviewed.[19] The standard maintained the .2 milligram level in the opening to spin-ning areas of the mills, with compliance required within four years. The union complained that the standard set too high a permissible exposure limit and that the industry did not need four years to clean up the mills. The industry complained that the standard would lead to higher prices on products containing cotton and that it had neither the technological or the economic means to meet the standard.[20]

The U.S. Court of Appeals agreed to hear the industry's case, but ruled 3–0 in October 1979 that the textile industry did have both the technical and economic means to meet the new standard.[21] To delay further, the textile industry asked that enforcement be postponed until an appeal to the U.S. Supreme Court could be heard. This request was denied in January 1980, and the standard went into effect in March 1980. This meant that companies had until March 1984 to meet the .2 milligram level.[22]

For the next several months, the early requirements of the standard were implemented. These basically included provision of respirators until permissible levels were reached, employee education and training programs, medical surveillance programs, initial dust-level monitoring, and written compliance programs. The industry, however, kept up its campaign to protest the standard as too costly and technologically impossible. On October 6, 1980, the U.S. Supreme Court agreed to take the industry's case, although the standard would remain in effect until the Court's decision. The industry's appeal was based not only on the issue of excessive costs, but also on the argument that OSHA had failed to complete a cost-benefit analysis of the standard.

Cost Benefit Analysis

Cost benefit analysis is a method of decision-making based on the economic efficiency of competing alternative actions. It has been used in the United States since the early part of the present century, primarily to make decisions about government works projects. Its use in determining the feasibility of regulations, particularly regarding safety and health, has only recently been advanced. One of the requirements of doing a cost benefit analysis is the systematic enumeration of all benefits and costs, tangible and intangible, that will accrue to all members of society if a particular project is to be adopted.[23]

At the very heart of this process is the problem of putting a value on human life. According to a recent editorial in the *American Journal of Public Health*, the debate no longer centers on whether we should attach a value to human life, but what method we should use to do this.[24] Two of the most currently used methods are the "human capital approach" and the "willingness-to-pay" approach.

In the human capital option, the value to society of an individual's life is measured by future production potential, usually calculated as the discounted value of expected labor earnings.[25] Workers' compensation for industrial accidents and diseases is generally calculated on this model. However, by its emphasis on the economic potential, not only are many people in our society left out of consideration (the retired, the disabled, etc.), but other dimensions of illness and death that may be more important to an individual than simple economic loss are ignored. An alternative model, the willingness-to-pay approach, suggests that we look at what individuals are willing to pay for a change that will affect loss of life. Although in theory this concept would take into consideration any aspect of life, the practical implementation would generally not allow that decision to be made by the individuals themselves, but by the broader population assessing the lives of a certain aggregate.[26]

Placing a value on human life is not just a theoretical concept. It is a task undertaken every day by judges and juries who must make decisions on how much to compensate victims of man-made tragedies and by governments who make decisions on spending public money. The textile industry invoked this argument in its defense of the need for a cost benefit analysis of the cotton dust standard, suggesting that decisions on how many police or firemen to hire, whether to modernize roads, and how fast we allow people to go on highways are decisions concerning health and safety that are tempered by consideration of costs and benefits.

On January 21, 1981, the Supreme Court heard arguments from both sides of the cotton dust controversy. The industry side, represented by ATMI, twelve individual cotton companies, and most of the cotton trade associations, was argued by Robert Bork, a Yale University law professor and former U.S. Solicitor General. His basic argument was that human life was not at stake in this case and that OSHA had failed to show that the benefits to workers outweighed the costs to industry of cleaning up the mills.[27] His testimony was witnessed by thirty disabled members of the Brown Lung Association who later held a press conference to protest the argument: "Would the officials and lawyers who have argued today that this is too high a price to pay to protect a person's health trade that money to live and suffer as we do? What price would they put on their own lives? You can't put a price tag on human life."[28]

Before the Supreme Court was able to reach its decision, however, the new administration embarked upon an unprecedented move to block the standard. One month after President Reagan took office, he signed an executive order requiring all regulatory agencies to send any proposed new rules and standards costing $100 million or more to the Office of Management and Budget (OMB) for cost benefit analysis.[29] The debilitation of OSHA was a top priority for the Reagan administration, and the cotton dust standard, which had provided a principal thrust behind the creation of OSHA in 1970, became a leading symbol of its regulatory counterrevolution.[30] On March 27, 1981, Thorn Auchter, the newly appointed Assistant Secretary of Labor and head of OSHA, announced that OSHA was withdrawing the cotton dust standard to take another look at it and asked the Supreme Court to delay its ruling until OSHA had more time for the review process. The major argument underlying this move was that it was necessary to make a more "objective analysis."

Because there was no precedent for this type of action, no one was certain whether the Supreme Court would grant OSHA's request. The Brown Lung Association, however, began plans for a trip to Washington to protest the action. On May 4, several hundred active millworkers and victims of brown lung demonstrated at the Department of Labor in what was called a "moral crusade."[31] It was one of the most militant actions ever taken by the Brown Lung Association, and one of the few in conjunction with the AFL-CIO and ACTWUA. The demonstrators, many of them in wheelchairs and accompanied by nurses, demanded to see either Labor Secretary Raymond Donovan or Auchter. Donovan was out of town, and Auchter would only meet with union leaders, not rank and file workers. The protestors were blocked at the entrance to the Labor Department by local police. However, about a dozen people managed to enter the building through a side door and make their way to a second story window, where they waved banners and signs which proclaimed, "Not Another Generation," "Clean Up the Mills," and "We Have a Right to Live." Although temporarily arrested, the group were let go when they agreed to leave the building. It was a symbolic victory. On that same day, protests were staged in thirty-six cities across the United States, most of them organized by state Community Occupational Safety and Health (COSH) groups, supportive unions, and the Brown Lung Association.[32]

Six weeks after the demonstration, the U.S. Supreme Court upheld the cotton dust standard, thereby nullifying the new OSHA
administration's request and rejecting the industry's appeal. In writing the 5–3 majority opinion, Justice William Brennan, Jr., declared,
"The legislative history demonstrates conclusively that Congress was
fully aware that the act would impose real and substantial costs of
compliance on industry and believed that such costs were part of
the cost of doing business."[33] He ruled that the Occupational Health
Act required the Secretary of Labor to set the standard "which most
adequately assures, to the extent feasible, on the basis of the best
available evidence" that no employee suffers material impairment
of health. Therefore, OSHA was not required to determine that the
costs of the standard bore a reasonable relationship to its benefits;
that is, cost benefit analysis was not required, although feasibility
analysis was.[34] Congress itself, then, according to Brennan, defined
the basic relationship between costs and benefits by placing the
"benefit" of worker health above all other considerations. The only
limitations on feasibility should be whether the technology existed
to achieve the standard, and whether its cost would be so high that
the ultimate survival of the industry would be threatened.[35]

Beulah Moore, then President of a North Carolina chapter of the
Brown Lung Association, summarized the reaction of retired and
disabled textile workers to the ruling:

It proves that you can't put a dollar value on human life in this country.
The cotton dust standards came too late to help people like me. . . . My
breath can't be saved now, and there are thousands in the same condition.
But for many thousands more, the cotton dust standard may mean that they
can look forward to a healthy future. We, in the Brown Lung Association,
are going to do everything we can to make sure that brown lung becomes
a disease of the past, like smallpox or polio. We are overjoyed that the
Supreme Court has supported the position that we have held all along: that
cotton mills shouldn't just worry about their profit margins, they should be
worrying about the health of their workers as well. We have been fighting
for this cotton dust standard for over five years, and we feel now that our
hard work has been justified. American textile workers now know that their
health and safety won't be sacrificed in the name of "cost-benefit" analysis.
That makes our struggle worthwhile.[36]

Beulah Moore's enthusiasm, and that of thousands of disabled
millworkers, was short-lived, however. On January 13, 1982, OSHA

announced again its intent to review and perhaps change the cotton dust regulations. The justification for this review was based on an interpretation of the term "feasibility," with the term "cost-effectiveness" replacing the concept of cost benefit analysis. Although OSHA recognized that the application of cost benefit analysis was precluded by the Supreme Court's decision, the agency concluded that it was totally appropriate to reexamine new health data and alternative compliance approaches to allow the agency to set "a more technically accurate and cost effective standard."[37] In addition, it suggested that this review could result in a reconsideration of the then current exposure levels.[38]

Over the next year and a half, OSHA conducted hearings to determine what changes would be necessary, in effect reopening the scientific debate about the evidence supporting the cotton dust standard. The controversy continued, and thus prompted the House Science and Technology Committee to hold its own hearings into how the recent research on cotton dust and byssinosis was being used by the Reagan administration to question the standard approved by the Supreme Court.[39]

Although the textile industry continued to argue for a relaxation of the standards, the majority of the mills, especially the larger ones, had already met the .2 milligram limit—a limit they were not required to meet until 1984. A report released by ACTWUA (based upon data provided by ATMI to OSHA) revealed that 81 percent of the workers in the sample now worked in areas that met the standard. In addition, the report showed that the companies studied reported an average return on investment of 9.9 percent in 1980, compared with 8.6 percent for the industry as a whole. It was a strong argument for the success of the standard in terms of both technological capability and economic feasibility.[40]

The debate over the revision of the standard took a new twist in early 1983 as the President's Office of Management and Budget, through its Director, David Stockman, argued that expensive engineering controls would offer workers no more protection than if they simply wore protective masks. At this point, OSHA had reached the decision that engineering controls still should be required, even if other standards were eased. The conflict continued until May 1983, when the Reagan administration reversed itself and supported the retention of ventilation control equipment in the standard. It was a significant departure from Reagan's commitment to ease federal rules that required costly, extensive changes in the workplace. However, there was not widespread support from industry, which argued that it had already spent too much. OSHA estimated that 80 percent of the textile mills covered by the engineering controls requirement had spent about $143 million altering their plants.[41] It was also suggested by one observer that Reagan's upholding the standard was an attempt to show he cared about health and safety issues and to counteract many of the recent revelations of poor enforcement at the Environmental Protection Agency.[42]

Although the Reagan administration upheld the standard, less than three weeks later OSHA announced another proposed change which, if inacted, would weaken the standard by extending the deadline for compliance in certain areas by two years and provide for "action levels" below which training, monitoring, and medical surveillance would be eliminated.[43] Hearings were held in Columbia, South Carolina, on October 4, 1983, at which representatives of both the ACTWUA and the Brown Lung Association testified in opposition to the proposed changes. But by this time the association was merely a shell of the organization it had once been, and only a few members came to testify. Even more revealing of a more militant strategy by the industry was the presence at these hearings of a lawyer, hired by ATMI and reportedly experienced in compensation cases for brown lung, who directly challenged the testimony of the members of the Brown Lung Association and their supporters. It resembled a court of law more than a public hearing.[44]

Interestingly, OSHA has yet, almost two years later, to act on its proposed changes or the testimony from the hearings. On March 27, 1984, at least fourteen years after the government first proposed it, the standard went quietly into effect. The reality of the effectiveness of the cotton dust standard, however, lies not in the program itself, but in its enforcement. The deregulation of OSHA during the Reagan administration has continued to take its toll. During the first year of the new administration (1981), the number of workplace inspections dropped by 18 percent. Follow-up inspections were down 73 percent, serious citations declined 37 percent, and fines were reduced by 65 percent. Prior to 1981, approximately 23 percent of all citations were contested by the employer; in 1981, only 8 percent were contested. During this same period, the backlog of unanswered complaints from workers rose 121 percent. On February 1, 1982, OSHA announced that it would no longer respond automatically to complaints from workers, as the 1970 Occupational Safety and Health Act required.[45]

Budget cuts for OSHA have also had an impact. In 1982, the agency's funds were reduced by 25 percent, forcing a 30 percent reduction in OSHA inspectors. NIOSH, OSHA's research arm, had its budget cut by 40 percent, and its training and education centers were completely closed in 1982 for lack of funds. The budget of the New Directions Program, whose purpose was to educate active workers about health and safety, was cut in half.[46]

THE RESPONSE OF THE SOUTHERN TEXTILE INDUSTRY

Let us interject our ready acknowledgement that some industries have, from time to time, performed and produced evils during the course of history. Industries have produced harmful products, and industries have exploited workers. The cotton textile industry is not among these industries.

Editor, *Southern Textile News*,
August 11, 1980

The response of the southern textile industry to the problem of cotton dust and byssinosis has not been uniform. Some companies began addressing the problem long before the Brown Lung Association came into existence. Others have yet to take action, perhaps in hopes that an extension of time or a lack of enforcement will save them the costs. What united the opposition of mill owners against the occupational health movement in general and against the Brown Lung Association in particular was ideology. The two major themes in this opposition were the historical struggle against the collective organization of workers through unionization and the need for the textile industry to remain free from government intervention, especially on the federal level.

The cotton textile industry in the southern United States is a large enterprise. It provides over half a million jobs, supplies more than $16.7 billion in products and services, and contributes more than $908 million in state taxes across the South. Cotton is the mainstay of 94,810 businesses concentrated in the South—including farms, gins, cottonseed oil mills, warehouses, raw cotton merchandising firms, and, of course, textile mills. The major portion of the textile industry is located in North and South Carolina, with 250,000 and 144,000 employees respectively, and Georgia, running a close third with 123,000. In South Carolina, 187 mills employ 73,000 cotton workers. In North Carolina, 327 textile mills run cotton and provide a total of 83,700 jobs. The greater number of mills and the relatively similar number of employees testifies to the existence of smaller mills in North Carolina.[47]

The textile industry is a relatively low profit industry, primarily because of its serious competition from foreign trade. Its profit after taxes on sales is only 2.5 percent, compared to 5.2 percent for all manufacturing. The industry also employs a large number of minorities and women. In 1979, 47 percent of its employees were female; 23 percent were minorities, as compared with 15 percent for all manufacturing. It is also relatively ununionized, with less than 10 percent of southern textile workers belonging to a union.[48]

Many mill owners viewed the Brown Lung Association in much the same way as they did the union—it was a "third party." Equally important, it was a group orchestrated by "outsiders" who presented themselves as adversaries. As one mill owner stated, "Our people don't need a damned outside source to come talk to us and they know it."[49] In interviews, many mill owners mentioned the continued significance of the "open door policy," a procedure by which shopfloor workers could come into the office of the president anytime they wanted to discuss a problem. This "individual" approach to problem solving had existed for years, and administrators wanted to keep it because it demonstrated their concern for the welfare of the people and the success of the cooperative approach.

The adversarial relationship between management and labor had its roots in actions taken by the government, according to one mill owner:

This has been the theory all along since the thirties—to separate the management, to put them over here, and the workers in the corner. . . . It's the dividing hand of government that's done that. You tax the hell out of both of them, kill 'em in the head, get them fighting each other and the government bureaucrats run the damn world. You get an adversarial relationship and then you get these kooks up in Washington who think they know more than we do about what we should do with our lives. We claim that the people out here put their britches on the same way that we do, and it just happens that I am President. I wasn't put here by some dictator.[50]

The textile industry was particularly opposed to federal intervention, and at least one mill owner saw the battle in broader political terms:

This is simply not a fight against so called "brown lung." This fight is as old as civilization: the unending war of a free people with inalienable rights granted by God, against those tyrannical power hungry politicians intent on the establishment of a totalitarian government. This is what the fight is all about. What we are facing is the downfall of the free enterprise system. Everything we substitute for it is socialism.[51]

Although not all mill owners were as adamant as these two, statements by ATMI suggest that they did not want decisions to be made by "federal bureaucrats many miles away with little idea of local health and industry problems."[52]

Of course, the industry had a powerful lobby on the state level. In 1979, the South Carolina Textile Manufacturers Association spent $28,252 in the General Assembly session, more than twice as much as any of the 220 other registered lobby groups. Although the North Carolina Textile Manufacturers Association (NCTMA) only spent $1500 in 1979, it did not need a strong lobby. The Chairman of the Senate Committee on Manufacturing and Wages was a former President of NCTMA.[53]

Mill Owners and Brown Lung

One of the controversial issues regarding the industry's handling of brown lung was that of determining the point in time at which it first became aware of the disease. The Brown Lung Association publicized a 1940 issue of *Textile World*, a trade publication, in which an industrial hygienist for the North Carolina Industrial Commission wrote about a disease called "card-room fever" and the need for strict control of dust to eliminate this health hazard from low-grade cotton.[54] However, some twenty-four years later, a major textile leader explained why nothing had been done:

If this disease were prevalent among cotton textile employees, it would seem to me that some time during my 37 years in this industry that fact would come to my attention during the hundreds of meetings and conferences of textile manufacturing employers which I have attended and at many of which employee health, plant working conditions, and disease prevention programs have been discussed. I believe the employers who work with them everyday would have knowledge of that fact.[55]

This denial approach was reflected even more strongly in a 1969 editorial in *America's Textile Reporter* which referred to byssinosis as "a thing thought up by venal doctors who attended last year's [International Labor Organization] meeting in Africa where inferior races are bound to be afflicted by new diseases more superior people defeated years ago."[56]

Not all industries took this approach, however. In the same year, Burlington Industries, the largest textile company in the country, embarked upon a study supported by federal and state funds. In concluding that byssinosis could be clinically diagnosed and was directly attributable to cotton dust, Burlington became the first major textile company to publicly acknowledge the job-related aspects of the disease and to call for some form of compensation for those suffering from the disease.[57]

This positive step by Burlington was overshadowed, however, by the activity (or inactivity) of other mills and by the work of ATMI. Following its study which concluded that byssinosis was not as widespread as had been previously assumed, ATMI, along with two cotton trade associations (Cotton, Inc., and the Cotton Council, Inc.), formed an industry-wide cotton dust committee to coordinate their counterattack. Representatives of this committee met repeatedly with Secretaries of the Departments of Agriculture and Labor. The committee also provided staff assistance to many textile firms in successful fights against OSHA citations under the old standard between 1972 and 1979. In 1974, the committee testified before the Senate Labor Committee on a national workers' compensation bill. When the bill was reintroduced, cotton dust was excluded. And, by its own admission, the committee's efforts were instrumental in a reduction of nearly $2 billion from a $3.2 billion price tag for the initial cotton dust standard proposed by OSHA.[58]

The basic idea behind the industry's position was to dispel many

of what it called "myths" about byssinosis. The first had to do with
the name "brown lung." The term originated in an article by Ralph
Nader,[59] and was used to demonstrate its relationship to coal miner's
black lung. The industry considered the term a misnomer invented
purely for its emotional impact, and argued that not only was there
no discoloration of the lungs, but that no pathological evidence
existed to distinguish byssinosis from other chronic lung diseases.[60]
Industry's argument against both compensation and the cotton dust
standard was based on the lack of agreement among experts as to
what constituted a valid diagnosis of the disease. When the issue of
apportionment was advanced, however, the industry argued that it
was possible to identify byssinosis.

The second "myth" had to do with the prevalence of the disease.
One OSHA study had indicated that 84,000 cotton textile workers
had byssinosis. Based on its own research, the textile industry suggested that the figure was much lower, around 2,330, or one percent
of the total textile population.[61] Another study by ATMI in 1982
suggested that only 1,330 active workers suffered from chronic byssinosis. By that time, OSHA had also reduced its figure to approximately 30,000, with 18,000 of these residing in North and South
Carolina.[62]

In addition to attacking the studies which had already been done,
primarily on the basis of their limited scope and dated information,
the industry embarked on a campaign to identify certain millworkers
as "reactors" to cotton dust, shifting the responsibility for the illness
onto workers. As one top executive explained:

I kind of liken it to an allergy, you know. . . . You have seen people who
are allergic—they say everybody is allergic to something—but an asthmatic
gets along fine until all of a sudden something they contact triggers it. . . .
Now I think that byssinosis is not nearly so severe as that, but I think that
we call them reactors because . . . whenever they are exposed to whatever
it is in cotton lint or dust . . . they react.[63]

During the 1970s, the industry's response to the problem of cotton
dust was relatively low-key, mostly behind the scenes lobbying and
some congressional testimony. Little had appeared in the news media, and the industry took the position that the less said the better.

In 1980, when the *Charlotte Observer*, the largest newspaper in the Carolinas, began an investigation (after much encouragement from the Brown Lung Association), the newspaper requested that ATMI submit a statement about byssinosis. Even though ATMI declined, the newspaper ran its series "Brown Lung: A Case of Deadly Neglect"[64] for eight days in February of 1980, in twenty-four pages of newsprint. It was a monumental piece of investigative reporting, which had the effect of forcing the textile industry to bring its side of the story to the public. Larry Christiansen, editor of *Textile World*, responded that "justly or not, the series did light a fire under textiles to tell its own story, not to the *Observer*, but to the public."[65] According to Christiansen, the industry had consistently failed in its attempts to convince the media because it "never got its act together." The attempts had been piecemeal, primarily because most companies never really believed in the problem or were unwilling to release information.[66]

Unlike the Brown Lung Association, which had to create newsworthy events for media coverage, the textile industry ran a series of full-page advertisements in eleven newspapers across North Carolina in May of 1980. A committee of sixteen textile officials working through ATMI had constructed the ads, which cost $31,905.[67] The theme reflected the most consistent strategy taken by the industry, that is, that cotton dust was not the only cause of breathing problems among textile workers. Building on statistics provided by a county medical society in North Carolina,[68] the advertisements pointed out that one in five Americans had a chronic lung condition. More specifically, they stated that cigarette smoking had been linked to the vast majority of lung disease, and this raised "real questions about the role of cotton dust as a causative factor in byssinosis."[69] This approach had a negative aspect, however, because it produced a continuing struggle between the textile industry and the state's second-largest industry, tobacco.[70]

The industry-wide cotton dust committee also conducted a two-day Cotton Dust Tour for media representatives in June of 1980. Reporters from several southern states were not only provided guided tours of various plants but were given packets of information about the importance of cotton textiles to each southern state. In August of 1980, *Southern Textile News*, a weekly trade publication, published a twenty-eight-page special edition on cotton dust. Its extensive summary of the cotton industry's position was written to "be of value in answering some of the questions in the minds of Americans concerning moral, health, economic and technological issues of the cotton dust problem."[71]

Part IV

REFLECTIONS AND INTERPRETATIONS

10

On Insiders and Outsiders: The Making of a Social Movement

> To use only a language that is understood by graduates in law and economics, you can easily prove that the masses have to be managed from above. But . . . if you are not obsessed by the perverse desire to spread confusion and rid yourself of the people, then you will realize that the masses are quick to seize every shade of meaning and to learn all of the tricks of the trade. . . . Everything can be explained to the people, on the single condition that you really want them to understand.
>
> Franz Fanon, *The Wretched of the Earth*

This exploration of the Black Lung and Brown Lung Associations is guided by their designation as social movement organizations. Consequently, it is couched within the general study of social movement theory, particularly within the field of sociology. More specifically, it is influenced by an emerging approach to the study of social movements called "resource mobilization."[1] Although still primarily in the conceptual stage of development, this perspective is challenging many of the traditional ideas about social movements.[2] According to Mayer Zald and John McCarthy, two of its proponents, the resource mobilization approach deals in general terms with the dynamics and tactics of social movements' growth, decline, and change.[3] Whereas traditional approaches view social movements as based upon aggrieved populations which provide the resources and labor for the movements,[4] the new perspective "deemphasizes grievances and focuses upon societal supports and constraints of movements, tactical dilemmas, social control, media usage, and the interplay of external supports and elites."[5]

The present analysis attempts to follow the framework of the resource mobilization approach by giving attention to (1) the environment in which these movements emerged, including occupational health within the context of the broader health system in America, as well as the historical experiences of the workers themselves, (2) the roles of medical and legal institutions and the practitioners within them, (3) the significance of government, on both the state and federal level, (4) the influence of the news media, (5) the importance of external funding sources, and (6) the prominence of professional organizers within the movements. It is unlikely that coal miners and textile workers could have achieved as much as they did without a number of outside resources. This statement, however, may say less about the abilities of miners and millworkers and more about the complexity of issues that surround the problems of occupational health.

Still, we are left with the haunting suspicion that few, if any, of these advances were made until the workers themselves, particularly the retired and disabled coal miners and millworkers, were brought into the struggle. In effect, the struggle never really began until significant numbers of workers became knowledgeable about the diseases that afflicted them, what caused them, and what could be done. The 1969 Federal Coal Mine Health and Safety Act was passed only one year after the formation of the West Virginia Black Lung Association. The Black Lung Benefits Program, a part of this act, was not even under consideration by the legislators until it was pushed by miners and their supporters. The 1972 and 1977 amendments to the FCMHSA, which liberalized the benefits program, were generally attributed to the efforts of the Black Lung Association and the union. Even though there was a compensation law for brown lung as early as 1950, no claims were awarded in South Carolina until the Brown Lung Association began organizing over twenty-five years later. The majority of the over 3,000 cases filed for brown lung compensation in North Carolina by 1985 were filed during the peak years of the Brown Lung Association. Although the cotton dust standard had been proposed in 1966, it was not until the Brown Lung Association and the union pushed OSHA that a standard was finally instituted.

Other researchers have reached similar conclusions about the impact of these movements. Daniel Fox and Judith Stone, writing about the black lung issue, conclude that

angry miners persuaded public officials to accept their definition of disease, respiratory impairment resulting from work, and to reject prevailing opinion among pathologists, epidemiologists, and internists. The miners' anger and its translation into effective politics was a result of a series of events which persuaded a significant number of them that they had been betrayed by their employers, their union and their government.[6]

Historian George Hopkins's description of the movement is similar:

The Black Lung Association spearheaded the efforts of disabled and retired miners to . . . establish unprecedented federal involvement in occupational health and safety issues. The Federal Coal Mine Health and Safety Act of 1969 paved the way for the Occupational Safety and Health Act [of 1970].[7]

A comparable assessment of the Brown Lung Association is made by political scientist Robert Botsch:

By the fall of 1981, relatively strict standards [had] been set and upheld by the Supreme Court, a considerable number of disabled workers [had] collected awards, and state laws in both Carolinas [had] changed to somewhat ease the way for future claims. The BLA was actively producing input into all of the political bodies that made decisions to bring about these changes from the Department of Labor's cotton dust hearings . . . to Senate and House hearings on workman's compensation reform in 1978, 1979, and 1980.[8]

Retired and disabled workers were able to persuade public officials to reject, or at least supplement, the prevailing opinion of the medical establishment and their definitions of diseases. By "offering themselves as evidence," they contributed a necessary element to the successful movement action that resulted in reform of state compensation programs and federal intervention into the occupational health issues.

But coal miners and textile operatives are not the only American workers to experience serious occupational diseases.[9] Why, then, are they the first, and perhaps the only, workers to have created broad-based social movements in occupational health?[10] How were they able to achieve so many significant changes in the occupational health system? In other words, why did these movements emerge and why were they successful?

The answers to these questions are obviously complex. The resource mobilization perspective, however, is not only of theoretical significance, but has much to contribute to solving the practical problems of social movement decision-makers, particularly in terms of their attempts to resolve strategic dilemmas. As a result of the growing availability of resources and personnel who have made movement participation a lifelong pursuit, external resources and outside involvement were important issues of grass-roots organizations of the last two decades.[11] Both the Black Lung and Brown Lung Associations had to deal with these supports and/or constraints. Many who reacted negatively to both movements accused them of being orchestrated by "outside agitators" and supported by external organizations and foundations which had no real conception of the problems in either industry. Supporters, and particularly outside organizers, of both movements tended to minimize the significance of outside involvement, pushing the idea that these were totally "workers' movements" and that the roles of outsiders were secondary. While these distinctions may serve the political rhetoric of the radical left or the conservative right, they merely blur the reality that the social scientist hopes to understand. To comprehend both the successes and the failures of these movements, we must look more closely at the relationship which existed between the members and the various outsiders who made major contributions to the accomplishment of the movements' goals.

THE SIGNIFICANCE OF OUTSIDE INVOLVEMENT

The phrase "outside agitator" is familiar to both Appalachian mountaineers and Southerners, for those so labeled defined the framework for many of the changes, or attempted changes, which have been introduced into both regions. Appalachia has held a certain fascination for outsiders and has, according to one author, been rediscovered at least four times during its history. It was invaded by a literary movement in the post–Civil War period, by missionaries and mission schools in the first two decades of the twentieth century, by liberal groups adopting the coal miners as a cause in the 1930s, and by the War on Poverty in the 1960s.[12] In addition, industrialization brought on by coal mining, the absentee ownership of mines, and the mechanization of the mines all contributed to continued outside interference.

The intervention of the Union Army during the Civil War, the reconstructionists, the civil rights activists, and the federal government caused the South to develop a peculiar sensitivity to outside influence on the region. As historian Sheldon Hackney observes, "Almost every significant change in the life of the South has been initiated by external powers."[13] More to the point, however, is novelist Lillian Smith's lament that "outside interference became a compulsive cry to every suggestion of change. Always the outsider did the evil."[14] The sentiments about outside labor organizers specifically are captured in the early research of Harriet Herring on mill villages:

The paternalistic system is still quite generally approved in the South. The public, therefore, sees no need for organization. It disapproves heartily of strikes and the attendant disruption of the community. It disapproves of "outside agitators." These facts are plain enough in any labor trouble in the South; they were strikingly evident in the recent instances where literally hundreds of citizens of North Carolina were examined for jury duty and expressed their opinions on this subject.[15]

Recent empirical support for this theme is provided by sociologist John Shelton Reed, who found in survey research that 52 percent of a sample of North Carolinians who had high regional consciousness (that is, thought about regions of the country at all) agreed that most of the things that happen in the South are the result of forces outside of the South over which Southerners have little control. He also found that 47 percent of the southern whites in this sample agreed that the South could solve its own problems if the rest of the country would leave it alone. However, only 29 percent of non-southern whites felt the same way.[16]

Since both the Black Lung and Brown Lung Associations were

supported by outside funding and/or personnel, much opposition to them focused on these factors. But equally significant was the fact that the health of both miners and millworkers was not an isolated phenomenon. It was linked to the broader economic, political, social, and cultural systems of each of these regions. An attack on one part of this system posed serious problems for the maintenance of the stability of the other parts. Sociologist Neil Smelser argues that when the social institutions of a society are tightly integrated, and particularly when they are connected to a broader value system, the conduciveness for movements that challenge the foundation of that society increases,[17] which obviously influences the level of response for those who defend the system. Occupational health was an issue with ramifications for many parts of the broader social system, if not the system itself.

The success or failure of both movements was, at least in part, dependent on the leaders' ability to understand and work within this broader system. In an excellent analysis of the how the distribution of power prohibited attempts at social change in an Appalachian mining community, John Gaventa identifies the complex relationship between the powerful, the powerless, and the outsider who attempts to seek social change:

Those who sought to alter the oppression of the miner—the northern liberal and the Marxist radical—failed partly because they did not understand fully the power situation they sought to change. The northern liberal sought to allow freedom of expression for the miners by challenging the barriers to the exercise of his civil rights; yet the consequence was the transformation of the substance and the arenas of the issues away from those originally expressed and felt by the miners. The radical sought to develop a revolutionary class consciousness, but he misunderstood the prior role of power in shaping the consciousness which he encountered. It was the local mountain elite, who knew best the uses of power for control within their culture, who effectively capitalized on the mistakes of the others. The toll can be measured by the effects upon the miners, who faced the loss of control and the ultimate failure of the rebellion, with a consequent increase of a sense of powerlessness. For them newly shaped symbols—"communist," "outsiders," "dual unions"—had been added as resources to the prevailing mobilization of bias, to be used to re-instil labour acquiescence again in the future.[18]

It is this misunderstanding of the prior role of power and culture in shaping consciousness that outsiders in both Appalachia and the South have many times demonstrated in their attempts to mobilize the members of the working class. The organizers of both the black lung and brown lung movements faced similar situations. They were labeled anarchists, radicals, communists, hippies, damn Catholics, and labor union agitators. It is significant that these charges came not only from representatives of industry but from conservative elements in a wide range of institutions, suggesting that the response was a cultural reaction as much as a ploy on the part of industry to debunk the movement. Even regional natives who identified with the movements were labeled as outsiders, an indication that outsiders are not just identified by geographical boundaries but rather by their relationship to basic traditions, values, and beliefs that supposedly reflect the dominant culture. For example, supporters of both movements fell outside a culture which defines illness in such a way that those who fall victim to a disease, particularly an occupational disease, run the risk of being labeled as deviant in a production-oriented society.

Still, the fact that both movements were either initiated or heavily supported by outside influence raises the question: why was such intervention necessary? Retired and disabled workers anywhere are unlikely candidates for mobilizing the necessary resources to produce a social movement. Poor physical health, low pensions, limited mobility, and age seriously inhibit their efforts. But why did most of the resources *and* personnel that supported both of these movements come from outside their respective regions? If it is true that change in the South has been generally initiated from the outside, then is the South not producing institutions and people that are seriously interested in social change? It may be, as sociologist John Shelton Reed has suggested, that social activists, like sociologists, are inclined to examine or question things that many Southerners would just as soon leave unexamined.[19] Perhaps this is one of the reasons that the South produces so few of either.

A major contribution of outsiders to both movements, then, was an orientation toward change and a questioning attitude about traditional practices in established institutions. They challenged the social stability and harmony that had become a goal valued above everything else.[20] A second contribution of outsiders was a knowledge of medical and legal issues surrounding occupational disease. Both miners and millworkers experienced the symptoms of pulmonary disease and created their own names for them: "miner's con," "miner's phthisis," or "the black spit" for black lung, and "mill fever" "weaver's cough," or "weaver's asthma" for brown lung. Although these names indicated an awareness of the occupational link to disease, this "folk" knowledge was not considered legitimate to those in authority. In addition, according to Dan Berman, there may have been an actual conspiracy to minimize access to information that may have contributed to a better understanding of the true nature of both diseases.[21] The fact that access to medical records was an important part of both struggles suggests some support for this thesis. The Black Lung and Brown Lung Associations generally provided this information free, at least in areas where they organized. Otherwise, workers often had to pay for it. In South Carolina, where workers were responsible for the costs of medical exams, the number of workers who filed for compensation was reduced.

A similar situation existed in the legal arena. Not only did the miners of the original West Virginia Black Lung Association have to collect $10,000 just to draft a compensation bill, but miners in Kentucky had to pay attorneys an average of over $4,000 between 1971 and 1973 under the Black Lung Benefits Program. Equally important, when the attorneys' fees were later reduced by the government, the number of compensation claims dropped dramatically. The abuses were not so great in textile communities, where attorneys generally received from 20 to 25 percent of the final settlement or award. By June of 1985, a total of 1,554 cases had been found compensable in North Carolina for a total of $22,729,016 paid to brown lung victims.[22] If one conservatively applies the lower percentage, then the average attorney's fee was $2,925 on an average claim of $14,626.14.

The point here is not necessarily to raise an ethical issue for lawyers or doctors who handle compensation cases, but simply to indicate that the professional assistance workers needed to negotiate the occupational health system is, even if available, expensive. And, as Thomas Mancuso, Professor of Occupational Health at the University of Pittsburgh, has recently observed, much information is not available:

How can a worker file a claim for occupational disease . . . when the worker doesn't know the hazardous substances to which he has been previously exposed during his employment . . . when his own doctor doesn't know the chemicals and hazards in the workplace—what the working conditions are. . . . How can the worker know the harmful effects on the job if there is no plant doctor . . . or if there is no system of medical recognition of occupational diseases . . . where all essential information, even if in existence, is not available to the worker. . . . How can the worker hope for compensation when the worker does not have the professional consultants, the industrial medical experts, the industrial hygienist, the chemists, and laboratory to turn to for evaluation and testimony, when the entire burden is placed upon the worker to prove his case?[23]

A third major contribution of outsiders was funding. During the last two decades, many institutions not usually thought of as movement supporters—churches, foundations, and the government—provided financial backing to grassroots efforts for social change. Churches, particularly where northern liberal clergy were located, continued to be involved in social action projects.[24] There was also a dramatic increase in the funding available from foundations. One analysis of foundation grants from 1962 to 1969 found an increase in spending from $315 million to $677 million. Even more important was an increase in the amount which went to "social participation grants" (money which frequently went to social movement organizations) from 1.1 percent of the total ($3.7 million) to 8.1 percent ($54.9 million) in 1969.[25]

Substantially greater funds for the Brown Lung Association had a tremendous influence on the development of the movement. It was not only able to maintain a large professional staff, but also to hire specialists in medical research, legal issues, accounting, and external fundraising. At the same time, funding sources frequently established guidelines for continued support. The Campaign for Human Development made funding contingent upon the creation of a worker-controlled movement; OSHA funds permitted staff to work only with active workers (which at times created conflict with the union); VISTA volunteers were restricted in their lobbying activities; and CETA grants placed extensive restrictions on the hiring of staff. External funding also required an extensive time commitment to preparation of proposals which, in effect, became a major part of the movement's activities. The impact of this was realized by one staff member after the external funding, which supported the staff, the offices, and the association meetings, was dramatically reduced:

> The other thing about the government money was that it created a bureaucratic overlay. Suddenly there were meetings. One of the biggest complaints of the staff was that they were also having to drive people to meetings. People started to confuse all of those meetings with making decisions about how this or that grant money was going to be spent, with the movement, with making changes, with actually achieving goals. It did a lot of good because members were involved and they learned how committees functioned. They learned how to make decisions; they got involved in the organization. It had a lot of pluses, but I also think that with the ending of that, people think "well, we are not making progress anymore, because we don't have all of these activities."[26]

The loss of funds, staff, and offices removed many of the symbols of the movement that the membership had been accustomed to seeing and upon which much of their relationship with the movement was based. But it also removed real resources upon which the organization was heavily dependent. A better balance between external and internal funding might have reduced the dramatic impact of the loss of external funding, but this was not a pattern which either the staff or members encouraged. Less than 10 percent of total funding came from inside the organization.

A fourth external influence was the news media, particularly television and the press. Literally thousands of articles on both black lung and brown lung appeared in local, regional, and national newspapers. McCarthy and Zald suggest that since the invention of printing and the growth of widespread literacy, "social movement organizations have employed mass communications to build membership commitment, to garner support for movement goals, and to influence decision makers."[27] They also point out that the universality and immediacy of these forms allow movement organization leaders to manipulate images of social problems with great impact and to influence the public's perception of a movement's intensity of action.[28]

Both movements did this through press conferences and press releases. An analysis of twenty-seven press releases by the Black

Lung Association between January 1970 and November 1971 revealed that 88 percent (twenty-four) of these were attempts to arouse sympathy for the association's efforts or with the population of coal miners in general, a process sometimes referred to as "grievance portrayal."[29] Of these twenty-four, eleven were directed at specific bystander publics the association wanted to bring into its confrontation with the Social Security Administration.

The response of the news media to the problem of occupational disease was not automatic, however. It was not until the cotton dust hearings in Washington, D.C., in 1977 that national press attention to the problem of brown lung was evident. National television and press coverage in turn legitimized the story for local papers. Coverage in the local media, those most intimidated by industry, gave the millworkers an opportunity to see themselves in the news, particularly on television, which, according to one journalist, gave them a "sense of confidence and solidarity, of not being alone."[30] The local media also forced the industry to abandon its strategy of silence, particularly in the case of the publication of the *Charlotte Observer*'s "Brown Lung: A Case of Deadly Neglect."[31]

An analysis of the number of articles about brown lung published by the *Charlotte Observer*, the Carolinas' largest newspaper, from 1975 to 1982 revealed a high correlation between the number of staff in the Brown Lung Association and the number of articles published each month. As the size of the staff increased, shortly thereafter followed an increase in the number of articles published. Peak staff level and publications were reached at approximately the same time in 1980, after which time there was a substantial reduction in both.[32]

In sum, then, outside forces contributed to the growth and development of both the black lung and brown lung movements. First, outside organizers brought with them an ideology of social change and confrontation to challenge the prevailing power structure in both regions. Second, professionals contributed the medical, legal, and political knowledge to make that change viable. Third, outside funding agencies provided the financial resources for staff and offices which facilitated communication and interaction within the movements. Finally, regional and national news media provided a vehicle by which grievances could be portrayed and third parties could be brought into the struggle.

INSIDERS: THE DYNAMICS OF MOVEMENT PARTICIPATION

The discussion up to this point may give the reader the impression that both of these movements were essentially "professional social movements," orchestrated by outside forces that involved the membership in only marginal ways. On the contrary, retired and disabled miners and millworkers were actively involved in both movements, holding leadership positions and making the major policy decisions. The relationship between the membership and external supports, particularly staff, however, is a complex issue that is at the heart of many modern social movements and of theoretical perspectives which attempt to explain them.

The issue is sometimes discussed theoretically with regard to the incentives which encourage people to participate. The economist Mancur Olson argues that people are more likely to become involved in collective action if they are provided an individual selective incentive for participation.[33] He suggests that it is too difficult to mobilize people on the basis of some ill-defined, abstract collective good that may not necessarily benefit them personally. McCarthy and Zald, while accepting the validity of Olson's analysis, deflect the importance of the argument by advancing the thesis that "individual citizen participation may be unimportant to movement vitality."[34] They suggest that the mobilization of the resources important to the growth and survival of a movement may more effectively be carried out by a small group of professional entrepreneurs who use their skills to manipulate images of relevance and support through the communications media. The "modern" social movement, then, is generally composed of a small professional staff, which controls the movement's goals, strategies, and tactics, and a very small or nonexistent membership base which, although it will benefit from the movement, contributes very little to the actual functioning or success of the movement organization.[35]

There is certainly some support for this interpretation of the two movements discussed in this analysis, particularly the Brown Lung Association. Outside funding, professional staff, and the importance of news media may point to this conclusion. However, a weakness in this image is that it assumes a static view of movement organizations, and of the internal relationships of their participants. A more dynamic approach might suggest that retired and disabled workers changed as a result of participation in these movements, and that change not only affected their incentives for continued participation, but also their roles in the movement organization and the internal balance of power.

What encouraged most of the retired and disabled coal miners and millworkers to join these movements was a very individual, or selective, goal: monetary gain through the state compensation or federal benefits system. Mostly retired, living on fixed incomes with substantial medical expenses, they sought a way to supplement their meager incomes. If this motivation for participation remained static, we would expect that members who received or were denied benefits would at that time dissociate themselves from the movement. This was certainly the case for a number of participants. But, although no accurate figures exist, many people remained in the movements for years after this point. They did so because these movements produced change, not just in the societal structures to which their goals were directed, but within the participants themselves.

From their initial participation, retired and disabled workers were exposed to the ideas of lawyers, physicians, and activists who contributed a new perspective to their work, their health, and their communities. This helped to formulate an emerging ideology, but one which was being taught, not necessarily learned. The acceptance of an ideology of change was facilitated by involvement within the movement organization itself. Initially, this could be something as simple as gaining or renewing acquaintances with people who had similar life experiences. An ideology of change required that they recognize that their illness was something shared by others. This encouraged them to look at their plight not as a "personal trouble" but as a "public issue."[36] In addition, the movement provided opportunities to gain prestige and respect from holding leadership positions, talking to important government personnel, or from appearing in the news media.

These were important incentives for participation, but they also sensitized the membership to the possibility of collective organization for social change.[37] Coal miners and textile workers began to move from individualization of their plights (conditioned in part by cultural norms) to articulation of their problems in a broader context. It is only when people think in terms of the collective (be it family, community, occupation, region, or society) that we can expect them to acknowledge common goals.[38]

Exposure to outside ideas of change and experiences within movement organizations could carry this process of transformation only so far. It was not until the retired and disabled workers became involved in the actual struggles of the movements that they were able to fully comprehend the nature of the broader social, cultural, economic, and political systems that had controlled their lives. For the coal miners, this struggle began with the union, proceeded to the West Virginia state legislature, then to the federal government, the Social Security Administration, and the Department of Labor. For textile workers, it began with state compensation programs, then OSHA, then the federal legislature. Along the way, confrontations occurred with the medical community, the educational community, the insurance industry, the coal and textile industries, and a number of other institutions that were linked in some way to these struggles.

Each struggle was an educational and a group-building experience, reinforcing the importance of both collective action through the movement and the relationship of common goals to the achievement of individual goals. Historian George Rude is correct when he states, after an analysis of several revolutionary periods, that there is "no such thing as an automatic progression from 'simple' to more sophisticated ideas."[39] Sociologists Bruce Fireman and William Gamson express a similar thought in their statement that "people's allegiance to the goals of a collective actor cannot be taken for granted as arising spontaneously from their social conditions."[40] At the same time, much can be learned by looking at the dynamic processes internal to movements which may facilitate the acceptance of a common good, consequently resulting in increased levels of participation at different incentive levels.[41]

PROFESSIONAL STAFF AND MEMBERSHIP: TOWARD A PARTICIPATORY DEMOCRACY

Professional organizers could not teach these experiences or struggles; they could only attempt to provide opportunities for them to occur. From a practical standpoint, this was referred to as the process of "empowering workers." The basic goal of empowerment is to provide opportunities for those who have been powerless in the past to control their own destinies.[42] But this goal is sometimes independent of the other goals of a movement, and can actually impede their attainment. Although staff members in both movement organizations sought the goal of empowerment, it was frequently sacrificed for quicker and more efficient attention to other goals. The demands of funding agencies, the need for quick and accurate response to the news media, and the requirements of legislative testimony often necessitated that staff members abdicate an opportunity for empowering to achieve the "stated goals" of the movement.

A history of successful unionization facilitated the process of empowering coal miners, who were already accustomed to struggle within that context. Bonds between miners, encouraged by a dangerous work environment and traditional Appalachian values, contributed to a sense of collective identity and decision-making. Black Lung Association chapters were also able to meet frequently because of the relatively small geographical region in which they were located. Finally, the absence of a large staff required that the miners themselves do significant work.

Retired and disabled textile workers presented a greater challenge. Although some members of the Brown Lung Association had prior union experience, the majority did not, and many expressed negative opinions about the union, asserting strongly that the association was not affiliated with it. Work in textile mills also had a different effect than mining. Rather than unifying workers, it seemed to do the opposite, and strife frequently carried over into the Brown Lung Association:

There is a lot of hypocrisy there. There's backstabbings, there's jealousies, little petty jealousies, and I think a lot of this carried over into the organization. . . . It exists because of the fear—"The boss man is better to her than he is to me," or "he is better to him than he is to me"; "they always give him help but they don't give me any" [or] "that is the boss's pet." It is sort of like school . . . childishness things.[43]

The chapters of the Brown Lung Association were also spread out over a wide geographical area, making interaction difficult, as organizer Si Kahn has pointed out:

The Brown Lung Association first organized in widely separated towns in North and South Carolina. The chapters were separated by as much as nine hours driving time. When the board met, even at the most central location, some board members were traveling nearly five hours in each direction. Since board meetings only lasted for four hours, this meant that the people spent more time traveling than they did at the actual board meetings. This resulted in a great deal of frustration for the board members. It also meant that business was rushed, that new business could rarely be taken care of, and that people on the board had no time to make friends with each other.[44]

All of these factors inhibited the participation of retired and disabled workers and encouraged the staff to play a greater role in decision-making. Other factors were more subtle, having to do more with differences between the staff and the membership. There was strong tendency for members of both movements to defer to the staff in both task activities and decision-making. Although much of this may have evolved from the fact that staff were generally paid for their participation, interviews with members reveal consistent references to the education of the staff. Comments such as "[the staff] know how to deal with paperwork, but I know how to deal with people," or "I haven't got the education, [but] I have some experience and wisdom that they ain't got, that you need . . . it takes both," reflect a division of labor between the membership and staff. Others were more optimistic: "In years to come, we might have people that have an education to do the work that they [the staff] do," and "I believe that the time will come when mill people are going to be just as highly educated as anybody else, and they will have a clean place to work, and they will be treated as decent citizens."

The staff were aware of the educational differences between themselves and the membership and frequently acknowledged their failure to fully empower the membership with knowledge and skills to carry on the movement. At the same time, it was considered insulting to think that a worker had not fulfilled his role as a member if he could not, for example, write proposals to funding agencies. Writing proposals, interpreting research, etc., were skills that the staff brought to the organizations. Workers provided an understanding of the industry and the community and legitimized the activities of the whole movement. It was a "marriage," as one person called it, but one in which the staff sometimes robbed the membership of their roles. As one staff member of the Brown Lung Association indicated, "When we take on their role, and try to speak for them, or push them, we confuse the role of organizer and member."[45]

CONCLUSION

The struggle for occupational health confronts a complex set of problems. Coal miners and textile workers who entered into this battle did not have all of the necessary resources to engage the political and economic structures that controlled them. Four significant elements to this struggle were provided by outsiders: an ideology of social change and confrontation, a knowledge of occupational health issues, funding for movement organizations, and a vehicle for grievance portrayal. Assisted by these external factors, miners and millworkers were able to construct movements that challenged those institutions which had previously controlled both the knowledge and the politics of occupational health issues.

The black lung and brown lung movements, then, were neither totally workers' movements nor revolts orchestrated by a professional cadre of outside organizers. The complex nature of occupational health required social change organizations that reflected a particular fusion of the experiences of retired and disabled workers with the knowledge and expertise of many supporters. Participation within these movements, however, resulted in the transformation of not only the external environments, but the memberships as well. Although the process of empowerment was certainly not complete, many retired and disabled workers held important positions of leadership, planned innovative strategies for change, enhanced their knowledge of the world around them, and began to view the problem of occupational health as a public issue, not just a personal trouble.

11

The Future of Occupational Health

In August of 1981, the Brown Lung Association and the Black Lung Association came together at a three-day conference on occupational lung disease convened by the Appalachian Research and Defense Fund. They were joined by members of the White Lung Association, which had been organized in 1979 by victims of asbestos exposure, primarily from the Los Angeles–area shipyards. In addition to retired and active workers, several doctors, lawyers, and community organizers attended the conference. They formed a new coalition called the Breath of Life Organizing Campaign (BLOC); its goals were adequate compensation for disabled workers and safer work environments for active workers.[1]

Over the next two years, the coalition drafted a proposed federal compensation program to address many of the problems that all three occupational health organizations had experienced in their struggles. The proposal was revolutionary in almost every respect. It recommended the creation of a nonprofit corporation, run by a policy making board composed primarily of workers, which would administer a program financed by a trust fund from industry. No employer would be involved in the adjudication process, and no adversary use of attorneys by government agencies would be permitted. Presumption would be the basic procedure for determining illness, and disabled workers would receive 100 percent of wages and fringe benefits.[2]

Although the proposal has not been given serious consideration by Congress as yet, the formation of BLOC reflects a growing strategy toward coalition building (perceived as necessary because of threats to the survival of OSHA and attacks on gains made during recent years), the need for federal intervention in the compensation system, and the recognition that the successful accomplishment of these goals requires the skills and expertise of a wide variety of professionals. The involvement of a number of professionals reflects a definite change from a little more than two decades ago, when few even knew about the conditions in American industries, much less cared to participate in a struggle to change them.

But institutionalization and professionalization of the occupational health movement raises a number of questions about its future and how problems of workplace illnesses will be resolved. Although it may be that emerging coalitions have the needs of active and retired workers as their primary concerns, the strategies for addressing these needs are likely to reflect the broad and diverse ideologies of the various participants. Workers and professionals may have different incentives for involvement, ranging from simple compensation for disabled workers to a rekindling of the labor movement for active workers and union organizers, from purely financial considerations for compensation attorneys to the advancement of scientific knowledge for researchers and physicians, and from reform efforts for those who work directly with victims of occupational disease to socialist revolution based on safety and health for radical organizers. Some of these are laudable incentives for participation in an occupational health coalition. But will such coalitions necessarily lead to healthier and safer workplaces? Will they serve to empower workers to gain greater control over their lives and their health?

The real answers to these questions, of course, lie in the future. But there is much that we can learn from the experiences of coal miners and textile workers that might provide us a better understanding of what the future holds.

THE OCCUPATIONAL HEALTH STRUGGLE: SUCCESS OR FAILURE?

Both the black lung and brown lung movements were successful in accomplishing their goals of compensation for disabled workers.

Since 1969, the federal government and coal companies have paid more than $19 billion to more than 500,000 retired miners and their surviving dependents.[3] By 1980, the program cost approximately $1.8 billion annually.[4] Considering the original estimate in 1969 of a $50 million price tag for the program, the monetary benefits to miners have been beyond the most liberal expectations. The question, however, is whether this represents an extremely inadequate estimate of the problem of occupational disease in the coal industry or the increased liberalization of the requirements for obtaining benefits. The first option supports the fears of the occupational health movement that the problems of industrial disease are beyond even our current estimates. The second option leads to the conclusion that the issue of occupational health has been manufactured by government and political activists who view compensation and benefit payments as a way of redistributing America's wealth.

Southern textile workers had less financial success. By the summer of 1985, $22,729,000 had been awarded to 1,554 claimants in the state of North Carolina.[5] And, while over 80 percent of the miners and their widows who filed claims were eventually successful, only 51 percent of claimants for brown lung compensation were successful in North Carolina. This represents only 20 percent of the population who, according to research, suffer from byssinosis. There appears to be little indication that these people will file in the future. In 1981, the last year the Brown Lung Association had significant funding and staff, the average number of applicants for compensation for brown lung was forty-eight per month. The following year, the average had dropped to twenty-five per month. Although the industry argued that the reduction resulted from cleaner mills, the Brown Lung Association stated that it simply reflected a reduction of the efforts to find and persuade sick, and sometimes reticent, workers to file claims.[6]

Industry supported its argument with figures from its own research which indicated that only one-half of one percent of cotton textile workers in 1982 had the lung ailment known as byssinosis.[7] And even the Amalgamated Clothing and Textile Workers Union released figures in March of 1983 which indicated that 81 percent of workers in the textile industry worked in areas that met the cotton dust exposure limits.[8] Similar figures exist for the coal industry. In the latest NIOSH screening of coal miners, conducted in 1980, only

3.93 percent of active workers had coal worker's pneumoconiosis, compared to 10.6 percent in 1970.[9]

The Black Lung and Brown Lung Associations were also successful in encouraging the broader occupational health movement in the United States. An increasing number of individuals are choosing careers in this and related areas. From 1960 to 1968, only thirty-eight physicians completed three years of residency in occupational medicine. By 1981, NIOSH was providing grants for the three-year training of ninety-one physicians as occupational health specialists at twelve Educational Resource Centers (ERCs); in addition, twenty other physicians were receiving training at three other medical schools. Occupational health nurses and industrial hygienists were also being trained in increasing numbers at ERCs.[10] In 1983 the American Public Health Association reported a dramatic increase in the membership in its Occupational Safety and Health Section to over 1,000 members. They also reported a substantial increase in the educational and resource materials available as well as a number of coalitions developing among workers, health professionals, and others concerned about workplace health and safety. A number of Committees on Occupational Safety and Health (COSH) thrive in many states throughout the nation.[11]

There also seems to be evidence that, contrary to public opinion, business actually supports the idea of government regulation. A Louis Harris survey in the late 1970s found that 53 percent of the population favored either more regulation or the same amount, while only 30 percent favored less. Repeated polls have also shown wide popular support for measures to make the workplace safe.[12] A 1983 U.S. Justice Department survey of retired mid-level corporate executives reveals that 75 percent of them agree that American industry cannot police itself and therefore must be regulated by government. Two-thirds of this group specifically wanted the Occupational Safety and Health Administration to continue to regulate their businesses.[13]

Occupational health, then, has become a part of the nation's consciousness. Academics, public health officials, medical and legal personnel, government workers, and the organizations they represent, both public and private, are developing a vested interest in the pursuit of occupational health, a subject that attracted the attention of few people in any organization less than two decades ago.

In the sense that it is becoming institutionalized into the mainstream of American society, the occupational health movement must be considered successful. But can we integrate the demands for a healthy workplace into a production-oriented society facing serious competition from foreign industry? More to the point, will the institutionalization of the occupational health movement deflect more crucial issues that still must be resolved?

HUMAN LIFE: ITS VALUE AND PRICE

Like most issues, it is difficult to consider occupational health as an isolated phenomenon. Broader factors, many times ideological as well as structural, impinge on our ability to seek resolutions. As business professor Curtis McLaughlin recently queried, "How can we talk about health and safety when we haven't resolved whether an American worker even has a right to a job?"[14] Moreover, he points out, what is a reasonable risk to assume in order to bid for employment in a labor-surplus world? The occupational health movement had its beginning at a time in our society when labor was scarce and work was plentiful. World competition and the recent recession have encouraged the modernization of many companies that will leave us with a surplus of labor, even after the economy recovers from its present crisis.[15]

Since the value of labor, at least to industry, will probably change during these periods, will and should there be a change in the value of human health and life? The bottom line of this dilemma is cost, and who bears it. The regulation of health and safety is essentially the process of making costs external to the market into internal costs. Someone has to bear the monetary burden of these costs— government, industry, workers, or the American consumer—as prices are increased. The experiences of coal miners and textile workers suggest that these costs can be very high, if not in regulation, then in the costs of compensation and medical care.

But there are other costs that must also be considered. There are the costs to workers who develop occupational diseases and lose many years of their productive lives. There is the cost to their families, economic and otherwise, and the impact on the community, which must bear some of the responsibility for their care. Although these costs are difficult to quantify, we find ourselves forced in this direction as we attempt to evaluate the costs and benefits of any policy directed toward the solution of occupational health issues. Even more controversial is the possible requirement of putting a value on human life and differentiating the value of different people's lives. McLaughlin argues that putting the value of human life on the same economic scale as the dollar costs of implementing protective standards is necessary for at least two reasons: On the one hand, human life is a risky affair and there is no way of eliminating all risks; on the other hand, the material resources required for the prevention of risks are limited.[16]

Philosopher Anselm Min suggests that this process raises many of the complex moral issues and dilemmas of modern industrial capitalism. Is it technically possible to put a price on human life? Is it morally justifiable to do so? Under what conditions is it morally justifiable to risk health and life? And what is the moral right and responsibility of the community and its official expression, the government, in case of a conflict between the human and the economic costs of doing business?[17] Journalist Coleman McCarthy suggests that the political debate over government's role has put aside even more crucial questions of ethics: What is the moral obligation of an employer whose worker comes down with a work-related disease, and what is a socially acceptable risk "when what is gambled is the health of the worker next to the coke oven and not the owner in the boardroom?"[18] Underlying these questions are fundamental controversies about control over the workplace in general and decision-making in the area of occupational health in particular.

TOWARD WORKERS' CONTROL OF OCCUPATIONAL HEALTH

Workers' control over the workplace, a significant part of the European labor movement, has never become an issue considered worthy of serious debate in the American labor movement. Although there is some evidence of its existence in the middle 1800s, by 1890, the American labor movement was dominated by the philosophy of the American Federation of Labor and of leaders like Samuel Gompers. According to Daniel Zwerdling, it was generally argued that, rather than attempt to replace management and control the workplace, workers should form strong trade unions. These trade unions would concede to management the right to direct the workplace and then devote their energies to wresting various concessions from management in return. Workers' power evolved from the ultimate threat of shutting down production by going on strike. By the 1930s, this system, known as collective bargaining, had become the philosophy of all major unions in the United States.[19]

For the first half of this century, unions have endured often violent battles with management to develop what many consider to be the most elaborate, extensive, and complex system of collective bargaining in the world.[20] Labor union membership as a share of the total labor force has declined since 1950,[21] however, and today the American labor movement enrolls one of the smallest percentages of the labor force among industrialized countries.[22] Although the movement has been successful in numerous collective bargaining agreements and has been an important force for legislation on welfare, social insurance, and civil rights, it has never moved out of its production base to develop an overall political program.[23] As historian David Montgomery notes, the effects of the New Deal in the 1930s essentially completed a long process of reducing the American labor movement to a trade union movement, "an immobile and isolated aggregation of legally certified bargaining agents."[24]

Even though unions have spearheaded much of the recent occupational health movement, for most of their history there has been greater concern in collective bargaining for the more visible immediate problems of industrial safety, and perhaps even more for bread and butter issues like wages and benefits. Dan Berman suggests that the recent struggle for better health and working conditions, particularly with its emphasis on worker rights at the point of production, may help to rekindle the fledgling U.S. Labor movement.[25] The question is whether the issue of occupational health and safety will be simply integrated into the traditional framework of collective bargaining, or whether the struggle for industrial health will lead to new relationships between management and labor.

Part of this struggle encompasses a battle over the definition of occupational health and the conceptualization of the problem of illness. As Berman points out, this has been greatly influenced since the turn of the century by an overemphasis on compensation at the expense of prevention.[26] Vicente Navarro argues that this resulted primarily from a broader need within the capitalistic system for all struggles at the point of production to be shifted to the area of consumption, where attention is drawn to the cost of labor—personal and social wages—rather than control over the process of production. Not only did labor unions accept this shift, but, consequently, they accepted the unalterability of the process of work and perceived the damage created at the workplace as unavoidable. Compensation became the accepted alternative, and occupational medicine developed to define for management the nature and degree of damage which needed to be compensated.[27]

It is this traditional system by which occupational diseases have been identified, measured, and defined that is now being challenged. A crucial part of both the black lung and brown lung movements was the formulation of "political" definitions of occupational diseases that challenged the traditional scientific definitions. The scientific definitions were used primarily in medical diagnosis and treatment, while the political definitions were used to create and monitor health and safety regulations and make compensation eligibility determinations. Medical anthropologist Janet Bronstein suggests that while we must accept separate scientific and political definitions of occupational diseases, in reality these definitions are generally formulated in the context of constant interaction between scientists and politicians. Not only are political actions both stimulated and threatened by scientific findings, but the direction and credibility of scientific research are influenced by political interests.[28] With regard to both black lung and brown lung, the guiding questions for research were the by-products of political concern. Even though scientific facilities were available in the United States when Britain did much of its research in the 1930s, political interest did not exist here until the 1960s. Scientific findings also affected the political process, as research observations provided support for labor groups' claims that dust in both the coal mines and textile mills made them unhealthy places to work. Scientific findings were in turn affected by the political process because information gathered from workers was influenced by economic considerations. Coal miners were said to exaggerate their symptoms in order to win black lung benefits, while cotton workers were said to minimize their symptoms in order to avoid losing their jobs.[29] Bronstein concludes by suggesting that scientists and politicians must balance the pursuit of their unique goals with a mutual awareness of each other's activities and concerns.[30]

Others have suggested that the politicalization of defining occupational diseases must go much further. Vicente Navarro suggests that the understanding of the evolution and causality of black lung in the United States must come not from just the natural history of the disease, but from an understanding of the class power relations and how that class struggle shaped "both the scientific definition, recognition and knowledge of black lung in the United States and the actual production and distribution of that disease."[31] While Navarro recognizes the achievements of occupational health legislation based upon political definitions, he points out that the limitations of legislation result from manipulation by the components and strata of the capitalist class who are affected by the legislation. He argues that there needs to be not only continuous pressure from the working class on the legislative process, but also a working class science to complement traditional science.[32] This is necessary because "the power relations in society appear also within scientific knowledge, and the bourgeoisie ideological dominance appears and is being reproduced in the production of knowledge itself."[33] "Scientific" documents about both black lung and brown lung had concluded that either they did not exist in the United States or that they were not causally linked to the workplace. These findings were considered trustworthy because they were scientific, but the knowledge accumulated by generations of coal miners and textile workers, knowledge which appeared in their culture as folk songs and popular writings—that work in the mines or the mills was destroying their lungs—was considered "cultural, folksy, ideological, and, in summary, untrustworthy."[34] Consequently, not only was this knowledge not recognized as legitimate, but for decades little attention was given to the serious loss of health which resulted.

Navarro suggests that there must be a mass democratization in the process of the creation of knowledge and a deprofessionalization of science. This would result in a change in the method and creation of knowledge, i.e., "knowledge created not by the few—the scientists—but the many—the working classes and popular masses." This would require not only a change in the power relations in the creation of knowledge, "with the working class . . . being the agents and not the objects of that knowledge," but also a professional and political commitment by scientists to the working class. More importantly, it would require a struggle for democracy in the workplace and in our society, to include participation by the working class in all economic, political, and social institutions, including medical and scientific institutions.[35]

WORKPLACE DEMOCRACY: A SOLUTION TO OCCUPATIONAL DISEASE?

What Navarro is proposing from a fairly traditional Marxist or socialist approach has recently received some support, even if for different reasons, from more traditional, and perhaps conservative, elements within society. Although its initial proponents came from the academic community, many corporations have embraced at least some of the emerging ideas behind the concept of "workplace democracy," especially those centering around increasing the degree of worker participation in management and experimenting with worker ownership. According to sociologist Severyn Bruyn, the trend has generally developed at three levels of corporate activity: in the formation of quality circles and autonomous work groups at lower levels of management, in the establishment of labor management committees which are concerned with productivity and improving working conditions at middle levels of administration, and in the provision of opportunities for employee ownership and employee representation on boards of directors at top levels of management.[36] The more radical fringe of this movement has suggested that the transformation necessary is not simply workplace democracy but national economic democracy, which would transfer capital from the corporations to the public, so that people who work and consume can collectively and democratically decide what to do with it.[37] Workplace democracy and economic democracy do not necessarily coincide, however. Public ownership of industry and reforms that shift power over investment decisions to workers and consumers do not necessarily produce firms which are democratic and nonhierarchical in structure. Democratic decision-making, therefore, requires worker control at the plant level.[38]

Some of the strongest resistance to this movement has come from the leadership in American labor unions. In general, union repre-

sentatives have argued that workplace democracy, with its underlying theme of cooperation rather than conflict, is nothing more than
management's attempt to reduce or eliminate the power of established worker organizations, and to blur the distinctions between
employees and employers—the distinction which gives unions and
union officials their identity.[39]

Although still only an emerging perspective, the trend toward
workplace democracy adds an alternative approach to collective bargaining and government regulations as solutions to the problems of
occupational disease. The significance of government intervention
has been well established, particularly since the passage of the 1970
Occupational Safety and Health Act. Even if we accept the fact that
it may have been passed as only a symbolic gesture by the Nixon
administration to win support from labor,[40] its impact on the development of the occupational health movement has been substantial. As Lloyd McBride, President of the Steelworkers of America,
put it, "OSHA has uncorked a bottle of knowledge on workplace
hazards and unleashed an educational process which has awakened
workers to the dangers they confront on the job."[41] This knowledge
was even more rapidly disseminated under the New Directions
Program, which began in 1978 to fund colleges, unions and trade
associations for courses on occupational safety and health. These
training and education programs substantially increased the number
of union personnel working on occupational safety and health issues
in the United States from fifteen in 1978 to over one hundred profes-
sionally trained staff by 1981.[42]

However, a 1985 report by the congressional Office of Technology
Assessment (OTA) was extremely critical of the protection which
had been provided workers through OSHA. It pointed out that in
its thirteen years of existence, OSHA had issued only twelve new
or revised standards for chemical substances, and that its inspections
were extremely rare, even in the most dangerous types of workplaces. The agency was able to inspect only about 4 percent of the
4.6 million workplaces each year and only about 20 percent of manufacturing establishments, which are more hazardous.[43] Part of this
failure can be attributed to lack of resources and funds, which have
been cut substantially since the advent of the Reagan administration.
In effect, OSHA's situation points to the problem of a primary dependence on the government for protection, because, in a relatively

short period of time, changing administrations can undo much of what has been accomplished.

Can unions, which have recently gained both a consciousness and knowledge about occupational health, take over where the government leaves off? The major means by which workers have attempted to improve safety and health conditions since 1970 have been to amend and improve the law, expand standards, and improve administrative practices.[44] However, many OSHA proposals have infringed upon collective bargaining agreements, which has made OSHA more responsive to trade union programs for input into their process of rules, regulations, and enforcement programs. Also, the complexity of occupational health and safety issues has resulted in more sophisticated language during contract time, as workers have continued to use established forms of labor relations to address occupational hazards.[45] On the other hand, a survey done prior to OSHA's formation revealed that union leadership thought that money rather than working conditions deserved the most attention, although unionized rank and file workers felt that good health and safety practices and workers' compensation were top priorities. Similar studies have documented that employed persons in general stress the importance of health and safety conditions.[46]

Even if union leaders do begin to stress health and safety, the dwindling number of unionized employees not only limits the potential power to affect change, but also means that close to four-fifths of our nation's employed would not be able to avail themselves of this power. Furthermore, are the economic conditions always going to encourage bargaining for health, particularly in a recession economy with jobs in demand?

Although it is anticipated that government regulations and union activity will continue to play important roles in advancing the cause of occupational health, those who have been able to organize effectively around safety and health issues have increasingly found that the fundamental requirement for social change is democracy in the workplace.[47] They argue that workers have a right to know about dangers in the work environment but that they also need to be able to participate in the detection, evaluation, and reduction of workplace hazards.[48] The main goal of the Occupational Safety and Health Act of 1970, "to assure as far as possible every working man and woman in the nation safe and healthful working conditions and to preserve our human resources,"[49] is possible to achieve only if workers are active participants.

According to its advocates, workplace and economic democracy would encourage participatory involvement by large numbers of different consumer groups and worker groups in the society to counterpoise the autonomy in which managerial and corporate elite have made decisions.[50] Carnoy and Shearer suggest that the movement for economic democracy in the United States will not be in the European socialist tradition, but in the American radical tradition of populism, with a strong emphasis on applying the value of political democracy to the economic sector. In the same vein, class consciousness will not be the foundation for this struggle, but networks of mobilized citizens will recognize their mutual victimization by industrial hazards and waste.[51]

There is growing evidence of the emergence of many such groups across the United States,[52] and of programs within industry to encourage participation by workers and the local community in decision-making on the corporate level.[53] Will this have any impact on worker health and safety? Possibly, if it results in a shift in our priorities from profits and productivity to a concern for the health and welfare of our workers. Medical sociologist Elliot Krause reminds us that the reason many workers continue to work in settings which are dangerous to their health is that the alternative is welfare: "Work may mean sacrificing their own health, but the alternative will sacrifice not only theirs, but that of their children as well. This lack of choice is not an accident, but rather the consequence of the structure of a capitalist society which forces people into such jobs even at the cost of their health in order to preserve the profits of the employers."[54]

But an ideological shift must also be accompanied by creation of structures which encourage active worker participation, particularly in the identification of yet undiscovered hazards in industry. One of the most recent strategies for addressing this problem is the use by large companies in the United States of computer-based systems to store and integrate information on worker exposures and medical illnesses. As one observer has pointed out, these sophisticated systems were designed with input from a number of professionals: "industrial hygienists, epidemiologists, physicians, information scientists, programmers, systems analysts, toxicologists and nurses."[55]

Michael Reich and Rose Goldman observe that "noticeably absent
. . . [is] any mention of workers—the most intimately involved persons in the work process, whose experience could contribute significantly to the development of systems for gathering and using
the data."[56]

The significance of the active rank and file worker must be un-
derscored. Although the Black Lung and Brown Lung Associations
were important to advancing the occupational health movement, it
must be remembered that almost all of the members of both movements were retired and disabled workers. Their participation was
facilitated by the fact that they had very little to lose (such as their
jobs) and much to gain (workers' compensation). But neither the
black lung or brown lung movements had prevention as their primary goal. Although much attention was given to the cotton dust
standard, retired and disabled millworkers were more easily mobilized in the struggle for compensation. The Black Lung Association
was almost totally dedicated to the issues of workers' compensation
and the Black Lung Benefits Program. Sociologist Barbara Smith
suggests that, for miners, "this was partly due to the initial, erro-
neous view that the cost of state compensation, (financed by industry) would force the companies to improve health conditions in the
mines."[57] Essentially the same argument was made in the brown
lung movement. Upon reflection, however, Smith recognized that
industrial democracy might have been a better preventive strategy:

A lasting and effective preventive campaign would have required a tighter
alliance between working miners, disabled miners and widows; a much
firmer conviction that black lung [was] not inevitable, and, at least eventually, a political vision of how miners might improve their occupational
health by asserting greater control over the workplace.[58]

CONCLUSION

Would greater control over the workplace actually improve the
health of the nation's workers? It is certainly a subject worthy of
empirical investigation, although it will probably be many years
before we have substantial evidence. Logically, however, the argument has merit. First, it would mean greater control by workers
over the production process itself. A key characteristic of the current

international crisis is the conflict which appears between the demand for higher productivity at the workplace and the resistance by workers to that demand. Workers are becoming increasingly aware of the meaning of higher productivity—faster speeds of work, longer working hours, and shift work—and its impact on their health and their lives.[59] Second, worker control would mean influence over decisions about technology. The problems of both coal and cotton dust were greatly exacerbated by decisions regarding the use of certain technologies to which neither the rank and file miner nor millworker had significant input. Third, it would mean greater control over the introduction of new chemicals into the workplace. State and federal "right to know" laws have contributed greatly to this process, but the length of time for both development and detection of many of these diseases may mean that a large percentage of the working population will serve as guinea pigs for occupational illnesses. In some cases, the most that we can do is establish surveillance programs. For these to be effective, there must be significant worker involvement. Although the emergence of a working class science may be unrealistic, the knowledge which workers possess about their bodies and their environments can be increasingly integrated into the existing structures.

The conflict over industrial health is a condition that will not easily be resolved in the industrial mode of production. As sociologist/historian Carl Gersuny has projected, "The struggle over work hazards will be an endless quest for compromise, rather than for a definitive solution."[60] The nature of that compromise will depend on whether the workers who are exposed to the greatest risks have significant influence over the decisions about production, technology, and medical surveillance and data collection. The experiences of coal miners and textile workers suggest that the political struggle for occupational health is an important part of this overall process.

The compromise will also involve a continuing strain between the societal needs for a healthy economy and healthy workers. This is not necessarily to suggest that these are incompatible goals, although the pressures for higher production and maximization of profit inherent in industrial capitalism do not appear to be subsiding. At the same time, there seems to be an increased consciousness and concern on the part of American workers about their health and about the potential damage from the work environment. Although the emerging coalitions and organizations may not rekindle the American labor movement, it appears doubtful that future workers will tolerate the same working conditions that their predecessors were forced to endure.

Notes

CHAPTER 2

1. R. Dobos, *Mirage of Health* (New York: Harper Brothers, 1959).

2. For more on this see: P. Conrad and J. Schneider, *Deviance and Medicalization: From Badness to Sickness* (St. Louis: C.V. Mosby, 1980); E.W. Ackernecht, *Short History of Medicine* (New York: The Ronald Press, 1955); and Alice Hamilton, *Exploring the Dangerous Trades* (Boston: Little, Brown and Company, 1943).

3. Vicente Navarro, "Work, Ideology and Science: The Case of Medicine," *International Journal of Health Services* 10 (1980): 523–50.

4. M. Baxter, "Diagnosis as Category and Process: The Case of Alcoholism," *Social Services and Medicine* 12A (1978): 9–17.

5. R. Dobos, *Man Adapting* (New Haven: Yale University Press, 1965).

6. A.N. Kleinman et al., "Culture, Illness and Care: Clinical Lessons from Anthropological and Cross Cultural Research," *Annals of Internal Medicine* 88 (1978): 251–58.

7. H.S. Loft, *The Economic Causes of and Consequences of Health Problems* (Cambridge, Mass.: Ballinger Press, 1978).

8. John R. Butler, "Illness and the Sick Role: An Evaluation on Three Communities," *British Journal of Sociology* 21 (1970): 241.

9. Talcott Parsons, *The Social System* (London: Routledge and Kegan Paul, 1951), p. 440.

10. Butler, "Illness and the Sick Role," p. 242, and see Talcott Parsons,

"Definitions of Health and Illness in the Right of American Values and Social Structure," Chapter 20 in E.G. Jaco, *Patients, Physicians and Illness* (New York: Free Press, 1957), p. 167.

11. David Mechanic, "Illness and Social Desirability: Some Problems in Analysis," *Pacific Sociological Review*, Spring 1959: 38.

12. Butler, "Illness and the Sick Role," p. 242.

13. Mechanic, "Illness and Social Desirability," pp. 38–39.

14. Butler, "Illness and the Sick Role," p. 244.

15. Ibid.

16. E. Friedson, *The Professions of Medicine* (New York: Dodd, Mead and Company, 1970).

17. R.H. Roblee, "Medico-Legal Aspects of the Coverage of Occupational Diseases under Worker's Compensation: Changing Concepts of Causation and the Case of Byssinosis," reprinted in *Occupational Diseases*, Hearings before the Subcommittee on Labor, Senate Committee on Human Resources, Session 95–1 (Washington: U.S. Government Printing Office, 1977), pp. 134–209.

18. Lorin Kerr, "The Neglect of Occupational Health: A National Scandal," presented at British National Tuberculosis and Respiratory Disease Association, October 1972, p. 2.

19. Ibid.

20. George C. Guenther, "Workmen's Compensation for the Coal Miner," in *Papers and Proceedings of the National Conference on Medicine and the Federal Coal Mine Health and Safety Act of 1969*, June 15–18, 1970 (Washington: U.S. Government Printing Office, 1970), pp. 257–63 (hereafter *Papers and Proceedings*).

21. Kerr, "The Neglect of Occupational Health," p. 1.

22. "Council on Occupational Health: Some Objectives and Functions of Occupational Health Programs," *Journal of the American Medical Association* 174 (1960): 533–36.

23. Ibid., p. 533.

24. Eugene Mittelman, testimony in *Papers and Proceedings*, p. 53.

25. Dan Berman, *Death on the Job* (New York: Monthly Review Press, 1978), p. 4.

26. Ibid., p. 15.

27. Ibid., pp. 75–76.

28. Ibid., p. 95

29. Karen Rothmyer, "Washington Moves Slowly," *Wall Street Journal*, June 7, 1976.

30. Berman, *Death on the Job*, p. 95.

31. Kerr, "The Neglect of Occupational Health," p. 12.

32. Irving R. Tabershaw, "How Is the Acceptability of Risks to Health of the Workers to Be Determined?" *Journal of Occupational Medicine*, October 1976: 674–76.

33. Berman, *Death on the Job*, p. 5.

34. Ray Davidson, *Peril on the Job* (Washington: Public Affairs Press, 1970), p. 112.

35. Ibid., p. 142.

36. Nicholas A. Ashford, *Crisis in the Workplace* (Cambridge: MIT Press, 1976), p. 5.

37. Carl Gersuny, *Work Hazards and Industrial Conflict* (Hanover, N.H.: The University Press of New England, 1981), p. 37.

38. Ibid., p. 3.

39. Ibid.

40. Lorin Kerr, "The UMWA Looks at Occupational Health," *American Journal of Public Health* 61 (May 1971): 972–78.

41. Lorin Kerr, "Physicians Involvement in Industrial Productivity," *The Journal of the Tennessee Medical Association* 63 (December 1970): 1024.

42. Reported in Berman, *Death on the Job*, pp. 44–46.

43. *An Interim Report to Congress on Occupational Disease*, submitted by the U.S. Department of Labor to the U.S. Congress (Washington: U.S. Government Printing Office, June, 1980) p. 1.

44. Ashford, *Crisis in the Workplace*, p. 4.

45. Ibid., p. 15.

46. Ibid., p. 6.

47. Ibid.

48. *An Interim Report*, p. 112.

49. Ibid.

50. Ibid., p. 114.

51. Ibid.

52. Ibid., p. 111.

53. Ibid., p. 123.

54. Ashford, *Crisis in the Workplace*, p. 7.

55. J.L. Castrovinci, "Prelude to Welfare Capitalism: The Role of Business in the Enactment of Worker's Compensation in Illinois, 1905–1912," *Social Services Review* 50 (1976): 80–102.

56. Ashford, *Crisis in the Workplace*, pp. 388–89.

57. Jacob Javits, Opening Statement to *Hearing on National Workers Compensation Standards Act of 1978*, September 19, 1978, Subcommittee on Labor of the Committee on Human Resources, United States Senate. (Washington: U.S. Government Printing Office), p. 50.

58. Ashford, *Crisis in the Workplace*, p. 388.

59. *Occupational Diseases and Their Compensation, Part 3*, Congressional Hearings in Washington, D.C., April 4–June 21, 1979 (Washington: U.S. Government Printing Office, 1980), p. 107.

60. Ibid.

61. G. Rosen, *The History of Miner's Diseases* (New York: Schuman, 1943), p. 194.

62. Lorin Kerr, "Coal Workers and Pneumoconiosis," *Archives of Environmental Health* 16 (April 1968): 579.

63. Martin Agronsky, "The Public and the Act," in *Papers and Proceedings*, p. 323.

64. Ibid.

65. Kerr, "Coal Workers and Pneumoconiosis," p. 599.

66. Henry N. Doyle, "Pneumoconiosis in Bituminous Coal Miners," in U.S. Lainhart et al., *Pneumoconiosis in Appalachian Coal Miners* (Ohio Public Health Service: Columbus, 1969), p. 16.

67. Kerr, "Coal Workers and Pneumoconiosis," p. 581.

68. Ibid.

69. Ibid., p. 579.

70. Ibid.

71. Robert Murran, "International Overview of Coal Worker's Pneumoconiosis," in *Papers and Proceedings*, p. 114.

72. Kerr, "Coal Workers and Pneumoconiosis," p. 579.

73. Doyle, "Pneumoconiosis," p. 15.

74. Ibid.

75. *Black Lung*, report produced by the United Mine Workers of America, not dated, p. 6.

76. Ibid.

77. Ibid.

78. Doyle, "Pneumoconiosis," p. 16.

79. Ibid., p. 18.

80. Ibid.

81. Ibid.

82. Richard Naeye, "Soft Coal Worker's Pneumoconiosis: A Quantitative Postmortem Study," in *Papers and Proceedings*, p. 63.

83. Irving R. Tabershaw, "The Health of the Coal Miner—An Expendible Resource," in *Papers and Proceedings*, p. 8.

84. Edgar Collins, "Industrial Pneumoconiosis," reprinted from *Public Health* (The Society of Medical Offices of Health, Milvoy Rectuns, 1915).

85. Lorin Kerr, quoted in *Coal Mine Health and Safety Act of 1969*, Hearings before the Subcommittee on Labor and Public Welfare, U.S. Senate, 91st Congress, February 27, 1969 (Washington: U.S. Government Printing Office, 1969), pp. 675–76.

86. Lorin Kerr, in *Legislative History of the Federal Coal Mine Health and Safety Act of 1969*, U.S. Senate, August 1975 (Washington: U.S. Government Printing Office, 1975), p. 340.

87. Bernardino Ramazzini, *Diseases of Workers* (New York: Hafner Publishing Company, 1964), p. 257.

88. *Senate Hearings on Brown Lung*, December 9, 1977, (Washington: U.S. Government Printing Office, 1977), p. 5.

89. T. Reginald Harris et al., "Byssinosis and Respiratory Diseases of Cotton Mill Workers," *Journal of Occupational Medicine* 14 (March 1972): 200.

90. Ibid.

91. *Occupational Diseases and Their Compensation*, p. 493.

92. Richard Robblee, "The Dark Side of Workers Compensation," *Industrial Relations Law Journal*, Winter 1978: 612–24.

93. Ralph Nader, "The Cotton Mill Worker," *The Nation*, March 15, 1971, p. 335.

94. Mimi Conway, "Brown Lung Disease Now a Major Issue," *Boston Sunday Globe*, July 17, 1977, p. 52.

95. Reported in statement of Sol Stetin in *Senate, Hearings on Brown Lung*, (Washington: U.S. Government Printing Office, Dec. 9, 1978), pp. 63–64.

96. Charles C. Johnson, Administrator of the Consumer Protection and Environmental Health Service, quoted in statement of Sol Stetin, p. 64.

97. R.S.F. Schilling, *Hearing Before the Committee to Make a Study of Byssinosis*, South Carolina Legislature, April 5, 1972.

98. Nader, "The Cotton Mill Killer," p. 336.

99. *National Worker's Compensation Standards Act of 1978*, Committee on Labor and Human Resources, U.S. Senate, Hearings held September 19, 20, and 22, 1978, p. 127.

100. *Senate Hearings on Brown Lung*, p. 65.

101. Quoted in Harris et al., "Byssinosis and Respiratory Diseases," p. 201.

102. Arend Bouhuys, quoted in *Senate Hearings on Brown Lung*, p. 121.

103. Referenced in Kay H. Kilborn et al., "Byssinosis: Matter from Lint to Lungs," *American Journal of Nursing* 73 (November 1973): 1954.

104. Robblee, "The Dark Side," pp. 612–24.

105. Quoted in "Washington Moves Slowly on Tough Controls," *Wall Street Journal*, June 7, 1976.

106. Robblee, "The Dark Side," pp. 612–24.

107. Arend Bouhuys et al., "Editorial: Byssinosis in the Textile Industry," *Archives of Environmental Health* 21 (1970): 475–76.

108. Testimony at Hearings before the Subcommittee on Labor Standards, House of Representatives, April 4, 1979.

109. Siegfried Heyden and Philip Pratt, "Exposure to Cotton Dust and Respiratory Disease," *Journal of the American Medical Association*, October 17, 1980: 1979.

110. Butler Derek, testimony in *Occupational Diseases and Their Compensation*, p. 2.

111. Edward E. Knipe and Helen M. Lewis, "The Impact of Coal Mining on the Traditional Mountain Subculture: A Case of Peasantry Gained and Peasantry Lost," paper read at the 1969 Meeting of the Southern Anthropological Society, New Orleans, March 14, 1969, p. 11.

112. Henry N. Doyle, "The Impact of Changing Technology on Health Problems in the Coal Mining Industry," in *Papers and Proceedings*, p. 195.

113. Ibid., p. 197.

114. Ibid.

115. Sol Stetin, in *Senate Hearings on Brown Lung*, p. 68.

116. R.S.F. Schilling, *Hearing before South Carolina Legislature*, April 15, 1972.

117. Stephen Sinclair, "The Cotton Dust Controversy," *Job, Safety and Health*, November 1976: 5.

118. Sol Stetin, in *Senate Hearings on Brown Lung*, p. 68.

119. Joseph Hughes, testimony in *Occupational Diseases and Their Compensation*, p. 103.

CHAPTER 3

1. Kai T. Erikson, *Everything in Its Path* (New York: Simon and Schuster, 1976), p. 68.

2. C. Vann Woodward, *Origins of the New South* (Baton Rouge, La.: State University Press, 1951).

3. David S. Walls and Dwight Billings, "The Sociology of Southern Appalachia" (unpublished paper, University of Kentucky, March 1977), p. 20.

4. Ibid.

5. For a number of articles on this approach see Helen Lewis et al., editors, *Colonialism in Modern America: The Appalachian Case* (Boone, N.C.: Appalachian Consortium Press, 1978). See also Dwight Billings, "Culture and Poverty in Appalachia: A Theoretical Discussion and Empirical Analysis," *Social Forces*, December 1974: 315–23.

6. Helen Lewis and Edward Knipe, "The Colonialism Model: The Appalachian Case," revised draft, October 1970, of article which appeared in Edward Storey, editor, *Uncertain America: Anthropological Approaches to Domestic Crises* (Boston: Little, Brown and Company, 1971). For a recent account of a similar process operating in the South see Robert Botsch, *We Shall Not Overcome: Populism and Southern Blue-Collar Workers* (Chapel Hill: University of North Carolina Press, 1980).

7. Norman Simpkins, from a speech given at Huntington Galleries Mountain Heritage Week in Huntington, West Virginia, June 19–24, 1972.

8. Helen Lewis, "The Subcultures of the Southern Appalachians: Their

Origins and Boundary Maintenance," paper read at the Institute for Southern Culture, Longwood College, Farmville, Virginia, February 17, 1967.

9. Ibid., p. 10.

10. Lewis et al., "The Colonialism Model," p. 11.

11. Erikson, *Everything*, p. 95.

12. James Watt Raine, quoted in Erikson, *Everything*, p. 94.

13. Lewis et al., "The Colonialism Model," p. 12.

14. Erikson, *Everything*, p. 104.

15. Edward E. Knipe and Helen M. Lewis, "The Impact of Coal Mining
on the Traditional Mountain Subculture: A Case of Peasantry Gained and
Peasantry Lost," paper read at the 1969 Meeting of the Southern Anthropological Society, New Orleans, March 14, 1969, p. 10.

16. Ibid., p. 11.

17. Lewis et al., "The Colonialism Model," p. 15.

18. Lewis, "The Subcultures," pp. 3–4.

19. Jack E. Weller, *Yesterday's People: Life in Contemporary Appalachia* (Lexington: The University Press of Kentucky, 1965), p. 28.

20. Lewis et al., "The Colonialism Model," p. 20.

21. Erikson, *Everything*, p. 103.

22. Tom Bethel, "Conspiracy in Coal," *The Washington Monthly*, March
1969: 16–23, 63–72. See also Melvyn Dobofsky and Warren Van Tine, *John
L. Lewis: A Biography* (New York: Quadrangle/The New York Times Book
Company, 1977) and Saul Alinsky, *John L. Lewis: An Unauthorized Biography* (New York: Vintage Books, 1970), for more on the history of Lewis
and the UMWA.

23. Ibid., pp. 16–23.

24. Ibid.

25. Ibid.

26. Ibid.

27. Brit Hume, "Coal Mining: The Union," *Atlantic Monthly*, November 1969: 23.

28. Bethel, "Conspiracy in Coal," p. 64.

29. Brit Hume, *Death in the Mines: Rebellion and Murder in the United
Mine Workers* (New York: Grossman Publishers, 1971), p. 22.

30. From testimony by Tony Boyle in *Coal Mine Health and Safety
Act, Part 1*, Hearings before the Subcommittee on Labor and Public Welfare, U.S. Senate, February 27, 1969 (Washington: U.S. Government Printing Office, 1969), p. 458.

31. Joseph Brennan, "Technology and the Coal Miner," in *Papers and
Proceedings of the National Conference on Medicine and the Federal Coal
Mine Health and Safety Act of 1969*, June 15–18, 1970, Washington (Wash-
ington: U.S. Government Printing Office, 1970), p. 203.

32. Ibid., p. 201.

33. James R. Garvey, "Technology and the Coal Industry," in *Papers and Proceedings*, p. 208.

34. Brennan, "Technology," p. 203.

35. See Todd Gitlin and Nanci Hollander, *Uptown: Poor Whites in Chicago* (New York: Harper and Row, 1970).

36. Erikson, *Everything*, p. 109.

37. Ibid., p. 111.

38. Ibid., p. 112.

39. Bethel, "Conspiracy," p. 64.

40. Hume, *Death in the Mines*, p. 36.

41. Ibid., pp. 39–40.

42. Ibid., p. 22.

43. Ibid., pp. 40–41.

44. Melton McLaurin, in *Paternalism and Protest* (Westport, Conn: Greenwood Press, 1971), p. 11, used this phrase to characterize the approach of Broadus Mitchell in *Rise of the Cotton Mills in the South* (Baltimore: John Hopkins Press, 1921).

45. Liston Pope, *Millhands and Preachers: A Study of Gastonia* (New Haven: Yale University Press, 1942), pp. 14–15.

46. Quoted in Pope, Millhands, p. 25.

47. Ibid., p. 25.

48. McLaurin, *Paternalism*, pp. 12–13.

49. Paul D. Escott, *Many Excellent People: Power and Privilege in North Carolina, 1850–1900* (forthcoming, University of North Carolina Press), Chapter 9, p. 313.

50. Escott, in *Many Excellent People*, p. 314, challenges W.J. Cash's argument to this effect.

51. Tom Tippett, *When Southern Labor Stirs* (Huntington, W.Va.: Appalachian Movement Press, 1978) p. 13.

52. Ibid., p. 14.

53. Pope, *Millhands*, p. 11.

54. Ibid., pp. 49–69. See also Kenneth Moreland, *Millways of Kent* (New Haven: College and University Press, 1958).

55. Harriet Herring, *Welfare Work in Mill Villages: The Story of Extra-Mill Activities in North Carolina* (Chapel Hill: University of North Carolina Press, 1929), pp. 268–69.

56. Mitchell, *Rise of the Cotton Mills*, p. 80.

57. Moreland, *Millways*, p. 96.

58. McLaurin, *Protest*, pp. 23–24.

59. Ibid., p. 23.

60. Herring, *Welfare Work*, p. 100.

61. Pope, *Millhands*, p. 276.

62. Moreland, *Millways*, p. 247.

63. Ibid., p. 32.
64. Ibid., p. 23.
65. Ibid., p. 247.
66. McLaurin, *Protest*, p. 56.
67. Pope, *Millhands*, pp. 68–69.
68. McLaurin, *Protest*, p. 203.
69. Ibid., p. 211.
70. John Earle, Dean Knudsen, and Donald Shriver, Jr., *Spindles and Spires: A Restudy of Religion and Social Change in Gastonia* (Atlanta: John Know Press, 1976), p. 177.
71. For an account of these strikes see F. Ray Marshall, *Labor in the South* (Cambridge: Harvard University Press, 1967).
72. Glen Gilman, *Human Relations in the Industrial Southeast* (Chapel Hill: University of North Carolina Press, 1956), p. 235–37.
73. Marshall, *Labor in the South*, p. 118.
74. Earle et al., *Spindles and Spires*, pp. 177–78.
75. Bob Dennis, "Bitter Labor Saga," *Charlotte Observer*, September 25, 1980.
76. *Fabrics of Injustice: The Struggle at J.P. Stevens* (Resolution and Background Report adopted by the National Council of Churches of Christ, November 1977), p. 10.
77. Ibid.
78. Joann S. Lubin, "Union Organizer Faces Harder Job Than Ever in Recession-Hit South," *Wall Street Journal*, August 3, 1982, p. 1.

CHAPTER 4

1. Quoted in interview with Joe Malay, conducted by Thomas Rhoddenbaugh, 1969.
2. Ibid.
3. William N. Denman, "The Black Lung Movement: A Study in Contemporary Agitation," unpublished dissertation, Ohio University, August 1974, p. 31.
4. Dr. Isadore Buff, quoted in *Coal Mine Health and Safety, Part 1*, Hearings before the Subcommittee on Labor of the Committee on Labor and Public Welfare, U.S. Senate, February 27, 1969 (Washington: U.S. Government Printing Office, 1969), p. 641.
5. James Castro, "Dr. Buff," *Huntington Herald Dispatch*, March 1974, editorial page.
6. Brit Hume, *Death in the Mines* (New York: Grossman Publishers, 1971), p. 94.
7. O. Norman Simpkins, "Appalachian Culture," Marshall University, undated lecture notes, p. 11.

8. Phillip Trupp, "Dr. Buff vs. Black Lung," *Reader's Digest*, June 1969: 101–5.

9. Brit Hume, "Coal Mining: The Union," *Atlantic Monthly*, November 1969: 106.

10. Earl Stafford, interviewed in Matewon, West Virginia, July 1973.

11. Hume, *Death in the Mines*, p. 109.

12. *Legislative History of the Federal Coal Mine Health and Safety Act of 1969*, U.S. Senate, August 1975, U.S. (Washington: U.S. Government Printing Office, 1975), p. 133.

13. Denman, "The Black Lung Movement," pp. 51–52.

14. *Legislative History*, p. 134.

15. Reprinted in Denman, "The Black Lung Movement," p. 58.

16. Quoted in Trupp, "Dr. Buff," p. 102.

17. Hawey Wells, quoted in Denman, "The Black Lung Movement," p. 71.

18. Hume, *Death in the Mines*, p. 111.

19. Hank Burchard, "Coal Miners Lobby for Black Lung Aid," *Washington Post*, January 30, 1969, pp. C–1, C–3.

20. Reprinted in Burchard, "Coal Miners," p. C–1.

21. Russ Lilly, "3500 Yell Demand for Black Lung Law," *Huntington Herald-Dispatch*, January 27, 1969, pp. 1, 2.

22. Ralph Nader, reported in Lilly, "3500 Yell," p. 5.

23. Quoted in Edward Peeks, "UMW, Doctors, Operators Act," *Charleston Gazette*, January 29, 1969, pp. 1, 8.

24. Quoted in George W. Hopkins, "Occupational Health and the Miners: The Black Lung Revolt," paper presented at the 1982 Annual Meeting of the Organization of American Historians, Philadelphia, April 2, 1982, p. 10.

25. Ibid.

26. Don Marsh, "House Shows Mixed Coal Strike View," *Charleston Gazette*, February 22, 1969, pp. 1, 2.

27. Denman, "The Black Lung Movement," p. 76.

28. Hume, *Death in the Mines*, p. 134.

29. Marsh, "House Shows," pp. 1–2.

30. Denman, "The Black Lung Movement," pp. 150–60.

31. Ibid., p. 160.

32. Charles Ryan, "Report to West Virginia: The 1969 Legislature," *The West Virginia Hillbilly*, March 1969: 1, 6.

33. "Black Lung Bill Close to Demands," *Charleston Gazette*, February 27, 1969, p. 1.

34. Ibid., p. 2

35. See Hopkins, "Occupational Health," p. 11, and Hume, *Death in the Mines*, p. 150.

CHAPTER 5

1. Brit Hume, *Death in the Mines* (New York: Grossman Publishers, 1971), p. 21. See also Paul J. Nyden, "Miners for Democracy: Struggle in the Coal Fields," unpublished dissertation, Columbia University, 1974.

2. Ward Sinclair, "Coal Seeks New Health and Safety Laws," *Louisville Carrier Journal*, March 23, 1969, p. F9.

3. Ben A. Franklin, "Senate Favoring Mine Safety Reforms," *New York Times*, June 22, 1969, p. 51.

4. R.D. McGillicuddy, "The Legislative History of the Black Lung Reform Efforts," in *Black Lung Benefits Reform Act*, February 1979 (Washington: U.S. Government Printing Office, 1979), p. 1228.

5. Ibid.

6. *Report on Federal Coal Mine Health and Safety Act of 1969*, Committee on Education and Labor, U.S. House of Representatives, 1969 (Washington: U.S. Government Printing Office, 1969), pp. 13–14.

7. Congressman Daniels of New Jersey, in *Legislative History of the Federal Coal Mine Health and Safety Act of 1969*, U.S. House of Representatives, March 1970 (Washington: U.S. Government Printing Office, 1970), p. 815.

8. Congressman Dent, in *Legislative History*, p. 654.

9. McGillicuddy, "The Legislative History," p. 1230.

10. "Miners Invite UMW Chief to Aid Black Lung Battle," *Charleston Daily Mail*, January 27, 1969, p. 17.

11. Tony Boyle, testimony in *Coal Mine Health and Safety, Part I*, Hearings before the Subcommittee on Labor of the Committee on Labor and Public Welfare, February 27, 1969 (Washington: U.S. Government Printing Office, 1969), p. 782.

12. Hume, *Death in the Mines*, p. 69.

13. "The Black Lung Controversy," *Mountain, Life and Work*, October 1969: 20.

14. William N. Denman, "The Black Lung Movement: A Study of Contemporary Agitation," unpublished dissertation, Ohio University, August 1974, p. 40.

15. Ward Sinclair, "Mine Health and Safety Bills Evoke Storm Signs," *Louisville Courier Journal*, January 24, 1969, p. A–1.

16. According to records of the Black Lung Association.

17. Federal Coal Mine Health and Safety Act of 1969, Public Law 91–173, 91st Congress, approved December 30, 1969.

18. Arthur E. Hess, "Disability Procedures: Statement of Steps and Rationale for Action Taken by Department of HEW," *Papers and Proceedings of the National Conference on Medicine and the Federal Coal*

Mine Health and Safety Act of 1969, Washington, June 15–18, 1970, pp. 41–50.

19. Ibid., pp. 41–42.

20. *Achievements, Administrative Problems and Costs in Paying Black Lung Benefits to Coal Miners and Their Widows* (Washington: Security Administration, Comptroller General of the United States, September 5, 1972), p. 16.

21. Ibid., p. 16.

22. "Red Tape Ties Up Black Lung Benefits," *Black Lung Bulletin*, October 1970: 1.

23. *Black Lung Benefits Reform Act*, February 1979, p. 6.

24. David V. Hawpe, "Poor Demand Better Black Lung Aid," *Washington Post*, November 26, 1970, p. L–1.

25. *Achievements*.

26. Ibid.

27. Testimonies in *Black Lung Legislation, 1971–72*, U.S. Senate Subcommittee on Labor of the Committee on Public Welfare, 1971.

28. *Black Lung Bulletin*, October 1971: 2.

29. Quoted in Hawpe, "Poor Demand," p. 4.

30. See George W. Hopkins, "Occupational Health and the Miners: The Black Lung Revolt," paper presented at the 1982 Annual Meeting of the Organization of American Historians, Philadelphia, April 2, 1982, p. 10; and Hume, *Death in the Mines*, p. 121.

31. Hopkins, "Occupational Health."

32. Hume, *Death in the Mines*, p. 121.

33. Interview with Thomas Rhoddenbaugh, April 1973.

34. Hopkins, "Occupational Health," p. 14.

35. "The Charleston Office Crew," undated document in files provided by the Black Lung Association, pp. 1–2.

36. "Memo: What We're Here For," undated document in files provided by the Black Lung Association, pp. 1–2.

37. From files provided by the BLA.

38. For a discussion of this see John D. McCarthy and Mayer Zald, *The Trend of Social Movements in America: Professionalization and Resource Mobilization* (Morristown, N.J.: General Learning Corporation, 1973).

39. The significance of VISTA to the black lung movement is discussed in K.W. Lee, "Catalyst of the Black Lung Movement," in David Walls and John Stephenson, editors, *Appalachia in the Sixties* (Lexington: The University Press of Kentucky, 1972), pp. 201–9.

40. Jack E. Weller, *Yesterday's People* (Lexington: The University Press of Kentucky, 1965), pp. 110–14.

41. Quoted in David Whisnant, *Modernizing the Mountaineer* (Boone, N.C.: Appalachian Consortium Press, 1980), p. 212.

42. Ibid.

43. "Statement of Purposes," undated document from files provided by the Black Lung Association.

44. Leo Kramer, *The Health Impaired Miner Under Black Lung Legislation* (Washington: Kramer Research, March 1973), pp. 31, 47, and 166.

45. Ibid., p. 106.

46. "Bureaucrats vs. People," *Black Lung Bulletin*, September 1971: 1.

47. For a discussion of this see Ron E. Roberts and Robert M. Kloss, *Social Movements: Between the Balcony and the Barricade*, 2nd ed. (St. Louis: C.V. Mosby Company, 1979), p. 85.

48. Statement by Kate Currie, BLA representative from Beckley, West Virginia, at BLA State Meeting, Charleston, West Virginia, March 15, 1974.

49. Interview with Gibbs Kinderman, Director of the Mountain Family Health Plan, Inc., a health program which supported the miners' efforts, March 15, 1974.

CHAPTER 6

1. Arnold Miller, testimony in *Black Lung Amendments of 1973*, Committee on Education and Labor, House of Representatives, July 11, 17, and August 2, 1973 (Washington: U.S. Government Printing Office, 1973), p. 203.

2. Leo Kramer, *The Health Impaired Miner Under the Black Lung Legislation* (Washington: Kramer Research, March 1973), p. 35.

3. From undated newspaper clippings in files provided by the Black Lung Association.

4. "Black Lung Group Makes Demand List," *Charleston Gazette*, April 14, 1971, p. 1.

5. Quoted in Jim Calfee, "Black Lung Delegation Demand Rights in March on SS Office," *Bluefield Daily Telegraph*, April 29, 1971, pp. 1–2.

6. Information on the march came from the files provided by the Black Lung Association.

7. Ibid.

8. Hank Burchard, "Coal Miners Lobby for Black Lung Aid," *Washington Post*, June 8, 1971, p. C–1.

9. Ben Franklin, "Miners Assail Black Lung Benefits Plan," *New York Times*, June 8, 1971, p. C–1.

10. "Proceedings: Washington Trip," *Black Lung Bulletin*, June 6, 1971: 1.

11. "Fight for Clinics," *Black Lung Bulletin*, February 1972: 1.

12. "What Happened to Clinics," *Black Lung Bulletin*, September/October 1972: 4.

13. Ibid.

14. E.E. Cody, in *Black Lung Legislation, 1971–72*, U.S. Senate Subcommittee on Labor of the Committee on Public Welfare, December 1, 1971, p. 92.

15. *Black Lung Legislation*, p. 223.

16. Harrison Williams, in *Legislative History of the Federal Coal Mine Health and Safety Act of 1969*, Committee on Public Welfare and Labor, August 1975 (Washington: U.S. Government Printing Office, 1975), p. 2035 (hereafter *Legislative History, 1975*).

17. Senator Jennings Randolph, in *Legislative History of the Federal Coal Mine Health and Safety Act*, Committee on Education and Labor of the House of Representatives, March 1970 (Washington: U.S. Government Printing Office, 1970), pp. 325–27 (hereafter *Legislative History, 1970*).

18. Ibid.

19. R.D. McGillicuddy, "Legislative History of the Black Lung Reform Efforts," *Black Lung Benefits Reform Act*, February 1979 (Washington: U.S. Government Printing Office, 1979), p. 1241.

20. Ibid., p. 1233.

21. *Black Lung Benefits Eligibility*, (Oversight) Hearing before the General Subcommittee on Labor at the Committee on Education and Labor, House of Representatives, Eastern Kentucky, June 23, 1973 (Washington: U.S. Government Printing Office, 1973), p. 23.

22. Paul Kaufman, quoted in *Black Lung Legislation, 1971–72*, pp. 186–87.

23. "RDF Public Interest Report No. 7," reprinted in *Black Lung Legislation, 1971–72*, p. 189.

24. Ibid., p. 190.

25. Congressman Ken Hechler, quoted in *Black Lung Legislation, 1971–72*, p. 224.

26. Ibid.

27. McGillicuddy, "Legislative History," p. 1233.

28. Comptroller General's Report in *Black Lung Benefits Reform Act, 1976*, Hearings Before the Subcommittee on Labor, U.S. Senate, March 23, 26, and April 2, 1976 (Washington: U.S. Government Printing Office), pp. 446–447.

29. *Black Lung Bulletin*, December 1970: 2.

30. *Legislative History, 1975*, p. 2032.

31. Ibid., p. 235

32. Ibid., p. 248.

33. Ibid., pp. 254–55.

34. Ibid., p. 237.

35. McGillicuddy, "Legislative History," p. 1235.

36. Senator Jennings Randolph, in *Black Lung Legislation, 1971–72*, p. 85.

37. Senator Lowell Schweiker, in *Legislative History, 1975*, pp. 2014–2015.

38. "Nixon Gives In," *Black Lung Bulletin*, May 1972: 1.

39. McGillicuddy, "Legislative History," p. 1235.

40. "Black Lung Benefits: Miners Make Demands," *Mountain Life and Work*, June/July 1972: 24–30.

41. Ibid., p. 33.

42. "Black Lung Association Wins a Major Battle," *Mountain Life and Work*, September 1972: 23.

43. Ibid., p. 23.

44. "The New B.L. Regs," *Black Lung Bulletin*, September 1972: 1.

45. Nancy Snyder and Mark Solomon, "Black Lung: A Study in Occupational Disease Compensation," *Black Lung Benefits Reform Act, 1976*, pp. 476–77.

46. McGillicuddy, "Legislative History," p. 1236.

47. Snyder and Solomon, "Black Lung," p. 521.

48. McGillicuddy, "Legislative History," p. 1236.

49. *Black Lung Bulletin*, February 1974: 1.

50. Ibid. See also McGillicuddy, "Legislative History," p. 1238.

51. Snyder and Solomon, "Black Lung," p. 479.

52. Ibid., pp. 510–12, 515.

53. McGillicuddy, "Legislative History," p. 1240.

54. Ibid.

55. *Wall Street Journal*, March 18, 1981, p. 28.

56. W. Keith Morgan et al., "Respiratory Disability in Coal Miners," *Journal of the American Medical Association*, June 20, 1980: 2401–4.

57. Dr. Morgan had replaced Dr. Rasmussen as the principal Public Health Service investigator on coal worker's pneumoconiosis in 1966. See Chapter 2.

58. William R. Barclay, "Black Lung Benefits," *Journal of the American Medical Association*, June 20, 1980: 2427.

59. *Mountain Life and Work*, September 1980: 10.

60. Press release of the Chicago Area Black Lung Association, June 18, 1980 (provided by Paul Siegel).

61. *Mountain Life and Work*, March 1981: 14.

62. Paul Siegel, Secretary of the Chicago Area BLA, Editorial in *Chicago Sun Times*, March 16, 1981.

63. "UMW Calls for 2-Way Strike Protesting Black Lung Cuts," *The Saturday Herald and Leader* (Lexington, Kentucky), February 28, 1981, p. 1.

64. "Black Lung Protest Draws Thousands to Washington," *Mountain Life and Work*, April 1981: 9–12.

65. From information provided by the Chicago Area Black Lung Association.

66. Ibid.

CHAPTER 7

1. From interview with Pearl Hartgrove, January 21, 1981.

2. See A. Bouhuys, "Byssinosis in a Cotton Weaving Mill," *Archives in Environmental Health* 6 (1963): 465–68; A. Bouhuys et al., "Byssinosis in the United States," *New England Journal of Medicine* 277 (1967): 170–75; and R.S.F. Schilling, "Epidemiological Studies of Chronic Respiratory Disease among Cotton Operatives," *Yale Journal of Biological Medicine* 37 (1964): 55–74.

3. "History of the Cotton Dust Standard," provided by the Carolina Brown Lung Association.

4. *New York Times*, September 24, 1969, p. 93.

5. *Textile News*, August 11, 1980, p. 1

6. See *Textile World*, May 1971: 31.

7. Patrick R. Atkins, "Impact of Governmental Environmental Regulations upon Industrial Activities," in Lester V. Cralby et al., editors, *Industrial Environmental Health* (New York: Academic Press, 1975), p. 330.

8. See Bob Hall, "The Brown Lung Controversy," *Columbia Journalism Review*, March/April 1978: 28.

9. Interview with Mike and Kathy Russell, May 24, 1982.

10. Fran Ansley, who had been working through the Center for Health Services at Vanderbilt University on a grant from the Youth Project, an organization based in Washington, D.C., was attempting to locate retired textile workers in Knoxville, Tennessee. Although the mills had been closed too long then to locate many people, her work on this project was the foundation for much of the early work of the Brown Lung Association (from interview with Charlotte Brody, March 8, 1981).

11. Thad Moore, a student at the University of North Carolina at Greensboro, was working through the campus PIRG (Public Interest Research Group), a Nader-founded organization, to expose the problem of byssinosis in North Carolina.

12. Most of this work was being done by Thad Moore, Mike Spazk, and Frank Blechman (interview with Charlotte Brody).

13. The main work by this group was conducted by Joseph ("Chip") Hughes, Charlotte Brody, and Bill Finger (interview with Charlotte Brody).

14. From *Planning a Clinic; Planning Preparation and Follow-Up;*

Building the Organization Through Screening Clinics, undated pamphlet provided to organizers and staff in the Brown Lung Association.

15. Interview with Charlotte Brody.

16. *Campaign for Human Development Newsletter,* November 1976: 3.

17. Undated application for funding (circa 1975) by the Brown Lung Project to the Campaign for Human Development.

18. Interview with Charlotte Brody.

19. This was ascertained through interviews with several members of the Brown Lung Association.

20. From *Planning a Clinic.*

21. "Brown Lungers Ride to Arouse Interest," *Greensboro Daily News,* November 13, 1975.

22. "Retirees File en Masse for Brown Lung Benefits," *Raleigh News and Observer,* October 7, 1976.

23. From *Planning a Clinic.*

24. Hugh Macaulay et al., "The Question of Damage and Compensation," *The Greenville News and Piedmont,* October 27, 1979.

25. Interview with Lizzie Hardy, President of the Brown Lung Association Chapter, Anderson, South Carolina, March 14, 1981.

26. Siegfried Heyden and Philip Pratt, "Exposure to Cotton Dust and Respiratory Disease," *Journal of the American Medical Association,* October 17, 1980: 1797–98.

27. Interview with Lizzie Hardy.

28. Interview with Lyn Haskett, then President of the Bi-State Board of the Brown Lung Association, January 26, 1981.

29. Interview with Stella Turner (one of the few former textile workers who became a staff member), February 27, 1981.

30. See John McCarthy and Mayer Zald, *The Trend of Social Movements in America: Professionalization and Resource Mobilization* (Morristown, N.J.: General Learning Corporation, 1973).

31. Bea Norton, then President of the Brown Lung Association, interviewed by Fran Lynn, 1977.

32. These figures were determined from proposals sent for funding to foundations, 1981.

33. Specialization of roles was determined by looking at the records of the association and role assignments of all staff members in the spring and summer of 1981.

34. This was ascertained by repeated observations of meetings from 1975 to 1985.

35. Interview with Charlotte Brody.

36. Interview with Charlotte Brody and other staff members and from personal observation.

37. Interview with James Martin, March 18, 1981.

38. From personal observation.

39. Interview with Charlotte Brody.

40. From applications for funding in 1981.

41. From "Brown Lung: Case of Deadly Neglect," special supplement to the *Charlotte Observer*, Feb. 3 to Feb. 10, 1980, p. 18.

42. Frank Goldsmith and Lorin E. Kerr, *Occupational Safety and Health: The Prevention and Control of Work-Related Hazards* (New York: Human Sciences Press, 1982), pp. 101–3.

43. Although the Brown Lung Association received substantial funding from OSHA, the present administration of OSHA is currently seeking the return of most of the money on the grounds that it was misused. Interview with Eileen Hansen, part-time bookkeeper for the Brown Lung Association, April 27, 1985.

44. An application for funding in 1981 revealed that while $668,643 of the association's income for the previous five years came from foundations, churches, and the government, only $61,700 came from grassroots fundraising.

45. This process is sometimes referred to as the "defunding of the left," and was aimed particularly at organizations like VISTA which supposedly organized poor people in a confrontational mode. See Charles Babington, "Greensboro Lawyer Nominated to Direct VISTA," *Greensboro Daily News*, undated article in files of the Brown Lung Association.

46. See "Byssinosis Group Spent No Money to Aid Victims," *Charlotte Observer*, February 14, 1983; and "N.C. Bars Brown Lung Fundraising," *Charlotte Observer*, October 29, 1983.

CHAPTER 8

1. Interview with Joe Roberts, attorney and later State Representative, 1981, Gaston County, North Carolina.

2. *Occupational Diseases and Their Compensation*, Part 3, congressional hearings held in Washington, D.C., April 4 to June 21, 1979 (Washington: U.S. Government Printing Office, 1980), p. 447.

3. Peter S. Barth and H. Allan Hunt, *Worker's Compensation and Work-Related Illnesses and Diseases* (Cambridge: MIT Press, 1980), p. 4.

4. Hugh Fisher, "A Summary of How Workmen's Compensation Systems in Four Southeastern States Affect Byssinotic Claimants," paper prepared for Legislative Services, Commonwealth of Virginia, October 14, 1981.

5. Joseph T. Hughes, "Brown Lung Disablity: Costs, Compensation and Controversy," research paper for Institute for Southern Studies under a grant from the U.S. Department of Labor, June 1979, p. 6.

6. Statement by South Carolina Industrial Commission Chair Sarah Leverette, in "Brown Lung Victims Told Were Misled," *The State*, September 21, 1976.

7. Brown Lung Association representative quoted in *Mountain Life and Work*, April 1977: 15.

8. Ibid., p. 16.

9. Ibid.

10. Douglas Maudlin, "SC Brown Lung Compensation Fight Nears Proverbial Light," *The State*, March 23, 1977.

11. "The 1977 Legislative Program of the South Carolina Brown Lung Association," October 1975, provided by the Brown Lung Association.

12. "Brown Lung Association Seeking Aid," *The State*, October 21, 1976.

13. *Mountain Life and Work*, April 1977: 17.

14. "Brown Lung Legislation OK Likely," *Charlotte Observer*, April 17, 1977.

15. Henry Eichel, "SC Legislature Approves Brown Lung Compensation Bill," *Charlotte Observer*, May 15, 1977.

16. Senator Isadore Loure, quoted in Eichel, "South Carolina Legislature Approves."

17. *National Workers Compensations Standards Act of 1978*, Committee on Human Resources of the U.S. Senate, September 19, 20, 22, 1978 (Washington: U.S. Government Printing Office, 1978), p. 264.

18. Olive Pankey, quoted in Jack Betts, "Brown Lung Association Gets Help for Claims," *Greensboro Daily News*, March 15, 1978.

19. Report of the Brown Lung Study Committee to Governor James B. Hunt, Jr., April 10, 1980, p. 3.

20. Fisher, "A Summary of Workmen's Compensation."

21. *Greensboro Daily News*, November 13, 1975, p. B–1.

22. Rick Nichols, "Retirees File en Masse for Brown Lung Benefits," *Raleigh News and Observer*, October 7, 1976.

23. Ted Vaden, "Brown Lung Claims Filed," *Raleigh News and Observer*, August 21, 1977, p. 37.

24. David Tomlin, "Claim System Strained by Brown Lung Cases," *The Daily Times News*, February 20, 1978.

25. Susan Jetton, "Textile Workers Seek Payments for Brown Lung," *Charlotte Observer*, March 15, 1978, p. B–1.

26. Jetton, "Textile Workers"; see also E. Tomquest and R. Brown, "Brown Lung Group Opens Up Logjam on Claims," *The North Carolina Anvil*, March 31, 1978.

27. Statement of Byssinosis Policy of the North Carolina Industrial Commission, February 19, 1980, reprinted in *Asbestos Health Hazards Compensation Act of 1980*, August 26–27, 1980 (Washington: U.S. Government Printing Office, 1980), p. 156.

28. Howard Covington, "Hunt Orders Investigation of Brown Lung Complaints," *Charlotte Observer*, September 13, 1979.

29. Howard Covington, "Hunt Backs Brown Lung Proposals," *Charlotte Observer*, April 19, 1980.

30. Florence Sandlin, "Minority Report of the Governor's Brown Lung Study Committee," in unpublished *Report of the Brown Lung Study Committee* to James B. Hunt, Governor of North Carolina, April 10, 1980.

31. Interview with James Martin, March 18, 1981.

32. G.J. Beck et al., "A Prospective Study of Chronic Lung Disease in Cotton Textile Workers," *Annual of International Medicine* 97 (1982): 645–774; and A. Bouhuys et al., "Epidemiology of Lung Disease in a Cotton Mill Community," *Lung* 154 (1977): 167–86.

33. For more on the textile industry's response to the brown lung issue see *Textile News*, August 11, 1980; *Facts About Cotton Dust, Byssinosis and the Textile Industry* (American Textile Manufacturers Institute, Washington, D.C., March 20, 1980); *Cotton Dust and Occupational Diseases* (Dan River, Inc., Danville, Va., May 1980); and *Workers' Compensation: A Question of Fairness* (North Carolina Textile Manufacturers Association, Raliegh, North Carolina, not dated).

34. *Report of the Brown Lung Study Committee*, p. 11.

35. The concept of a "legal" disease was advanced by Nancy Snyder and Mark Solomons in "Black Lung: A Study in Occupational Disease Compensation," *Black Lung Benefits Reform Act, 1976*, pp. 476–77. More recently medical anthropologist Jan Bronstein has written about political and medical definitions of both black lung and brown lung in "Science and Policy: Controversies in the Definition of Black Lung and Brown Lung," paper presented at the American Association for the Advancement of Science meetings in Detroit, 1983.

36. Marion A. Ellis, "The Brown Lung Battle: Into the Courtroom," *North Carolina Insight*, June 1981: 17.

37. Marion Ellis, "Brown Lung Claims Can't Include Cigarette Damage, Court Rules," *Charlotte Observer*, October 7, 1981.

38. Ellis, "The Brown Lung Battle," p. 17.

39. "Elsie Morrison Court Decision Was Wrong," *Charlotte Observer*, October 11, 1981, editorial.

40. "North Carolina Ruling a Precedent on Benefits," *Charlotte Observer*, April 6, 1983.

41. "No Retreat on Fairness," *Raleigh News and Observer*, May 6, 1983, editorial.

42. From participant observation.

43. Quoted in Mimi Conway, *Rise, Gonna Rise: A Portrait of Southern Textile Workers* (New York: Anchor Press/Doubleday, 1979), p. 86.

44. Howard Covington, "Court Expands Limits on Byssinosis Compensation," *Charlotte Observer*, May 7, 1980).

45. "Brown Lung Group Raps Claim Delay," *Charlotte Observer*, September 4, 1980.

46. Ibid.

47. Charlotte Brody and Bill Adler, "BL Organizers Say: Give Us Compensation or Give Us Breath," *Labor Notes*, September 2, 1980, p. 1.

48. Quoted in Michael Ginsberg, "Byssinosis Claim Tied Up in Court," *Greenville News-Piedmont*, June 18, 1981.

49. Ibid.

50. *Cotton Dust and Occupational Illnesses: A Dan River Position Paper*, (Dan River, Inc., May 1980), pp. 9–10.

51. Ginsberg, "Byssinosis Claim."

52. Ibid.

53. Scott Sinde, "Brown Lung Protest Aimed at Company," *Greenville News*, January 27, 1981.

54. Quotes in Michael Ginsberg, "Brown Lung Victim Agrees to $12,000 Settlement Offer," *Greenville-Piedmont*, February 16, 1981; and "Byssinosis Victim Accepts Dan River Settlement," *Greenville News*, February 17, 1981.

55. Fisher, "A Summary of Workmen's Compensation."

56. Quoted in Sharon Hudson, "Brown Lung Hearing," *Gastonia Gazette*, February 17, 1981.

57. *Brown Lung*, Hearings in the U.S. Senate, Committee on Appropriations, December 9, 1977 (Washington: U.S. Government Printing Office).

58. Quoted in Sharon Hudson, "Astonishing Testimony: Brown Lung Victims Don't Want Government Money," *Gastonia Gazette*, April 8, 1979.

59. Quoted in Jerry Shinn, "Brown Lung Bill Could Put Law Makers on the Spot," *Charlotte Observer*, May 2, 1977.

60. Robert Hodierne, "Brown Lung: What's Been Done, What's Yet to Come," *Charlotte Observer*, August 29, 1977.

61. Testimony in *Brown Lung*, p. 39.

62. Testimony in *Brown Lung*, p. 47.

63. Ibid., p. 48.

64. Testimony in *Brown Lung*, p. 53.

65. Vinnie Ellison, speaking for her husband, Elliott, in *Brown Lung*, pp. 59–60.

66. Testimony in *Brown Lung*, pp. 40–41.

67. Testimony in *Brown Lung*, p. 57.

68. Senator Ernest Hollings, quoted in "Brown Lung: Raising the Costs," *Charlotte Observer*, February 14, 1978.

69. Statement of Senator Harrison Williams, *National Worker's Compensation Standards Act of 1978*, September 19, 20, and 22, 1978 (Washington: U.S. Government Printing Office, 1978), p. 1.

70. Ibid.

71. Testimony of Essie Briggs, *National Worker's Compensation Standards Act of 1978*, p. 120.

72. Statement of Robert Flockhart, Council for American Insurance Association, *National Worker's Compensation Standards Act, 1978*, p. 205.

73. *National Worker's Compensation Standards Act of 1978*, p. 415.

74. Ibid., pp. 223–59.

75. *Occupational Diseases and Their Compensation, Part 3*, Hearings from April 4 to June 21, 1979, U.S. House of Representatives (Washington: U.S. Government Printing Office, 1980).

76. Letter sent by ATMI to Congressman Beard, reprinted in *Occupational Diseases*, pp. 354–55.

77. Congressman George Miller of California, in *Occupational Diseases*, p. 10.

78. Quoted in *Asbestos Health Hazards Compensation Act of 1980*, Hearings before the Committee on Labor and Human Resources, U.S. Senate, August 26–27, 1980 (Washington: U.S. Government Printing Office, 1980), p. 144.

CHAPTER 9

1. The Watergate investigations uncovered a memo from the federal Occupational Safety and Health Administration to the North Carolina OSHA which urged them not to make any controversial inspection visits until after the 1972 presidential election. From Rachelle Linner, "Breath and Justice," *Sojourners*, July 1977: 19.

2. Karen Rothmyer, "Washington Moves Slowly on Tough Controls to Prevent Long Ignored Cotton Dust Disease," *Wall Street Journal*, June 7, 1976.

3. Letter from files of the Brown Lung Association, dated October 1976.

4. J.A. Merchant et al., "Byssinosis and Chronic Bronchitis among Cotton Textile Workers," *Annual of Internal Medicine*, March 1972: 423–33.

5. From "Brown Lung: A Case of Deadly Neglect," special supplement to the *Charlotte Observer*, February 3 to February 10, 1980, p. 6.

6. Ibid., p. 7.

7. Allen Cowan, "S.C. Could Lose Right to Inspect Mills," *Charlotte Observer*, July 2, 1978, p. 4–A.

8. "Brown Lung: Case of Deadly Neglect," p. 6.

9. "CBLA's Position Statement on Federal OSHA's Proposed Cotton Dust Standard, *Mountain Life and Work*, April 1977: 21.

10. Reported in Paul Horvitz, "U.S. Proposes Fixed Levels of Cotton Dust," *Raleigh News and Observer*, January 16, 1977.

11. Mimi Conway, *Rise, Gonna Rise: A Portrait of Southern Textile Workers* (New York: Anchor/Doubleday, 1979), p. 59.

12. Ibid., p. 63.

13. *Mountain Life and Work*, April 1977: 21.

14. Quoted in Conway, *Rise, Gonna Rise*, p. 61.

15. Ibid.

16. Robert Hodiere, "Cotton Dust Standard for Textile Mills Still Not Ready," *Charlotte Observer*, February 19, 1978.

17. "Report Delay Angers State's Lung Group," *Greensboro Record*, May 25, 1978.

18. "Lung Group Claims Victory; Industry Sees Impossibilities," *Greensboro Daily News*, January 20, 1978.

19. Janet Guyon, "Cotton Dust Standards Draw Fire," *Raleigh News and Observer*, June 21, 1978.

20. Ibid.

21. "Court Allows Tougher Rules on Cotton Dust," *Charlotte Observer*, October 28, 1979.

22. "Textilists Hope Top Court Will Postpone Dust Limits," *Charlotte Observer*, January 17, 1980.

23. "American Textile Manufacturers Institute vs. U.S. Department of Labor," 101 *Supreme Court Reporter* 2478, (1981), p. 2489.

24. Dorothy Rice and Thomas Hodgson, "The Value of Human Life Revisited," *American Journal of Public Health*, June 1982: 536–37.

25. Steven Laudefeld and Eugene Seskin, "The Economic Value of Life: Linking Theory to Practice," *American Journal of Public Health*, June 1982: 556.

26. Ibid., p. 557.

27. "ATMI vs. U.S. Dept of Labor," p. 2488.

28. Brown Lung Association Press Conference, July 21, 1981.

29. Kitty Calavita, "The Demise of the Occupational Safety and Health Administration," *Social Problems*, April 1983: 441.

30. Linda Greenhouse, "U.S. Pulls a Switch on High Court," *New York Times*, April 5, 1981.

31. "Protest Called Moral Crusade," *Kannapolis Daily News*, May 4, 1981.

32. "Millworkers Defend Cotton Dust Standard," *Mountain Life and Work*, June 1981: 14–17. See also Phillip Shabecoff, "Hundreds in Capital Protest Plan," *New York Times*, May 5, 1981.

33. *Supreme Court Reporter*, pp. 2478–79.

34. Ibid.

35. *Mountain Life and Work* (July/August 1981): 23.

36. Quoted in "Local Brown Lung Members Rejoice Over High Court Ruling," *Richmond County Daily Journal*, June 19, 1981.

37. "Advance Notice of Proposed Rulemaking," Occupational Safety and Health Administration, February 9, 1982.

38. Ibid., p. 4.

39. Stephen Kelly, "OSHA Criticized in Hearings on Brown Lung," *Charlotte Observer*, September 23, 1982.

40. Amalgamated Clothing and Textile Workers Union press release, March 17, 1983; see also Marion Ellis, "Cotton Dust Rules Help Industry, Union Study Says," *Charlotte Observer*, March 18, 1983.

41. Joanne S. Lublin, "OSHA Upholds Exposure Rules for Cotton Dust," *Wall Street Journal*, May 20, 1978.

42. Bill Arthur, "Some See EPA Follies as Key," *Charlotte Observer*, May 21, 1983.

43. U.S. Labor Department press release, June 7, 1983.

44. Personal observation at OSHA hearings in Columbia, South Carolina, October 4, 1983.

45. Calavita, "The Demise," p. 443.

46. Ibid.

47. Statistics provided by the American Textile Manufacturers Institute.

48. Ibid.

49. Interview with James Martin, President of TiCaro, Inc., March 18, 1981. Martin later became President of the American Textile Manufacturers Institute.

50. Ibid.

51. William Pitts, then President of Heritage Mills, quoted in "Brown Lung: A Case of Deadly Neglect," p. 8.

52. Statement of the American Textile Manufacturers Institute, in *National Workers Compensation Standards Act of 1978*, Hearings before the Subcommittee on Labor of the Committee on Human Resources, U.S. Senate, September 19, 20, and 22, 1978 (Washington: U.S. Government Printing Office, 1978), pp. 415–25.

53. "Brown Lung: A Case of Deadly Neglect," p. 13.

54. M.F. Trice, "Card Room Fever," *Textile World*, March 1940.

55. T.M. Forbes, in a letter to the President of Emory University, June 2, 1964 (personal copy).

56. *America's Textile Reporter*, July 10, 1969, referenced in Ralph Nader's "The Cotton Mill Killer," *The Nation*, March 15, 1971.

57. *Textile World News*, May, 1971: 31.

58. "Highlights: National Cotton Council's Cotton Dust Activities," undated material provided by the Cotton Council, Inc.

59. Nader, "Cotton Mill Killer," pp. 335–36.

60. From statement by Joe L. Lanier, Chairman, Safety and Health Committee of ATMI, to Southern Governors' Conference, September 20, 1978.

61. Ibid.

62. Robert Conn and Marion Ellis, "Textile Study Disputes Government Figures on Brown Lung, *Charlotte Observer*, January 19, 1982.

63. Interview with James Martin, March 18, 1981.

64. "Brown Lung: A Case of Deadly Neglect."

65. Editorial appeared in the March 1980 issue of *Textile World*, reprinted in *Charlotte Observer*, March 22, 1980.

66. Ibid.

67. Don Bedwell and Marion Ellis, "Textile, Tobacco Industries Clash on Smoking Risk," *Charlotte Observer*, June 1, 1980.

68. "Doctors Look at Byssinosis," *Charlotte Observer*, June 21, 1980, p. A–15.

69. "Byssinosis: Some Medical Facts," paid advertisement for ATMI in *Charlotte Observer*, May 8, 1980.

70. See Bedwell and Ellis, "Textile, Tobacco Industries Clash on Smoking Risk."

71. "Cotton Dust: A Special Report," *Southern Textile News*, August 11, 1980.

CHAPTER 10

1. The resource mobilization perspective is reflected in John D. McCarthy and Mayer Zald, "Resource Mobilization and Social Movements: A Partial Theory," *American Journal of Sociology*, May 1977: 1212–39; John Wilson, *Introduction to Social Movements* (New York: Basic Books, 1973); Anthony Oberschall, *Social Conflict and Social Movements* (Englewood Cliffs, N.J.: Prentice-Hall, 1973); and Mayer Zald and J.D. McCarthy, editors, *The Dynamics of Social Movements* (Cambridge, Mass.: Winthrop Publishers, 1979).

2. James L. Wood and Maurice Jackson, *Social Movements: Development, Participation and Dynamics* (Belmont, Calif.: Wadsworth Publishing, 1982), p. 143.

3. Zald and McCarthy, *The Dynamics*, p. 1.

4. McCarthy and Zald, "Resource Mobilization."

5. Zald and McCarthy, *Dynamics*, p. vii.

6. Daniel M. Fox and Judith F. Stone, "Black Lung: Miners' Militancy and Medical Uncertainty," *Bulletin of the History of Medicine*, Spring 1980: 43.

7. George W. Hopkins, "Occupational Health and the Miners: The Black Lung Revolt," paper presented at the 1982 Annual Meeting of the Organization of American Historians, Philadelphia, April 2, 1982, p. 26.

8. Robert E. Botsch, "Organizing the Breathless: The Politics of Brown

Lung," paper presented at the 1982 Southern Labor History Conference, Atlanta, pp. 29–30.

9. For information on other occupational diseases see Peter S. Barth and H. Allen Hunt, *Worker's Compensation and Work-Related Illnesses and Diseases* (Cambridge: MIT Press, 1980); Joseph A. Page and May-Win O'Brien, *Bitter Wages* (New York: Grossman Publishers, 1973); Donald Huner, *The Diseases of Occupations*, 6th edition (London: Hodder and Stoughton, 1978), and Elizabeth Sue Pease, *Occupational Safety and Health: A Sourcebook* (New York: Garland Publishing, 1985).

10. This is not to imply that other worker groups have not pushed for occupational health but, with the possible exception of workers in asbestos, none have established movements and received the national attention of coal miners and textile workers.

11. John D. McCarthy and Mayer Zald, *The Trend of Social Movements in America: Professionalization and Resource Mobilization* (Morristown, N.J.: General Learning Press, 1973), pp. 12–17.

12. Robert F. Munn, "The Latest Rediscovery of Appalachia," in David Walls and John Stephenson, editors, *Appalachia in the Sixties* (Lexington: The University Press of Kentucky, 1972), pp. 26–27.

13. Sheldon Hackney, "Southern Violence," *American Historical Review* 74 (1969): 43.

14. Lillian Smith, *Killers of the Dream* (New York: Norton, 1969).

15. Harriet L. Herring, "Toward Preliminary Social Analysis: The Southern Mill System Faces a New Issue," *Social Forces* 8, no. 3: 54–55.

16. John Shelton Reed, *Southerners* (Chapel Hill: The University of North Carolina Press), pp. 136–69.

17. Neil J. Smelser, *Theory of Collective Behavior* (New York: The Free Press of Glencoe, 1963), pp. 278–81.

18. John Gaventa, *Power and Powerlessness: Quiescence and Rebellion in an Appalachian Valley* (Chicago: University of Illinois Press, 1980), p. 116.

19. John Shelton Reed, *One South* (Baton Rouge: Louisiana State University Press, 1982), p. 49.

20. John Earle et al.: *Spindles and Spires: A Restudy of Religion and Change in Gastonia* (Atlanta: John Know Press, 1976), Chapter 4.

21. Dan Berman, *Death on the Job* (New York: Monthly Review Press, 1978).

22. Report provided by Industrial Commission of North Carolina.

23. Thomas Mancuso, "Medical Aspects of Determining Causality," *Interdepartmental Worker's Compensation Task Force Conference on Occupational Diseases and Worker's Compensation*, University of Chicago, February 10–12, 1976, pp. 106–8.

24. See Jeffrey Hadden, *Gathering Storm in the Churches* (New York: Doubleday, 1969).

25. McCarthy and Zald, *The Trend*, p. 12.

26. Interview with Kathy Russell, May 24, 1982.

27. McCarthy and Zald, *The Trend*, p. 18.

28. Ibid., p. 19.

29. See John D. McCarthy and Mayer Zald, "Tactical Considerations in Social Movement Organizations," paper presented at the American Sociological Association, August 26–29, 1974.

30. Bob Hall, "The Brown Lung Controversy," *Columbia Journalism Review*, March/April 1978: 28.

31. "Brown Lung: A Case of Deadly Neglect," Special Supplement to *Charlotte Observer*, February 3–10, 1980.

32. The author counted the number of articles each month from 1975 to 1982 on the issue of brown lung which appeared in the *Charlotte Observer* and compared this with the number of staff in the Brown Lung Association at six-month periods during the same time. Graphing this comparison shows a correlation between the number of staff at each point and the number of articles appearing soon after.

33. Mancur Olson, *The Logic of Collective Action* (Cambridge: Harvard University Press, 1967).

34. McCarthy and Zald, *The Trends*, p. 20.

35. McCarthy and Zald, *The Trends*, p. 22.

36. C. Wright Mills, *The Sociological Imagination* (New York: Oxford University Press, 1959).

37. See P.B. Clark and J.Q. Wilson, "Incentive Systems: A Theory of Organizations," *Administrative Science Quarterly*, September 1961: 129–66.

38. See Reed, *Southerners*, Chapter 3, for the significance of group conciousness to group identification.

39. George Rude, *The Ideology of Protest* (New York: Pantheon Books, 1980), p. 28.

40. Bruce Fireman and W. Gamson, "Utilitarian Logic in the Resource Mobilization Perspective," in Zald and McCarthy, p. 26.

41. The ideas presented here were greatly influenced by George Rude in *The Ideology of Protest*, p. 158, where he discusses the importance of indoctrinaton, experience, and struggle to the development of revolution.

42. For a discussion of empowering, see Gale Miller, *It's a Living: Working in Modern Society* (New York: St. Martin's Press, 1981), Chapter 8.

43. Interview with Pauline Hansel, January 29, 1981.

44. S. Kahn, *Organizing: A Guide for Grassroots Leaders* (New York, McGraw Hill, 1982), p. 74–75.

45. Interview with Charlotte Brody, March 8, 1981.

CHAPTER 11

1. "Background Statement," provided by Breath of Life Organizing Committee.

2. "BLOC Outline of Platform for Compensation and Prevention of Occupational Diseases," adopted July 1983.

3. Lucinda Fleeson, "Law Fails to Cleanse Mines of Black Lung Danger," *Charlotte Observer*, November 25, 1984.

4. Richard Whitt, "Black Lung Program Is Costly for States, Lucrative for Miners," *Louisville-Courier Journal*, January 27, 1985.

5. Reports provided by North Carolina Industrial Commission.

6. Marion Ellis, "Byssinosis Claims Fall: Cleaner Mills or Reticent Victims," *Charlotte Observer*, January 23, 1983.

7. American Textile Manufacturers Institute press release, January 19, 1982.

8. Amalgamated Clothing and Textile Workers Union press release, March 1983.

9. Whitt, "Black Lung Program."

10. Frank Goldsmith and Lorin E. Kerr, *Occupational Safety and Health* (New York: Human Sciences Press, 1982), pp. 36–37.

11. *Occupational Health and Safety Newsletter*, American Public Health Association, June 1983.

12. Reprinted in Steven Kelman, "Regulation That Works," *The New Republic*, November 25, 1978.

13. Paul Maynussen, "Study Says Most Executives Favor Regulation," *Charlotte Observer*, May 16, 1983.

14. These questions and ideas emerged from comments by Curtis P. McLaughlin at a North Carolina Humanities Committee–sponsored conference titled "Perspectives on the Cotton Dust Standard, 1982," September 25, 1982, Durham, North Carolina.

15. Ibid.

16. Ibid.

17. Anselm Min, "Human Life: Its Value and Price," paper presented at "Perspectives on the Cotton Dust Standard, 1982," September 19, 1982, Charlotte, North Carolina.

18. Coleman McCarthy, "Industry's Assault on Workplace Safety," *Washington Post*, September 19, 1978.

19. Daniel Zwerdling, *Workplace Democracy* (New York: Harper and Row, 1980), pp. 169–70.

20. Thomas Donahue, Executive Assistant to the President of the AFL-CIO, quoted in Zwerdling, *Workplace Democracy*, p. 170.

21. Martin Carnoy and Derek Shearer, *Economic Democracy* (White Plains, N.Y.: M.E. Sharpe, 1980), p. 29.

22. Ibid.

23. Ibid.

24. David Montgomery, *Worker's Control in America* (Cambridge, England: Cambridge University Press, 1980), p. 171.

25. Dan Berman, *Death on the Job* (New York: Monthly Review Press, 1978), p. 117.

26. Ibid.

27. Vicente Navarro, "Work, Ideology and Science: The Case of Medicine," in V. Navarro and Daniel Berman, editors, *Health and Work Under Capitalism* (Farmingdale, N.Y.: Baywood, 1983), p. 17.

28. Janet M. Bronstein, "Science and Policy: Controversies in the Definition of Black Lung and Brown Lung," paper presented at the American Association for the Advancement of Science Meetings in Detroit, May 1983, p. 23.

29. Ibid., pp. 19–20.

30. Ibid., pp. 23–24.

31. Navarro, "Work, Ideology and Science," p. 30.

32. Ibid., p. 31.

33. Ibid.

34. Ibid., p. 25.

35. Ibid.

36. Severyn T. Bruyn, "On Becoming a Democratically Managed Firm," *The Social Report*, June 1983: 1.

37. Carnoy and Shearer, *Economic Democracy*, p. 3.

38. Ibid., p. 27.

39. Zwerdling, *Workplace Democracy*, p. 170–72.

40. Kitty Calavita, "The Demise of the Occupational Safety and Health Administration: A Case of Symbolic Action," *Social Problems*, April 1983: 437–48.

41. Quoted in Calavita, "The Demise," p. 444.

42. Ibid., pp. 444–45.

43. "OTA Report Is Critical of Workplace Protection," *The Nation's Health*, May/June 1985: 1, 5.

44. Goldsmith and Kerr, *Occupational Safety*, p. 143.

45. Ibid., p. 143.

46. Berman, *Death on the Job*, p. 119.

47. Calavita, "The Demise," p. 445.

48. Steven Deutsch, "Introduction: Theme Issue on Occupational Safety and Health," *Labor Studies Journal*, Spring 1981: 3–6.

49. Quoted in *All About OSHA*, Programs and Policy Series, U.S. Department of Labor, 1976, p. 1.

50. "If Not Now, When?" *Social Policy*, January/February 1981: 3.

51. Ibid., p. 4.

52. Charles Levenstein et al., "COSH: A Grass Roots Public Health Movement," *American Journal of Public Health*, September 1984: 964–65.

53. For more information on the movement toward workplace democracy, in addition to references already listed, see Karl Frieden, *Workplace Democracy and Productivity* (Washington: National Center for Economic Alternatives, 1980); Ronald Mason, *Participatory and Workplace Democracy* (Carbondale: Southern Illinois University Press, 1982); William Foote Whyte et al., *Worker Participation and Ownership* (Ithaca: ILR Press, New York State School of Industrial and Labor Relations, 1983); and Robert Jackall and Henry M. Levine, editors, *Worker Cooperatives in America* (Berkeley: University of California Press, 1984).

54. Elliott Krause, *Power and Illness: The Political Sociology of Health and Medical Care* (New York: Elsevier, 1977), pp. 318–19.

55. R.L. Joiner, "Occupational Health and Environmental Information Systems: Basic Considerations," *Journal of Occupational Medicine* 24 (Supplement, 1982): 863–66.

56. Michael R. Reich and Rose H. Goldman, "Italian Occupational Health: Concepts, Conflict, Implications," *American Journal of Public Health*, September 1984: 1038.

57. Barbara E. Smith, "Black Lung: The Social Production of Disease," in Vicente Navarro, editor *Health and Work Under Capitalism*, p. 51.

58. Ibid.

59. Navarro, "Work, Ideology and Science," p. 13.

60. Carl Gersuny, *Work Hazards and Industrial Conflict* (Hanover, N.H.: University Press of New England, 1981), pp. 142–43.

Bibliographical Essay

This book has attempted to integrate two fields: the sociology of social movements and occupational health. This essay includes materials from both areas (which have been useful as background reading and references) as well as some of the more recent research. It is organized into five parts: the sociology of social movements, the history of coal miners and textile workers, the black lung movement, the brown lung movement, and occupational safety and health.

THE SOCIOLOGICAL STUDY OF SOCIAL MOVEMENTS

The guiding framework for this research has been an emerging theoretical perspective called "resource mobilization." This model emphasizes the importance of societal supports and constraints on social movements, with a particular focus on tactical dilemmas, social control, and media usage. The concern is less with the beliefs and ideology of the movement and more with how people mobilize the resources necessary to develop a movement. Some of the earlier theoretical ideas in this area can be found in John D. McCarthy and Mayer Zald's *The Trend of Social Movements in America: Professionalization and Resource Mobilization* (Morristown, N.J.: General Learning Press, 1973), and in their article "Resource Mobilization and Social Movements: A Partial Theory," *American Journal of Sociology*, May 1977, pp. 1212–41. The resource mobilization perspective is also reflected in John Wilson's *Introduction to Social Movements* (New York: Basic Books, 1973); Charles Tilly's *From Mobilization to Revolution* (Reading, Mass.: Addison-

Wesley, 1978); Anthony Oberschall's *Social Conflict and Social Movements* (Englewood Cliffs, N.J.: Prentice-Hall, 1973); and William Gamson's *The Strategy of Social Protest* (Homewood, Ill.: Dorsey Press, 1975).

Some recent empirical research which has utilized this perspective can be found in Mayer Zald and John McCarthy, editors, *The Dynamics of Social Movements* (Cambridge, Mass.: Winthrop Publishers, 1979); Hank Johnston's "The Marketed Social Movement: A Case Study of the Rapid Growth of TM," *Pacific Sociological Review*, July 1980, pp. 333–54; Craig Jenkins and Charles Perrow's "Insurgency and the Powerless: Farm Worker Movements: 1946–1972," *American Sociological Review*, April 1977, pp. 249–68; Bennett M. Judkins's "The Black Lung Movement: Social Movements and Social Structure," *Research in Social Movements, Conflicts and Change* 2, (1979), pp. 105–29; and Edward J. Walsh's "Resource Mobilization and Citizen Protest in Communities Around Three Mile Island," *Social Problems*, October 1981, pp. 1–21.

COAL MINERS AND TEXTILE WORKERS

Kai T. Erikson's *Everything in Its Path* (New York: Simon and Schuster, 1976) is one of the best sociological books on coal mining communities, although its main focus is on the impact of a major flood. Brit Hume provides an excellent journalistic account of the United Mine Workers of America, particularly during the period just prior to and during the early stages of the black lung movement, in *Death in the Mines: Rebellion and Murder in the United Mine Workers* (New York: Grossman Publishers, 1971). In *Power and Powerlessness: Quiescence and Rebellion in an Appalachian Valley* (Chicago: University of Illinois Press, 1980), John Gaventa analyzes the forces of power which shape the actions and consciousness of people in the coal mining region. Several articles on the colonization of Appalachian miners can be found in Helen Lewis et al., editors, *Colonialism in Modern America: The Appalachian Case* (Boone, N.C.: Appalachian Consortium Press, 1978).

The most referenced work on southern textile workers is Broadus Mitchell's *Rise of the Cotton Mills in the South* (Baltimore: John Hopkins Press, 1921), although it has been challenged recently by a number of historians. An earlier, and somewhat less well known, work is Holland Thompson's *From the Cotton Field to the Cotton Mill* (New York: The Macmillan Company, 1906). Melton McLaurin's *Paternalism and Protest* (Westport, Conn.: Greenwood Press, 1971) is an excellent treatment of the early textile community, as is anthropologist Kenneth Moreland's *Millways of Kent* (New Haven: College and University Press, 1958). Although its focus is primarily on one strike in one community, Liston Pope's *Millhands and Preachers* (New Haven: Yale University Press, 1942) provides an important work on the role of religion in the early growth and development of mill communities. More intensive analysis of life in the southern mill community can be found in Harriet Herring's *Welfare Work in Mill Villages* (Chapel Hill: University of North Carolina Press, 1929).

THE BLACK LUNG MOVEMENT

Several doctoral dissertations have focused on the coal miners' occupational health movement as well as the reform movement in the UMWA at the same time. See historian George Hopkins's "Miners for Democracy: Insurgency in the United Mine Workers of America: 1970–1972" (unpublished dissertation, University of North Carolina, 1976); Paul J. Nyden's "Miners for Democracy: Struggle in the Coal Fields" (unpublished dissertation, Columbia University, 1974); William N. Denman's "The Black Lung Movement: A Study of Contemporary Agitation" (unpublished dissertation, Ohio University, 1974); and Bennett M. Judkins's "The Black Lung Association: A Case Study of a Modern Social Movement" (unpublished dissertation, University of Tennessee, 1975). Two recent articles which have focused on the social aspects of black lung are Daniel M. Fox and Judith F. Stone, "Black Lung: Miners, Militancy and Medical Uncertainty," *Bulletin of the History of Medicine*, Spring, 1980; and Barbara E. Smith, "Black Lung: The Social Production of Disease," in Vicente Navarro and Daniel Berman, editors, *Health and Work Under Capitalism* (Farmingdale, N.Y.: Baywood, 1983).

THE BROWN LUNG MOVEMENT

One of the best sources of comprehensive information about brown lung, compensation, the cotton dust standard, and the Brown Lung Association is the Charlotte Observer's Pulitzer Prize–winning series titled "Brown Lung: A Case of Deadly Neglect," which appeared February 3–10, 1980. Journalist Mimi Conway's *Rise, Gonna Rise: A Portrait of Southern Textile Workers* (New York: Anchor Press/Doubleday, 1979) contains some excellent interviews with members of the Brown Lung Association. Journalist Bob Hall analyzed how the media influenced the recognition of byssinosis in "The Brown Lung Controversy," *Columbia Journalism Review*, March/April 1978, pp. 27–35. See also Bennett M. Judkins's "Mobilization of Membership in Social Movements" in Jo Freeman, editor, *Social Movements of the Sixties and Seventies* (New York: Longman, 1982), and "Occupational Health and the Developing Class Consciousness of Southern Textile Workers," *Maryland Historian*, Spring/Summer 1982, pp. 55–71.

OCCUPATIONAL SAFETY AND HEALTH

One of the first works on occupational health in the United States was Alice Hamilton's *Exploring the Dangerous Trades* (Boston: Little, Brown and Company, 1943). A more recent work by Daniel Berman, *Death on the Job* (New York: Monthly Review Press, 1978), traces the history of occupational health from the turn of the century to the present. Carl Gersuny's *Work Hazards and Industrial Conflict* (Hanover, N.H.: University Press of New England, 1981) provides an interesting historical comparison between the period 1890–1910 and the 1970s which suggests that the ongoing adversary processes focused on safety and health hazards in the workplace are very much a part of the broader class divisions and conflict in society.

Sociological perspectives on health can be found in Talcott Parsons's *The Social System* (London: Routledge and Kegan Paul, 1951) and David Mechanic's "Illness and Disability: Some Problems in Analysis," *Pacific Sociological Review*, Spring 1959. Two labor-oriented works are Ray Davidson's *Peril on the Job* (Washington: Public Affairs Press, 1970) and Nicholas A. Ashford's *Crisis in the Workplace* (Cambridge: MIT Press, 1976).

For an overview and evaluation of the Occupational Safety and Health Administration from 1970 to 1981, see David P. McCaffrey's *OSHA and the Politics of Occupational Health* (New York: Plenum Press, 1982). An interesting interpretation of OSHA is found in Kitty Calavita's "The Demise of the Occupational Safety and Health Administration: A Case of Symbolic Action," *Social Problems*, April 1983, pp. 437–48.

A comprehensive sourcebook for a number of aspects of worker health and safety is Elizabeth Sue Pease's *Occupational Safety and Health: A Sourcebook* (New York: Garland Publishing, 1985). Frank Goldsmith and Lorin E. Kerr provide a recent overview in *Occupational Safety and Health: The Prevention and Control of Work Related Hazards* (New York: Human Sciences Press, 1982). Barry S. Levy and David H. Wegman are the editors of an excellent volume titled *Occupational Health: Recognizing and Preventing Work Related Disease* (Boston: Little, Brown and Company, 1983). Although intended primarily for health professionals, it is a volume easily read by the layperson. Lawrence White in *Human Debris: The Injured Worker in America* (New York: Seaview/Putnam, 1983) provides an account of industrial illnesses and injuries from the perspective of a lawyer who has handled many compensation cases. In *Bargaining for Job Safety and Health* (Cambridge: MIT Press, 1980), Lawrence S. Bacow provides an important look at how management and labor work together and against each other to abate occupational hazards.

For a more theoretical perspective, see Vicente Navarro and Daniel

Berman, editors, *Health and Work Under Capitalism: An International Perspective* (Farmingdale, N.Y.: Baywood Publishing Company, 1983). For an excellent monograph based upon interviews with workers in American industry to determine how they view the risk of working in a hazardous environment, see Dorothy Nelkin and Michael S. Brown's *Workers at Risk: Voices from the Workplace* (Chicago: The University of Chicago Press, 1984). A contrasting approach which argues that the market economy, not government, should regulate health and safety in the workplace is found in W. Kip Viscusi's *Risk by Choice* (Cambridge: Harvard University Press, 1983).

Index

About the Author

BENNETT M. JUDKINS is Professor and Chair of the Department of Sociology at Belmont Abbey College, Belmont, North Carolina. He has contributed chapters to *Social Movements of the Sixties and Seventies* and *Research on Social Movements, Conflicts and Change* and articles to such journals as *The Sociological Quarterly* and *The Maryland Historian*. He is currently serving as editor of a special issue of the *International Journal of Sociology and Social Policy* on work and health to appear in November, 1986. He has contributed papers (or chaired sessions) on work and health at the American Sociological Association, the Southern Sociological Society, the Organization of American Historians, and the American Popular Culture Association.